THE EUROPEAN UNION TREATY

THE
EUROPEAN UNION
TREATY

*Commentary on the draft adopted by
the European Parliament on
14 February 1984*

by

FRANCESCO CAPOTORTI
MEINHARD HILF
FRANCIS G. JACOBS
JEAN-PAUL JACQUÉ

CLARENDON PRESS · OXFORD

1986

Oxford University Press, Walton Street, Oxford OX2 6DP

Oxford New York Toronto
Delhi Bombay Calcutta Madras Karachi
Petaling Jaya Singapore Hong Kong Tokyo
Nairobi Dar es Salaam Cape Town
Melbourne Auckland

and associated companies in
Beirut Berlin Ibadan Nicosia

Oxford is a trade mark of Oxford University Press

Published in the United States
by Oxford University Press, New York

British Library Cataloguing in Publication Data

The European Union treaty: commentary on
the draft adopted by the European Parliament
on 14th February 1984.
1. European communities
I. Capotorti, Francesco
341.24′22   HC241.2
ISBN 0-19-825548-9

Library of Congress Cataloging-in-Publication Data

The European Union treaty.
Bibliography: p.
1. European Parliament. European Union treaty.
2. European communities.   I. Capotorti, Francesco.
II. European Parliament. European Union treaty.
KJE4442.5 1986   341.242   86-8680
ISBN 0-19-825548-9

Set and Printed in Great Britain by
Butler & Tanner Ltd,
Frome and London

Foreword

BY SIR GORDON SLYNN

*Advocate General, Court of Justice of
the European Communities*

When I first saw *Le Traité d'Union européenne—Commentaire du projet adopté par le Parlément européen*, published in 1985 by the Institute of European Studies, I wondered how four such distinguished but very busy lawyers could have produced so much, so quickly. The answer appeared at once. It was they who had been asked to prepare the Draft Treaty, giving effect to the principles and the details already laid down by the Committee on Institutional Affairs set up by the European Parliament. They were thus in a unique position to write a commentary on the aims and, line by line, on the text of the Draft.

The adoption of this text by the European Parliament was, on any view, a major event in the process of thinking out 'Europeanisation'. Fired by the vitality and persistence of Signor Spinelli and his colleagues meeting at 'The Crocodile', it went far beyond tinkering with the existing Treaties, even though, inevitably, it stopped far short of proposing anything resembling a federation. Coming at a time of gloom—economic because of the recession, institutional because so little progress seemed to be being made, individual because of fears that momentum would not be regained—it provoked new thinking and discussion against the background of Parliament's conviction that there was an urgent and vital need for a revival of European integration, to include 'a further development of existing policies, the introduction of new policies and the establishment of a new institutional balance'.

Much of the Draft is concerned with the structure of the Union—the creation of a citizenship, bringing in the European Monetary System and European political co-operation, reorganizing the Community's decision-making processes; but, no less important than seeking to make the institutions work more effectively, is the statement of the expanded objectives of the Union, wider in many ways than those of the existing Communities, and, in some respects, to be seen in a world context.

For a lawyer, two features are particularly striking: the acceptance in express terms in the Draft Treaty of what has already been achieved by the Court of Justice—direct effect, the supremacy of Community

law over national law, the recognition of fundamental rights and freedoms derived in particular from the common principles of the constitutions of the Member States and the European Convention on Human
Rights; and the changes proposed—wider jurisdiction for the Court,
particularly at the suit of individuals and in disputes between Member
States, equal treatment of the institutions, a right of appeal from a
refusal by a Court of last resort to make a preliminary reference, sanctions against Member States in default.

The great merit of the Commentary in relation to all these important
matters is that it explains lucidly both the factors that had to be weighed
before decisions were reached on particular points and the new concepts
involved—'subsidiarity' (surely, despite near-competitors, the ugliest of
Community adoptions), the distinction between 'co-operation' and
'common action', the division or sharing of competencies, the extent to
which the 'freedoms' of the EEC Treaty can be said to be extended, the
technical rules relating to the adoption and amendment of proposals for
legislation, the difference between organic and non-organic laws. All
these matters called for explanation. Where rules have not been made
precise, or further decisions have to be made, the views or suggestions
of the authors are given, and questions are raised.

Despite the apparently pellucid language of the Treaty, the Commentary adds greatly to comprehension of what lies behind and what
remains to be filled out.

The fact that the Treaty of Union was not adopted, but that the
Single European Act was, does not detract from the ultimate importance
of the Draft Treaty. The Act has taken some important steps and may
lead to greater enterprise in sectors so far little developed, technology,
environment, finance, though it does raise questions as to the powers
of Member States in relation to the free movement of goods, as to
voting procedures and the extent to which Parliament's position has
really been affected. It does not, however, as perhaps at this stage was
to be expected, go anywhere near the distance covered by the Treaty.
Nonetheless, in the evolution of Europe, the discussion provoked, the
enthusiasm generated, the idea crystallized by the Draft Treaty of Union
can in the long term only have a positive effect.

This commentary on the Draft Treaty is an essential aid for the
student of Community affairs; it will certainly provide a working document for future developments.

Preface

THIS commentary is offered both as a guide to the European Parliament's Draft Treaty establishing the European Union, and as an indication of the constitutional and legal issues raised by the task of developing the European Community beyond the stage reached under the existing Treaties.

We had the privilege, as a 'committee of jurists', of assisting the Parliament in the drafting of the Treaty. In the course of our work, we soon found that there were many questions of legal interest and importance which were not always obvious from the terms of the Treaty as it emerged. We have written this commentary so that those questions can be explored. We have sought to explain the provisions of the Treaty, giving some account of the reasons why the provisions were adopted, the legal difficulties to which they may give rise, and, at least in some cases, possible solutions.

We hope that our commentary will be of interest, not only in future work on this Treaty, but also to students of the European Communities and to those interested and engaged in their reform.

The commentary is a joint work: while each author has had initial responsibility for part of the work,[1] we have discussed the drafts together, have benefited from one another's contributions, and have endeavoured to reach agreed views.

We are grateful to the European Parliament for its assistance with the translation of our commentary.

F.C.
M.H.
F.G.J.
J.-P.J.

---

[1] F.C.: Articles 3–4, 30–2, 34, 42–54, 82–3; Conclusions.
  M.H.: Introduction, Section I; Articles 5-6, 8, 25–9, 33, 35, 63–9, 84–7.
  F.G.J.: Introduction, Section III; Articles 1–2, 7, 20–4, 55–62, 70–4.
  J.-P.J.: Introduction, Section II; Preamble; Articles 9–19, 36–41, 75–81.

Contents

Introduction

I. PLANS FOR EUROPEAN UNIFICATION IN AN HISTORICAL CONTEXT

A. Origins of the idea of unification

THE concept of European unification dates back in origin to the four-teenth century, when the medieval view of the world, with its more dynastic ideas of unity, was losing currency. The French lawyer, Pierre Dubois, is said to have drawn up the first plan for the political unification of Europe (1305-7).[1] Since then there have been at least 182 documented proposals for European unification,[2] but, until the end of the Second World War, there were none which specifically envisaged a federal union of states. The central aim was rather to establish a peace-ful association of European states.[3] The proposals of Abbé de Saint Pierre (*Mémoire pour rendre la paix perpétuelle en Europe*, 1713), Kant (*Zum ewigen Frieden*, 1795), and Johann Kaspar Bluntschli (*Die Organisation des europäischen Staatenvereins*, 1878) were limited in scope and adhered essentially to the concept of an association of states without recognizing the need for any more extensive limitation of national sovereignty.[4]

The First World War saw the break-up of Europe's power and supremacy. While it was also becoming separated ideologically from the Soviet Union, new plans were put forward for European integration. In his work *Paneuropa*, published in 1923, Count Richard Coudenhove-Kalergi argued in favour of a pan-European federation.[5] Together with Aristide Briand, the French Foreign Minister, he sought to put this project into effect. After a number of pan-European congresses, Briand

---

[1] On this and subsequent points, see Louis Cartou, *Organisations européennes*, 3rd edn. (1971), pp. xxxvi-xli; Denis de Rougemont, *Vingt-huit siècles d'Europe* (1961).

[2] Rolf H. Foerster, *Die Idee Europa 1300-1946: Geschichte einer politischen Idee* (1967), with a bibliography of 182 proposals for unification.

[3] Cf. A. Bleckmann, *Europäisches Recht*, 3rd edn. (1980), pp. 1 f. and Beutler/Bieber/Pipkorn/Streil, *Die Europäische Gemeinschaft-Rechtsordnung und Politik*, 2nd edn. (1982), pp. 28 ff.

[4] Cf. Léontin-Jean Constantinesco, *Das Recht der Europäischen Gemeinschaften*, i (1977), pp. 69 ff.

[5] Count Richard Coudenhove-Kalergi, *Paneuropa* (1923).

published in 1930 the most important proposal for European integration of the inter-war years: the Briand Memorandum.[6]

Briand's proposal was for a limited federal association of the states of Europe, with no encroachment on the sovereignty of its members. This proposal did not, however, receive any support from the other European states.

The economic and political role of the major powers of Europe was once again diminished by the Second World War. The new consciousness which fostered the idea of European union was essentially the result of the experiences of the war and the weakness of Europe in relation to the federations of the United States and the Soviet Union. There was growing uncertainty as to whether the individual sovereign states would be able to survive. This combination of circumstances provided a powerful stimulus to efforts to bring about European integration, which then, as now, were based on two differing principles.

The first five years after the end of the Second World War saw the conclusion of a number of treaties which provided for institutional co-operation between the European states in international organizations without affecting their national sovereignty (Western European Union, OEEC, North Atlantic Treaty, Council of Europe). Alongside this development were federalist proposals which called for the unification of Europe on a supranational basis.[7]

B. Treaties and draft treaties during the period 1951-70

The Treaty of 18 April 1951 establishing the European Coal and Steel Community (ECSC Treaty) marked the first step towards supranationality in the area of the present European Community.

Following the successful conclusion of this Treaty, several attempts were made to achieve closer union in the political field. Discussions on the European Defence Community (EDC)[8] began in 1951 and only after difficult negotiations was it possible to arrive at a compromise.[9] In

---

[6] Text in League of Nations, *Official Journal*, Special Supplement No. 75, *Acts of the Tenth Ordinary Session of the Assembly*, *Plenary Sessions* (1929), pp. 51 f.; see also Ellinor von Puttkamer, 'Der Briand-Plan: Vorbote der Europäischen Integration?', in *Festschrift für Carl Friedrich Ophüls* (1965), pp. 143-51.

[7] Cf. Cartou, op. cit., pp. xlii f.

[8] Treaty establishing the European Defence Community, published by the Press and Information Service of the Federal Government, 1952, pp. 5-60.

[9] Siegler, Heinrich, 'Europäische politische Einigung', *Dokumentation von Vorschlägen und Stellungnahmen, 1949-1968* (1968), p. 13, Doc. 21.

Article 38 of the Treaty establishing the EDC it was agreed that the controversial question of whether the long-term aim for the construction of Europe should be a confederation of states or a single federal state would be settled at a later stage by the 'ad hoc Assembly'. The Treaty establishing the EDC was signed in Paris on 27 May 1952 by the six Member States of the ECSC.

Encouraged by the signing of this Treaty, the Consultative Assembly of the Council of Europe proposed[10] to the Governments of the Member States of the EDC the drafting of a statute for a supranational political community. In their 'Luxembourg Decision' of 10 September 1952[11] the six Foreign Ministers of the ECSC Member States therefore called for the Assembly of the ECSC to draw up a draft treaty establishing a European Political Community (EPC) and to take as a basis, without prejudice to the provisions of the Treaty, the principles laid down in Article 38 of the Treaty establishing the European Defence Community. The proposals concerning the EPC and EDC were thus to a certain extent interrelated and could not be negotiated entirely independently. On 15 September 1952 the enlarged Assembly of the ECSC Treaty, consisting of seventy-eight members of the Common Assembly and nine appointed members of the Consultative Assembly of the Council of Europe, held its constituent meeting as the 'ad hoc Assembly'.[12] The drafting committee of this Assembly drew up the draft treaty on the statute of the European Community, which was adopted by the ad hoc Assembly at its final meeting on 10 March 1953.[13]

The basic aim of this draft treaty was to create a supranational European Community which would bring together the individual sectoral communities (Article 1).[14] The Community was thus intended to be an extension of the existing sectoral communities, the ECSC and the EDC. Article 56 specified that it would exercise the powers of the ECSC

---

[10] Text in Siegler, op. cit., pp. 16 f., Doc. 25.

[11] Text ibid., pp. 18 f., Doc. 29, section A, and in the *Digest of the Institutional Documents of the Community between 1950 and 1982*, published by the Committee on Institutional Affairs of the European Parliament (1982), pp. 48 ff.

[12] Siegler, op. cit., p. 21, Doc. 31.

[13] Text in Jurgen Schwarze/Roland Bieber (edd.), *Eine Verfassung für Europa* (1984), pp. 399–433, and in *Digest* (footnote 11), pp. 51 ff. See also Walter E. Genzer, 'Die Satzung der Europäischen Gemeinschaft', *Europa-Archiv* 1953, pp. 5653–64; Arthur H. Robertson, 'The European Political Community', *BYIL* 29 (1952), pp. 383–401.

[14] Cf. Hans-Ernst Folz, 'Das Modell der Europäischen Politischen Gemeinschaft von 1953/4', in *Rechtliche Probleme der Einigung Europas*, edited by Charles Zorgbibe, *Schriftenreihe des Institute fur Europäisches Recht der Universität des Saarlandes*, vol. 16, Series B: Dokumente (1979), p. 99.

and the EDC. The institutions of the European Community would also assume responsibility for the sectoral communities (Article 60). According to Article 57, the provisions of the Treaties establishing the sectoral communities would remain in force, subject, however, to any amendments necessary for adjustment to the organization of the European Community. The transitional period for integration was only two years (Article 59).

The institutions of the European Community (Article 9) were similar to those of the future EEC. There were, however, considerable differences in the provisions relating to the responsibilities of the Parliament and the Council. The Parliament of the EPC was to have two Chambers (Article 11). The Lower Chamber would consist of directly elected representatives of the Member States (Article 13), while the Upper Chamber would consist of senators elected by the national parliaments (Article 16). The Parliament would be empowered to issue laws, recommendations, and proposals, and to adopt the budget. It would also have extensive supervisory powers (Article 10). The main function of the 'Council of National Ministers' would be to ensure that the 'European Executive Council' and the governments of the Member States acted in harmony (Article 35). Both Chambers of the Parliament would be able to propose a vote of no confidence in the European Executive Council. If the motion was not carried by a qualified majority in the Lower Chamber, the European Executive Council could either resign or dissolve the Lower Chamber (Article 31). The Council would be responsible for the government of the Community. It would also have the power to propose legislation (Article 23) and the right to issue regulations required for the implementation of the laws of the Community (Article 53). In addition to the responsibilities acquired through the ECSC Treaty and the EDC Treaty, the Community was also to be responsible for the co-ordination of foreign policy and, in this connection, would be able to conclude international agreements which accorded with the aims and duties of the Community (Article 69). Article 82 specified that, in addition to the tasks allotted under the ECSC Treaty, the Community would also be responsible for the progressive development of a common market, based on the free movement of goods, capital, and persons.

With regard to finance, the European Community was to receive its own revenue from taxes, loans, and other income, together with contributions from the Member States (Article 77). While the ECSC Treaty was concluded for a period of fifty years and the EDC Treaty was to be concluded for the same period, Article 1 of this draft treaty specified that it was to be concluded on an 'irreversible' basis.

The draft treaty on the statute of the European Community was subsequently discussed at governmental level by conferences of the Foreign Ministers, and met with considerable resistance, as it was thought that it required the Member States to surrender too much sovereignty. It was this which gave rise to the demand for greater participation by the Member States in the formulation of Community objectives.[15]

At the same time the EDC Treaty was meeting with considerable opposition, particularly in France, because of continuing reservations about German rearmament and a further transfer of sovereign powers to a supranational organization. This was regarded as an unacceptable encroachment on national sovereignty. On 30 August 1954 the French National Assembly decided to postpone the discussions indefinitely, which meant in effect that the EDC Treaty was rejected.

As a result, the joint discussions on the European Community also had to be postponed indefinitely, since it was no longer possible to agree on a common political approach.

Efforts to achieve integration were not, however, abandoned. Following the 'relance européenne' of Messina (1955),[16] the Treaties establishing the European Economic Community (EEC) and the European Atomic Energy Community (EAEC) were concluded on 25 March 1957.

In the 1960s, efforts to achieve European political unity were resumed. In the Bonn Declaration of 18 July 1961[17] the Heads of State and Government of the EEC Member States expressed their readiness to bring about closer political co-operation and political unity. The Declaration itself provided only for regular meetings between representatives of the Member States and did not propose the establishment of institutions. It did, however, lead to the setting up of the Fouchet Committee, which was to draw up proposals for co-operation.

On 2 November 1961 the Fouchet Committee submitted to the governments of the EEC Member States the draft statute for a European Confederation of States.[18] It provided for the establishment of an indissoluble confederation of states, based on respect for the individuality of the peoples of the Member States. The draft no longer embodied the

---

[15] Ibid., p. 100.
[16] Digest (footnote 11), pp. 85 ff.
[17] Digest (footnote 11), pp. 97 ff. and in Heinrich Siegler, Dokumentation der Europäischen Integration, vol. 2 (1961-3), p. 10.
[18] Digest (footnote 11), pp. 103 ff. and in Siegler (footnote 17), pp. 43 ff.

'supranational' concept put forward in the 1953 draft of the *ad hoc* Assembly, but was intended essentially to provide an institutional basis for co-operation.[19] Its aims were common foreign and defence policies and co-operation in the areas of science, culture, and the defence of human rights, basic freedoms, and democracy (Article 2).

The institutions were the Council, the European Political Commission, and the European Parliament. The Council was composed of the Heads of State and Government of the Member States and had all decision-making powers. The European Political Commission was composed of senior officials of the Foreign Ministries, whose duty was simply to prepare and implement the decisions of the Council (Article 10). The European Parliament, which corresponded to the Assembly of the European Communities, was to have only powers of consultation and recommendation (Article 7). The statute made no mention of a Court of Justice. Provision was made for revision of the treaty after three years, with a view to strengthening the confederation (Article 16).

The Parliament of the European Communities approved the draft in principle on 23 November 1961, but criticized the absence of any supranational aspect. It considered that the Court of Justice of the European Communities should also be allocated responsibilities within the confederation and that the Parliament should have more extensive budgetary powers and the right to participate in the conclusion of treaties by the confederation.[20]

The draft was also examined by the Member States and, after discussions at governmental level, a second draft treaty establishing a confederation of states was submitted to the Fouchet Committee by the French representative.[21] The other delegations, however, were not prepared to accept the second draft as a basis for discussion.

No account had been taken of the proposals of the European Parliament and the other Member States and, furthermore, the responsibilities of the Council had been extended to include the economic sector, which meant that the Communities would have to surrender their responsibilities in this area. In view of this, on 25 January 1962 the other five

---

[19] Albert Bleckmann, 'Der Fouchet-Plan', in *Rechtliche Probleme der Einigung Europas* (footnote 14), p. 19.

[20] Siegler (footnote 17), p. 61, and Bleckmann (footnote 19), p. 20.

[21] Text in Schwarze/Bieber (footnote 13), pp. 436 ff, and in *Digest* (footnote 11), pp. 109 ff. See also Claus-Dieter Ehlermann, 'Vergleich des Verfassungsprojekts des Europäischen Parlaments mit früheren Verfassungs- und Reformprojekten', in Schwarze/Bieber, p. 275.

delegations submitted their own draft treaty.[22] This draft excluded the economic sector from the list of the Council's responsibilities and provided in particular for the financing of the confederation of states from its own revenue, the strengthening of Parliament through general direct elections, and the introduction of majority decisions in the Council.

No agreement could be reached between the Member States on these drafts and on 17 April 1962 the negotiations came to a standstill.

Although this meant the failure of another fundamental attempt at integration, further progress was achieved with the conclusion on 8 April 1965 of the Treaty establishing a single Council and a single Commission of the European Communities. The European Parliament in particular had called for this merger, following the establishment of a single Court of Justice and a single Parliament for all three Communities by an agreement of 25 March 1957.

C. Plans for amendment and further development of the Community Treaties

Following the failure of the Fouchet plans, there were no further proposals for fundamental revision of the Community treaties until the Spinelli initiative. The amending treaties of 22 April 1970 and 22 July 1975 simply increased the budgetary powers of the European Parliament and provided the Community with its own resources. Discussions on the nature of a future political union were continued on the basis of a number of reports and resolutions, some of them far-reaching.

The Werner Plan of 19 October 1970[23] put forward proposals for the gradual achievement of economic and monetary union, only one stage of which has so far been completed. At the same time, the heads of the political departments of the Foreign Ministries of the Member States drew up a first report on European Political Co-operation (EPC). This report, known as the Davignon Report and completed in Luxembourg on 27 October 1970, was drawn up on the instructions of the Heads of State and Government meeting in the Hague on 2 December 1969.[24]

The Vedel Report,[25] submitted on 25 March 1972 on the initiative of

---

[22] Cf. *Digest* (footnote 11), pp. 101 ff.

[23] Text in EC *Bulletin* supplement 11/1970, and in *Digest* (footnote 11), p. 150.

[24] Cf. with regard to the reports of 23 July 1973 (Copenhagen) and 13 October 1981 (London), *Europäische Politische Zusammenarbeit*, a publication of the Federal Government, 6th edn. (1982), pp. 31, 44, and 286.

[25] Report by the *ad hoc* working party on the extension of the powers of the European Parliament, 'Vedel Report', published by the Commission of the European Communities (1972).

the Commission, aimed to increase substantially the powers of the European Parliament, in view of the fact that the expanding competence of the Communities had caused the national parliaments to lose their powers, without those powers being replaced by any other form of democratic control. The report's main proposal was that Parliament should be given the right to participate in decisions within the Communities' competence in the areas of legislation, the budget, the appointment of the President of the Commission, and the ratification of treaties.

The Tindemans Report[26] of 7 January 1976 was drawn up on the instruction of the Heads of State and Government of the Member States who, following the summit conferences in Paris in October 1972 and in Copenhagen on 14 and 15 December 1973, had confirmed their common resolve to transform all their relations into a European Union by the end of the decade. The report contains a number of specific proposals to further the process of integration.

The Spierenburg Report[27] of 24 September 1979, drawn up on the instructions of the Commission, does not deal with the Communities as a whole but simply examines the internal structure of the Commission and its departments.

The report of the 'Three Wise Men',[28] which was submitted in October 1979 on the basis of instructions given by the European Council on 5 December 1978, discusses the functioning of the Community institutions within the framework of the existing treaties, in the light of the planned enlargement of the Communities to the south.

The European Parliament itself has repeatedly expressed opinions on the institutional development of the Communities and between 17 April 1980 and 18 February 1982 it adopted a total of eight resolutions providing a synopsis of its views on institutional matters (the step-by-step approach).[29]

The Draft European Act, submitted on 6 November 1981, represented a new initiative on the part of two Member States (the Genscher–Colombo Initiative).[30] It was originally intended to form the basis for a

---

[26] European Union, report to the European Council, EC *Bulletin* supplement 1/1976, and in Schwarze/Bieber (footnote 13), pp. 524 ff.

[27] Proposals for reform of the Commission of the European Communities and its services, published by the Commission (1979).

[28] Cf. *Digest* (footnote 11), pp. 392 ff.

[29] Cf. OJ No. C 234 of 14 September 1983, OJ No. C 66 of 15 March 1982 and OJ No. C 11 of 18 January 1982. Also in *Digest* (footnote 11), pp. 433 ff.

[30] Text in *Europa-Archiv*, No. 2, 1982, pp. D 50-5, and in *Digest* (footnote 11), pp. 460 ff.

treaty to be concluded by the Member States. The European Council was to assume central institutional importance as the controlling political organ within the framework of European union. In fact the initiative led only to the 'Solemn Declaration on European union' of 19 July 1983 (Stuttgart) which did not involve any obligations and failed to obtain the support of all the Member States in some important areas.[31]

On 9 October 1981, the French Government submitted a memorandum on the promotion and orientation of measures to revitalize the Community.[32] It did not propose any major institutional changes and concentrated on the socio-political sector. This memorandum also met with little response.

Before 1981, therefore, no significant action had been taken on any of the proposals and initiatives to further the progress of integration. Although the Merger Treaty had tightened the institutional structure and the Budgetary Treaties of 1971 and 1975 had increased Parliament's involvement in financial matters, no decisive step had been taken which would enable the Community to overcome its stagnation and enter a period of active integration. Before the end of its first term, the first directly elected European Parliament therefore had to consider whether a continuation of the step-by-step approach was likely to lead to success or if it should adopt a more global approach and draw up a more timely and forward-looking draft treaty on its own initiative.

II. THE ORIGINS OF THE DRAFT TREATY ESTABLISHING THE UNION AND ITS ADOPTION

Most of the Members of the European Parliament elected in 1979 probably had no idea at the beginning of their term of office that before the end of that term the Parliament would adopt a draft treaty establishing the European Union, which went beyond institutional reform and entailed a qualitative improvement in the process of European integration. Admittedly, Mr Willy Brandt had called, during the election campaign, for a European Constitution, but the newly elected Members were primarily concerned to fulfil the role assigned to them by the Treaties and remained detached from such considerations, even though some political

---

[31] EC *Bulletin* 6/1983, para. 1.6.1.
[32] EC *Bulletin* 11/1981, para. 3.5.1., and in *Digest* (footnote 11), pp. 470 ff.

groups had included institutional questions and the European Union in their programmes.[33]

Gradually, however, the Members of Parliament were persuaded of the inability of the existing structures to cope with the current problems of European integration and of the need for a comprehensive reform. In the exercise of their mandate they became convinced that, as matters stood, Parliament could not make a satisfactory contribution to the running of the Community, and also that the Council's operating methods prevented it from taking the necessary decisions.

The Community's inability to take decisions and the resumption of wheeling and dealing between governments, which seemed to threaten the very existence of the Community as an autonomous entity, were brought home to the Members of Parliament not just by the various turns taken by the budgetary disputes with the Council—which in fact had less to do with procedural matters than with the reform of the common agricultural policy and the question of the UK budget contribution—but also in the performance of their routine consultative duties.[34]

Altiero Spinelli described the situation as follows:

In other words, the existence of common problems is acknowledged, the need for common solutions is recognized and the ability to devise such solutions within a European political entity and a European administrative entity exists. However, so long as it favours and even gives pride of place to the individual national approach and encourages national consensus on the problems at hand, Community policy will make it difficult, if not impossible, to instil a European approach and fashion a European consensus.[35]

Just at the time when the draft Treaty was being prepared within Parliament, the difficulty of the negotiations and the disappointing content of the formal declaration on European Union issued by the European Council in Stuttgart finally convinced Members of Parliament of the futility of looking to traditional intergovernmental negotiation as a means of reviving the ideals of the Union.

However, the aspirations of Members would have come to nothing

---

[33] See J.-P. Jacqué, 'The institutional problem in the programmes drawn up by the political parties for the election of the European Parliament by direct universal suffrage', *Lo Spettatore Internazionale*, April–June 1978, pp. 131–42.

[34] Altiero Spinelli analysed the emergence of this conviction in his lecture to the European University Institute, Florence: *Towards European Union*, Jean Monnet Lecture, Florence, 1983.

[35] Op. cit., p. 16.

had there not been among them a group of men resolved to organize positive action. Before examining the various stages of the preparation of the draft Treaty within Parliament, we must call attention to the role played by the 'crocodile group'.[36]

A. The 'crocodile group'

The creator of this group was the spiritual father of the draft Treaty, Altiero Spinelli. Anti-fascist, founder of the European Federalist Movement, Member of the Commission of the Communities, Italian Deputy and, finally, Member of the European Parliament elected as an independent on the lists of the Italian Communist Party,[37] Altiero Spinelli was one of a small number of elected Members who were convinced from the outset of the need for Parliament to take the lead. On 25 June 1980, when it was clear that Parliament's strategy in rejecting the 1980 budget had failed, he sent a letter to Members and to the political groups or sub-groups with a positive attitude to European integration, proposing that a major debate should be held by Parliament on the institutional crisis of the Communities, that a working party should be appointed to prepare a draft institutional reform, that this should be debated and put to the vote in the form of a draft treaty, and that the national governments and parliaments should be formally recommended to adopt it. These proposals, which found favour with members of all the political groups, resulted in a meeting on 9 July 1980 of nine of the original supporters: Balfe (British Socialist), Giaotti de Biase (Italian Christian Democrat), Johnson (British Conservative), Key (British Socialist), Leonardi (Italian Communist), Lucker (German Christian Democrat), Visentini (Italian Liberal), von Wogau (German Christian Democrat) and, needless to say, Altiero Spinelli himself.

The group decided to call itself the Crocodile Club, a reference to the venue of its first meeting, a well-known Strasbourg restaurant, and to hold meetings thereafter during the part-sessions in a room used by Parliament in Strasbourg. Its discussions were to cover a variety of problems, the most important for the future being the choice between a return to the Treaties and the drafting of a new treaty. A minority of the Club's members believed that real progress could be made through

[36] For an appraisal of the events leading up to the draft Treaty, see P. V. Dastolis and A. Pierucci, *Verso una costituzione democratica per l'europa*, Marietti, Casole Monferrato, 1984.

[37] On the shaping of Spinelli's European ideals, see the first volume of his memoirs, *Come ho tentato di diventare saggio, io Ulisse*, il Mulino, Bologna.

a return to the application of the rules laid down by the Community Treaties, especially those applicable to voting within the Council, and that, for its part, Parliament should endeavour to take full advantage of the powers vested in it by the Treaties and pursue a policy which would slowly but surely broaden those powers. The view of the majority, however, was that the factors which had prompted a departure from the Treaty provisions would prevent a return to them, the best proof of this being that all past attempts to remedy the situation had failed. In particular, the proposals put forward in the report by the 'Wise Men' had had no practical effect whatever. To restore the decision-making capacity of the common institutions more fundamental reforms were needed, and these could only result from a new treaty.[38]

However, institutional change was not considered to be an end in itself. A reform of institutional procedures and practices had to be accompanied by a redefinition of the powers of the European Union, so that it would be possible both to bring existing policies to fruition and to develop new ones.

In the light of these considerations, the Crocodile Club, which now had seventy members, adopted, on 19 November 1980, a motion for a resolution calling on the European Parliament to prepare and adopt a draft reform and to submit it for ratification to the Member States. This motion was signed by 170 Members and debated by Parliament in July 1981. On 9 July 1981, Parliament decided to set up at the beginning of the second half of its term a committee on institutional affairs, with the task of modifying the existing Treaties.[39]

B. Preparation of the Draft Treaty establishing the European Union

This involved the following three exercises: establishing appropriate guidelines for reforming the Treaties, studying the content of the preliminary draft treaty, and preparing the draft treaty.

1. *Establishing appropriate guidelines for reforming the Treaties*

The committee, which consisted of thirty-seven Members reflecting the numerical strength of the groups, elected the Italian Socialist Mauro Ferri as its chairman. The vice-chairmen were Mr Jonker (Dutch Christian Democrat), Mr Nord (Dutch Liberal) and Mr Pannella (Technical

---

[38] On this matter, see *Le Parlement européen à la veille de la deuxième élection au suffrage universel direct: bilan et perspectives*, Bruges, De Tempel, 1984, particularly pp. 71-210.

[39] OJ No. C234 of 14.9.1981, p. 38. Resolution carried by 164 votes to 24 with 12 abstentions.

Co-ordination Group, Italy). Altiero Spinelli, assumed the duties of co-ordinating rapporteur.

The preamble of the resolution of 9 July entrusted the Committee on Institutional Affairs with a twofold task: to submit proposals for re-forming the functions of the Community and, hence, to submit propos-als for reforming the functions of its institutions. Institutional reform was a necessary consequence of a redefinition of the tasks of the Com-munity.

With a view to the successful completion of its mandate, the Com-mittee examined all previous plans for Community reform, which were brought together in a compendium of Community institutional docu-ments from 1950 to 1982.[40] It also took evidence from the President-in-Office of the Council (Mr Tindemans), the President of the Commis-sion (Mr Thorn), the Chairman of the Economic and Social Committee, and the Presidents of the European Trade Union Confederation, UNICE, and the European Movement.

On 6 July 1982, after six months' work, the committee submitted its general guidelines for the reform of the Treaties to Parliament, which accepted them.[41] The majority obtained was larger than in 1981 (258 votes to 37 with 12 abstentions). The resolution refers to the principle of subsidiarity, the yardstick adopted for the division of responsibili-ties between the Union and the Member States. This principle requires that 'the Union shall only undertake those tasks which can be executed more effectively in common than by the Member States separately, or those whose execution requires a contribution from the Union.'[42]

In this context, the broad objective must be to ensure that Member States' policies are compatible and convergent and to propose new initiatives:

— within the field of application of the existing Treaties;
— in economic policy and monetary policy;
— within the ambit of a policy for society, encompassing social, regional, environmental, cultural and information policy;
— in the fields of international relations and security.

The institutional reforms must preserve the Community structure but adjust relations between institutions, through the establishment of a new balance between them. In particular, there must be a fresh and

---

[40] Published by the European Parliament, Luxembourg.
[41] Resolution of 6 July 1982, OJ No. C 238 of 13 September 1982, p. 26.
[42] Ibid., paragraph 5.

more egalitarian sharing of powers between Parliament and the Council and a strengthening of the role of the Commission. The European Council must be brought into the institutional system, and the reforms must be based on the principle of the separation of powers and ensure democratic legitimacy and scrutiny of decisions.

The resolution concludes that all these modifications, which must preserve the Community patrimony, must form the basis of a series of proposals to be submitted to Parliament early in 1983 and subsequently embodied in a preliminary draft treaty to be submitted to Parliament in the autumn of 1983.

2. *Preparation of the preliminary draft treaty*

In the light of the guidelines mentioned above, the Committee on Institutional Affairs embarked on an exhaustive study of the relevant problems. To this end, rapporteurs were appointed for each of the main sectors identified by the committee:

- legal structure of the Union: Karel de Gucht (Belgian Liberal)
- economic policy: Jacques Moreau (French Socialist)
- policy for society: Gero Pfennig (German Christian Democrat)
- international relations: Derek Prag (British Conservative)
- finances of the Union: Michel Junot (French Gaullist), followed by Hans Seeler (German Socialist)
- institutions of the Union: Ortensio Zecchino (Italian Christian Democrat).[43]

The initial ideas and views of the rapporteurs were discussed at two meetings with experts in the autumn of 1982 at the European University Institute, Florence. The Committee on Institutional Affairs then examined the working documents prepared by each of the rapporteurs.

While the discussions ranged over many topics of differing importance, the subject most keenly debated was the institutional structure of the Union.

As far as the law of the Union was concerned, the focal point of the debate was the question of drawing up a charter of fundamental rights specific to the Union. This subject continued to be discussed right up to the point of the Treaty's final adoption, since, irrespective of the views put forward by its individual members, the committee found that it could not come up with a satisfactory body of provisions within the

---

[43] The working documents prepared by the rapporteurs are contained in Doc. 1-575/83/C.

excessively short time limits imposed upon it. The problem was auto-matically solved when it was realized during the final drafting stage that no final agreement could be reached on the matter, and it was accord-ingly entrusted to the organs of the Union (Article 4 (3) of the Treaty).

The discussions on economic policy were marked by disagreement between the rapporteur and the German Christian Democrats, who favoured economic liberalism. However, the approach finally adopted was not far removed from the principles enshrined in the existing Trea-ties.

As far as international policy was concerned, there was considerable support for the ideas evinced by the rapporteur, who proposed that the Union's activities should also be made to encompass political co-opera-tion but that, while preserving the present characteristics of such co-operation, there should be scope for development towards a more tightly-knit system.

As for the institutional issue, the provisions embodied in the draft Treaty are the product of a series of compromises: participation of the European Council and Parliament in the appointment of the Commis-sion; no change in the composition of the Council of Ministers, but the establishment of a single Council; balance between Parliament and the Council in the legislative procedure, with an active role being played by the Commission; maintenance during a transitional period of the right of a Member State to invoke its vital national interest, subject to the control of the Commission.

The various proposals put forward by the rapporteurs, brought to-gether by Altiero Spinelli in a motion for a resolution, were adopted on 5 July 1983 by the Committee on Institutional Affairs by 29 votes to 4 with 2 abstentions. The motion was submitted to Parliament on 14 September 1983 and adopted by 201 votes to 37 with 72 abstentions, those who abstained including the British Conservatives and the French Socialists.[44]

3. Drafting of the Treaty

In order to transform the resolution's 146 paragraphs into a draft treaty, Parliament appointed a committee of jurists, consisting of the four authors of the present text. In view of the prescribed deadlines, this committee set to work in July 1983, using as a basis the motion for a resolution drafted by the Committee on Institutional Affairs, but

[44] OJ No. C277 of 17 October 1983, p. 95.

reserving the right to amend its text in the light of the amendments adopted by Parliament.

The task of the committee was to give legal form to the proposals contained in the resolution and, where appropriate, to deal with specifically legal points, such as the question of the legal personality of the Union, to which Parliament had not given special consideration. In addition, it was required to assist the Committee on Institutional Affairs on the question of the entry into force of the Treaty, a matter not touched upon by the resolution of 14 September.

From October, the Committee on Institutional Affairs devoted its attention to an appraisal, article by article, of the text proposed by the Committee of Jurists. In this exercise, the rapporteurs and the members of the Committee of Jurists were entitled to submit their observations. The Commission was represented at the meetings of the Committee on Institutional Affairs.

At the end of this stage, each article of the resulting text was put to the vote. This involved an examination of countless amendments, but the Committee on Institutional Affairs had decided, on principle, to declare as inadmissible any amendment which appeared to call into question the content of the resolution of 14 September.

The final vote was taken on 13 December and the committee adopted the text by 31 votes to 2.

The plenary debate took place on 14 February 1984. Although many amendments were tabled (very few were adopted), only two key questions held the attention of the House. The first of these concerned the entry into force of the draft treaty following its ratification by a majority of States representing two-thirds of the total population of the Community. The compromise envisaged by Article 82, namely that entry into force would not be automatic, but would be on the date and in accordance with the procedure laid down by the States which had ratified the draft, was adopted by Parliament, despite the reservations of the Socialist Group. The second problem was to decide on the correct procedure once the draft had been adopted. The motion for a resolution had proposed that the draft be transmitted to the national governments and parliaments for approval by the national authorities. A compromise between all the political groups produced a more flexible arrangement, the European Parliament elected on 17 June 1984 being asked to gather together and take into account the observations and views of the national parliaments, in the expectation that the draft would then finally secure the support of all the Member States. This meant that, if necessary, the draft could be revised by its author, Parliament, with a view to facilitating the process of ratification.

In the light of the above considerations, Parliament adopted the draft by 237 votes to 31 with 43 abstentions.

III. GENERAL FEATURES OF THE TREATY

The first notable feature of the Treaty is that it is a single coherent structure. The European Community has developed piecemeal: the matters dealt with by the three legally distinct Communities (ECSC, EEC, EAEC) are each governed by a particular Treaty regime, and many important matters are dealt with outside the framework of those Treaties, on the basis of *ad hoc* co-operation. For many years efforts have been made, as outlined above, to develop the different systems into a European Union. The present Treaty boldly replaces the existing arrangements with a single and comprehensive constitutional text. It brings within a common institutional framework the affairs of the three Communities, the European Monetary system, European Political Co-operation, and a number of new policies.

The Treaty does not amend the previous treaties; instead, it makes a fresh start and creates a new entity. However, it takes as its starting point the 'Community patrimony', the *acquis communautaire*. Such provisions of the Community Treaties, of Community legislation, and of international agreements as are not amended or replaced by the Union Treaty itself remain in force until such time as they are modified under the procedures laid down in the Treaty. While the form is new, much of the substance is retained.

The institutional structure (Part Three of the Treaty) demonstrates a similar combination of continuity and change. The institutions of the Union include the Parliament, Council, Commission, and Court of Justice, corresponding to the four institutions of the Community; while the European Council, bringing together the Heads of State or Government of the Member States and the President of the Commission, becomes the fifth institution of the Union. But the powers of the institutions, and in some cases their composition and method of appointment, are altered so as to increase both the democratic character of the Union and the effectiveness of the decision-making process. Membership of the Union is limited to 'democratic' European States and the democratic quality of the Union is underlined by the increase in the powers of the directly elected European Parliament. The Council of the Union and the European Parliament constitute jointly the legislative authority. They also constitute jointly the budgetary authority, as is particularly appropriate, since the budgetary and fiscal powers of the Union (Part Five of the Treaty) are very great. The Parliament thus acquires legislative powers which it lacks in the Community system, and a great measure of control over the Union's finances. In both cases, its powers are shared with the Council. But, while the Council continues to exercise legislative and budgetary powers, it loses the ability to block development by inaction. Both the Council and the Parliament are required to act upon proposals within a specified time limit, after which the respective institutions are deemed to have approved the proposal in question. In addition, majority voting becomes the general rule in the Council, with a limited recognition of the national veto for a period of ten years. The composition of the Council is altered so as to introduce a greater degree of permanency in the representations of Member States.

The role of the Commission is strengthened and the method of its appointment altered; in addition, it is required to submit a programme acceptable to the Parliament before it takes office. The Commission retains the right of initiative;[45] it is given significant powers throughout the legislative procedure; and it becomes the sole executive body, having power to adopt subordinate legislation without the approval of the Council.

Taken together, the institutional arrangements will make the decision-making process more effective, while at the same time increasing the democratic accountability of the Union.

The Court of Justice retains the central constitutional functions which it has exercised under the Community Treaties; in certain respects its powers are increased, while provision is also made for its jurisdiction to be further enlarged. At the same time certain fundamental principles developed in the case law of the Community Court, notably the primacy and direct applicability of Community law, are entrenched in the Treaty, which expressly provides that the law of the Union shall be directly applicable in the Member States and shall take precedence over national law. In certain cases, the Treaty may be enforced by means of sanctions against Member States.

The legal system of the Union is designed to be more flexible than

---

[45] This right is shared, in certain cases, with the Parliament or the Council of the Union (Article 37 (2)).

that of the Community. The distinction made in the Community system between regulations and directives is replaced by a single type of Union law. However, the Treaty requires that laws should, as far as possible, restrict themselves to determining the fundamental principles, and entrust the responsible authorities in the Union or the Member States with setting out in detail the procedures for their implementation. The Treaty also allows differentiated application of laws during a transitional period. Special procedures are laid down for the adoption of organic laws.

Part Four of the Treaty, which sets out the policies of the Union, contains many notable departures from the Community Treaties. In contrast with the previous emphasis on economic questions, this Part contains three Titles of similar importance and similar length, dealing respectively with economic policy, policy for society, and international relations. Title I (economic policy) goes beyond the existing Treaties in a number of respects, incorporating the European Monetary System and a number of new sectoral policies, such as telecommunications and energy. Title II (policy for society) includes policies which are not expressly provided for in the Community Treaties, including consumer protection, the environment, education and research, and cultural policy. Title III (international relations) brings together matters previously handled separately under, for example, the common commercial policy and European Political Co-operation.

In every field of action, the Union is to act by one of two methods: either by common action, in the form of measures adopted by the Union institutions, or by co-operation, in the form of commitments undertaken by the Member States within the European Council. The Treaty determines, in every case, which of the two methods is to apply, and also makes provision for particular matters to be transferred from the method of co-operation to the method of common action.

While the Treaty confers greatly increased competences on the Union, in most cases the Union's competence is concurrent rather than exclusive. In fact, the only areas where the Union enjoys exclusive competence are, approximately, those where the EEC Treaty confers an exclusive competence on the Community. However, where the Treaty confers a concurrent competence, the Member States may no longer act once the Union has legislated.

Finally, the division of competences between the Union and the

Documents Quoted

Under the head *Preparatory documents*, before the commentary on each article, reference is made, as appropriate, to the following documents:

Resolution of 6 July 1982 on the European Parliament's position concerning the reform of the Treaties and the achievement of European union (OJ C238 of 13 September 1982, p. 25).

Document 1-575/83/B of 15 July 1983: reports on the substance of the preliminary draft Treaty establishing the European Union.

Document 1-575/83/C of 15 July 1983: working documents prepared by the rapporteurs and notes of Mr Spinelli, co-ordinating rapporteur.

Resolution of 14 September 1983 on the substance of the preliminary draft Treaty establishing the European Union (OJ C277 of 17 October 1983, p. 95).

Commentary on the Draft Treaty Establishing the European Union

Preamble

— With a view to continuing and reviving the democratic unification of Europe, of which the European Communities, the
  European Monetary System and European political co-operation represent the first achievements, and convinced that it is
  increasingly important for Europe to assert its identity;

— Welcoming the positive results achieved so far, but aware of
  the need to redefine the objectives of European integration,
  and to confer on more efficient and more democratic institutions the means of attaining them;

— Basing their actions on their commitment to the principles of
  pluralist democracy, respect for human rights and the rule of
  law;

— Reaffirming their desire to contribute to the construction of an
  international society based on co-operation between peoples
  and between States, the peaceful settlement of disputes,
  security, and the strengthening of international organizations;

— Resolved to strengthen and preserve peace and liberty by an
  ever closer union, and calling on the other peoples of Europe
  who share their ideal to join in their efforts;

— Determined to increase solidarity between the peoples of
  Europe, while respecting their historical identity, their dignity,
  and their freedom within the framework of freely accepted
  common institutions;

— Convinced of the need to enable local and regional authorities
  to participate by appropriate methods in the unification of
  Europe;

— Desirous of attaining their common objectives progressively,
  accepting the requisite transitional periods and submitting all
  further development for the approval of their peoples and
  States;

— Intending to entrust common institutions, in accordance with
  the principle of subsidiarity, only with those powers required
  to complete successfully the tasks they may carry out more
  satisfactorily than the States acting independently;

The High Contracting Parties, Member States of the European Communities, have decided to create the European Union.

Preparatory documents:

Resolution of 14 September 1983, points A to F and preamble.

The preamble to the Treaty seeks to give a formal definition of the Union by spelling out the objectives which are assigned to it and the principles which must underpin its activities.

1.   The first two recitals of the preamble contain both an acknowledgement of the progress made towards integration and an affirmation of the need to make further progress.

The need for Europe to assert its identity (first recital) was given greater weight by the resolution, which brought in Europe's relations with the great powers, the United States and the Soviet Union, its role in North-South relations and the importance of developing a specifically European political, economic, and social model of democracy. Hence, the identity of Europe must be strong enough to permit it not only to play a special role in international relations, but also to develop an original political model of democracy.

As the second recital shows, further progress is to be achieved through a redefinition of the objectives of European integration and an institutional reform based on a search for efficiency, coupled with respect for democracy. The fundamental objective of the authors of the Treaty is thus revealed: to create institutions capable of implementing new policies by democratic means.

The fourth, fifth, and sixth recitals enlarge on the ultimate objectives of European integration:

—To increase solidarity among the peoples of Europe while maintaining their diversity through the preservation of strong national structures. In this regard, a balance has to be struck between diversity and the loss of individuality likely to result from increased solidarity and common laws. From the legal point of view, this balance will be achieved through implementation of the principle of subsidiarity, but also by means of the active role to be played by the agencies representing the States within the common institutions. Increased solidarity will automatically open up the Union to the other peoples of Europe.

—Increased solidarity will promote peace and stability not just within Europe, but throughout the world. Hence the reference to the construction of an international society, an issue which is taken up and developed in the chapter on the international relations of the Union.

2. The preamble affirms that the Union shall be guided in its activities by the principles of pluralist democracy, respect for human rights, and the rule of law. These principles, which underpin the entire Treaty, figure predominantly in the provisions concerning human rights, the institutions and the rules governing judicial review. They are of fundamental importance, and only States which adhere to them may become members of the Union. They form the bedrock of the Union.

The preamble makes a more cautious reference to the need for appropriate local and regional authority participation in the unification of Europe. This requirement is scarcely touched upon in the body of the treaty, and the statement in the preamble is primarily intended as a reminder to the legislator that it must be taken into account in the legislation to be adopted.

The third principle, on the other hand, which states that the objectives of the Union must be attained progressively, is explicitly taken up by the provisions concerning the powers of the Union, for instance, those relating to the exercise of 'concurrent competence' (Article 12) and to the transition from co-operation to common action (Article 11). Furthermore, the principle that all further development shall be subject to the approval of the peoples and the States was taken into account by Parliament when drafting the clause on the revision of the Treaty (Article 84).

Finally, the principle of subsidiarity, which requires that the powers of the Union are subsidiary to those of the Member States and that, accordingly, the Union must only be entrusted with those tasks which it can carry out more effectively than the Member States, was of cardinal importance in determining the powers to be vested in the Union. It is applicable, for instance, where the Treaty confers 'concurrent competence' on the Union (Article 12); but it is fundamental to the entire Treaty.

PART ONE

THE UNION

Article 1

Creation of the Union

By this Treaty, the High Contracting Parties establish among themselves a European Union.

Preparatory documents:

Resolution of 14 September 1983, paragraph 2.

1. Article 1 of the Treaty is the corollary of the closing words of the preamble: 'The High Contracting Parties, Member States of the European Communities, have decided to create a European Union.'

The notion of a 'union' is found in the first recital of the preamble to the EEC Treaty, which states that the authors of that Treaty are 'determined to lay the foundations of an ever closer union among the peoples of Europe'. That reference to 'an ever closer union' itself recalls the preamble to the Constitution of the United States: 'We the people of the United States, in Order to form a more perfect Union, ... do ordain and establish this Constitution for the United States of America.'

However, it cannot be supposed that the term 'union' in the European context is used in the same sense as in the preamble to the Constitution of the United States; the term 'European Union' has acquired a significance of its own from proposals to develop the Community into a European Union.

The idea that the European Community should develop into a 'European Union' has been put forward in a variety of forms since the expiry of the 'transitional period' under the EEC Treaty on 31 December 1969. A Conference of Heads of State or Government meeting at The Hague in December 1969 called for the enlargement of the Community to be accompanied by the *'approfondissement'* of the Community and by the institution of an 'economic and monetary union',[1] but progress towards such a union has remained incomplete, the most significant step being the introduction of the European Monetary System.[2] A further

---

[1] *Third General Report on the activities of the Communities*, 1969.
[2] See below, Article 7 (4).

Conference of Heads of State or Government, held in Paris in October 1972, led to a further declaration on European Union,[3] embracing not merely economic and monetary affairs but the entirety of the relations between the Member States.[4] However, even in the European context, the term is not used in any precise legal sense, and politically also it is deliberately open-ended.

'The term "European Union", precisely because it is not specific, precisely because it implies movement in directions to be determined from time to time, is able to encompass Europe in a determination to build political unity in some form, but not necessarily in the image of existing constitutions.'[5]

However, the term 'union' does perhaps imply that the Union created by the Treaty is indissoluble; in any event, unilateral withdrawal by a Member State is excluded (as in the case of the European Communities).

2.   The formulation of Article 1, and the reference to the 'High Contracting Parties', are derived from the opening Article of each of the three Treaties establishing the European Communities (ECSC Treaty, Article 1; EEC Treaty, Article 1; Euratom Treaty, Article 1). However, the High Contracting Parties to the present Treaty are limited, as the closing words of the preamble make clear, to the Member States of the European Communities.

The Treaty is open for ratification, by virtue of Article 82, by all the Member States of the European Communities. The conditions of the entry into force of the Treaty are laid down by Article 82. Those conditions imply that the possibility of its entry into force is not excluded, even if not all the Member States of the European Communities ratify the Treaty.

Article 82 also makes it clear that the Treaty is not to be conceived as an amendment to the Community Treaties, and it is not intended to take effect by the procedures for amendments laid down in the Treaties establishing the European Communities (e.g. Article 236 of the EEC Treaty). Rather, the present Treaty is conceived as a new and independent treaty creating a new entity. While it takes over the Community patrimony (Article 7), it leaves open the question of the fate of the

---

[3]   Sixth General Report, 1972.
[4]   See above, p. 7.
[5]   Edmund Dell, letter to *The Times*, 1 November 1984.

European Communities if the Treaty enters into force without the participation of all the Member States.[6]

Once the Treaty has entered into force, and the European Union is thereby established, other States may accede under the conditions laid down in Article 2.

[6] See the commentary on Article 82.

Article 2

Accession of new members

Any democratic European State may apply to become a member of the Union. The procedures for accession, together with any adjustments which accession entails, shall be the subject of a treaty between the Union and the applicant State. That treaty shall be concluded in accordance with the procedure laid down in Article 65 of this Treaty.

An accession treaty which entails revision of this Treaty may not be concluded until the revision procedure laid down in Article 84 of this Treaty has been completed.

Preparatory documents:

Resolution of 14 September 1983, paragraph 13.

Provisions in force

ECSC Treaty, Article 98; EEC Treaty, Article 237; EAEC Treaty, Article 205.

1. Article 2 of the Treaty is based on Article 237 of the EEC Treaty. But, while the latter Article provides that 'any European State' may apply to become a member of the Community, only a 'democratic' European State may apply to become a member of the Union. The additional requirement reflects the existing practice of the Community. The requirement of a 'representative democracy' as an essential element of membership of the Community was affirmed by the European Council at Copenhagen on 8 April 1978.[1]

The commitment to democracy is reaffirmed in the preamble to the Treaty, which refers in the first recital to 'the democratic unification of Europe' and in the third recital to the commitment of the High Contracting Parties to 'the principles of pluralist democracy, respect for human rights and the rule of law'.

2. An important innovation is that any treaty of accession will be concluded between the applicant State and the Union, not, as under the

---

[1] See *EC Bulletin* No. 3/1978, pp. 5-6.

EEC and EAEC Treaties, between the applicant State and the Member States.

Article 237 of the EEC Treaty provides that an application to become a member of the Community shall be addressed to the Council, which shall act unanimously after obtaining the approval of the Commission. An accession treaty, after agreement between the Member States and the applicant State, then requires ratification by all the Contracting States in accordance with their respective constitutional requirements.

The present Treaty lays down entirely different procedures. In accordance with Article 65 (1), a treaty of accession will be negotiated by the Commission, under guidelines approved by the Council (Article 65 (2)). The Parliament will be kept informed (Article 65 (3)), and the treaty will be approved by the Parliament and the Council, both acting on an absolute majority (Article 65 (4)).

If the treaty of accession does not entail any revision of the present Treaty, it will not require ratification by the Member States. No revision of the Treaty will be required, for example, to enlarge the Union's institutions, since that will be done by organic laws (Article 34 (2)). Nor will revision be required to lay down the weighting of the votes of new Member States, since that will be done in the treaty of accession itself (Article 22).

If, however, the treaty of accession does entail a revision of the Treaty, then the draft amendment will be subject to the procedure laid down in Article 84, which requires that the draft must be approved by the Parliament and the Council, both acting in accordance with the procedure applicable to organic laws (Article 38), and that the draft thus approved must be ratified by all Member States.

It will therefore depend on the terms of the particular treaty of accession whether it can enter into force without ratification by all Member States.

Article 3

Citizenship of the Union

The citizens of the Member States shall *ipso facto* be citizens of the Union. Citizenship of the Union shall be dependent upon citizenship of a Member State; it may not be independently acquired or forfeited. Citizens of the Union shall take part in the political life of the Union in the forms laid down by this Treaty, enjoy the rights granted to them by the legal system of the Union and be subject to its laws.

Preparatory documents:

Doc. 1-575/83/A of 15 July 1983, p. 6.

Resolution of 14 September 1983, paragraph 4.

1. The concept of citizenship is generally defined as the bond between an individual and a state, although there are cases in which it has referred to certain unions of states (the British Commonwealth, for example). On the other hand, within the context of the European Communities the expression 'Community citizen' is already frequently used in an informal sense, that is, as an equivalent to 'citizen of one of the Member States', notably in connection with matters for which the approach adopted is based on that applied nationally (in particular, free movement of persons).

In the article under consideration, citizenship of the Union is acquired as a *status* formally recognized by Union law. The political importance of this status, however, far exceeds its legal significance. Politically, emphasis has been given to the idea that it is not only States but also their peoples who take part in the life of the Union, although the establishment of the Union requires a decision by the Member States. Clearly, the practical application of this idea is to be found principally in the election of Parliament by direct suffrage by the citizens of the Union (see Article 14). The legal position does not differ from that existing under Community law with regard both to the obligation to abide by the laws of the Union and to the enjoyment of the rights granted by these laws (insofar, of course, as they are directed only at citizens). It was perhaps because of the pre-eminence of the political aspect over the legal aspect that the resolution of 14 September 1983 dealt with this matter in the preamble.

2. That being so, the interpretation of the article does not raise any difficulties. The fact that the acquisition or loss of citizenship of a Member State is a prerequisite to the acquisition or loss of citizenship of the Union clearly indicates that each Member State retains unimpaired its fundamental freedom of choice between the various criteria (social or territorial) determining citizenship; in other words, Union legislation refers back in this matter to national legislation. The most important application of the right of citizens of the Union to participate in political life in the forms laid down by the Treaty is the right to elect the European Parliament. However, the electoral procedure will continue to be determined by national legislation, in accordance with the existing system, until an organic law is introduced laying down a uniform procedure (see Article 14, paragraph 2). The political rights of citizens explicitly laid down in the Treaty include that of addressing petitions to the Parliament (Articles 16 and 18). Although it is clearly the citizens of the Union who will be the principal holders of the other rights and obligations deriving from Union law, certain laws may also affect natural and legal persons who do not enjoy Union citizenship (for example the position of citizens of third countries living in the Union with regard to the rules on competition).

It is likely that the introduction of new Union legislation in the field of fundamental rights (in accordance with Article 4(3)) will in future increase the range of attributes characterizing citizenship of the Union. For example, in the context of its work on the special rights of European citizens, Parliament has frequently considered and called for the right to vote and to stand for election in national administrative elections in all the Member States. Connected with this is the question of equal treatment as regards access to public office, in the context of the various regional authorities below State level.[1] With a view to future agreements which realize these hopes, Article 46 states that national legislation should be co-ordinated, in accordance with the method of co-operation, 'to take measures designed to reinforce the feeling of individual citizens that they are citizens of the Union'. On the other hand, there are already unwritten rules on fundamental rights[2] and the vast majority of civil,

---

[1] See the Resolution of 16 November 1977 on the granting of special rights to the citizens of the European Community.

[2] See the commentary on Article 4 below.

social, economic, and cultural rights are conferred on all human beings, not only citizens.

Explicit reference is made to the citizens of the Union in other articles of the Treaty: Article 60, concerning education and research policy, whose aim is to 'create a context which will help inculcate in the public an awareness of the Union's own identity'; Article 61, concerning cultural policy, which provides for measures to 'promote cultural and linguistic understanding between the citizens of the Union'; and Article 62, concerning information policy ('The Union shall encourage ... access to information for its citizens').

f

Article 4

Fundamental rights

1.   The Union shall protect the dignity of the individual and grant every person coming within its jurisdiction the fundamental rights and freedoms derived in particular from the common principles of the Constitutions of the Member States and from the European Convention for the Protection of Human Rights and Fundamental Freedoms.

2.   The Union undertakes to maintain and develop, within the limits of its competences, the economic, social and cultural rights derived from the Constitutions of the Member States and from the European Social Charter.

3.   Within a period of five years, the Union shall take a decision on its accession to the international instruments referred to above and to the United Nations Covenants on Civil and Political Rights and the Economic, Social and Cultural Rights. Within the same period, the Union shall adopt its own declaration on fundamental rights in accordance with the procedure for revision laid down in Article 84 of this Treaty.

4.   In the event of serious and persistent violation of democratic principles or fundamental rights by a Member State, penalties may be imposed in accordance with the provisions of Article 44 of this Treaty.

Preparatory documents:

Doc. 1-575/83/B, De Gucht Report, p. 11.
Doc. 1-575/83/C, De Gucht working document, pp. 6-9.
Resolution of 14 September 1983, paragraphs 8-10 and 26.

1.   It should be noted at the outset that the undertaking to respect fundamental rights and freedoms has from the very beginning been one of the bases of the European Union and a constant concern of those seeking to foster it. For example, one of the points made in paragraph 4(a) of the European Parliament resolution of 6 July 1982 was that the tasks of the Union should be formulated with a view to the growing solidarity of its peoples 'in a context of respect for human (individual and

collective) rights and values and for democratic freedoms'. In addition, the third indent of the preamble to the Treaty states that the Contracting Parties should base their actions, when establishing the Union, 'on their commitment to the principles of pluralist democracy, respect for human rights and the rule of law'. However, the attempt to find the best way of ensuring that this undertaking was fully guaranteed raised considerable difficulties and revealed divergent opinions, leading finally to the compromise formula contained in Article 4.

Many Members of Parliament felt that the Treaty should have contained (or set out in an annex) a specific list of human rights intended, according to Mr De Gucht, rapporteur on the law of the Union, to provide the Union with the 'necessary legitimacy'.[1] In the course of his preparatory work, Mr De Gucht had already indicated all the rights to be included in the list, using as a basis for reference the European Convention on Human Rights, the European Social Charter, and the national constitutions. However, since this proposal did not obtain the necessary consensus (and indeed a different list was put forward by Mr van Aerssen), the resolution of 14 September 1983, apart from confirming the Union's commitment to protect fundamental rights, confined itself to stipulating that the Treaty should include civil, political, economic, social, and cultural rights, without actually specifying them. In the next phase of drafting the Treaty it was decided that, as set out in Article 4 (3), a declaration on fundamental rights would be adopted by the Union within five years of its entry into force, in accordance with the procedure for revision laid down in the Treaty. In the final debate, the plenary rejected an amendment seeking to delete the reference to this declaration, and a proposal for radical modification of Article 4, involving the addition of a detailed list of fundamental rights and freedoms (Amendment No. 29 by Mr Luster and others).

2.   There were essentially three factors which helped determine the majority decision. First, the protection of human rights in the Community has hitherto been based on unwritten principles derived from the Member States' constitutions and taking account of the European Convention. This approach, encouraged and developed by the European Court of Justice, was formally accepted by the other three institutions in the Joint Declaration of 5 April 1977. It may justifiably be questioned whether, given a flexible and balanced solution of this kind which has

---

[1] Doc. 1-575/83/C, p. 5.

proved satisfactory, it is really necessary to contemplate a different solution for the future. Second, the possibility of the Community adhering to the European Convention has been under discussion for a long time. For those who consider the principles of unwritten law to be inadequate, this would have the advantage of enshrining in a text which is already known and accepted by the Member States the protection of human rights at Community level (and in the future at Union level) and would render a new formulation of these rights unnecessary. Third, whenever an attempt is made to draft a new list—which must of necessity indicate not only the rights but also the limitations considered acceptable—delicate balances are called into question and the uncertainty inherent in the large number of laws to be applied is increased: there are countless national, European, and universal laws already in force. In this connection, it should not be forgotten that, in addition to the problem of the relationship between rules of different origin, there is that of the relationship between guarantee mechanisms of different kinds.

3. There is a further matter of major importance, which is on occasion resolved rather ambiguously. In the Community context, attention has been drawn to the need to protect human rights in connection with acts promulgated by the Community authorities or with the implementation of Community obligations, where these acts and obligations are not subject to national controls in relation to human rights. However, among those who have considered this problem in relation to Union law, there are those who favour a form of protection which, when applied to the citizens of the Union, would provide guarantees additional to those available at national or international level. These guarantees would include acts and obligations covered by national legislation and thus also by national mechanisms for the protection of human rights. The De Gucht report sought to distinguish between national and Union mechanisms, by providing that the fundamental rights recognized by the Member States, even if not recognized, wholly or in part, by the Union, would remain unaffected and, on the other hand, that the guarantees provided by the Member States' constitutions could not be invoked in relation to Union laws. However, what was not clarified was the question of fundamental rights which might be more fully recognized by the Union and which it was probably felt should also be applied even in connection with acts promulgated by national authorities or with legal relationships under national law.

In Parliament's resolution of 14 September 1983 (paragraphs 8, 9, and 10) it was not only the Union but also the Member States which undertook to protect fundamental rights. The different wording of Article 4, which places this obligation solely on the Union, in the context of its competences, suggests that a more restrictive view prevailed. Provisions for the protection of human rights adopted by the Union should not therefore interfere with the provisions in force in the Member States even if they are stricter in certain respects. Union and national provisions should coexist in accordance with the criteria which have hitherto governed the relationship between Community and national provisions in this delicate area.

4. Article 4 contains various provisions relating respectively to the direct protection of human rights by the Union, the possible accession by the Union to certain international agreements, and the future declaration to be made by the Union on this subject.

Direct protection is based on the common principles of the constitutions of the Member States and on the European Convention as regards civil and political rights, and on the Constitutions and the European Social Charter as regards economic, social, and cultural rights. The terminology used in Article 4 (1) is clearer than in Article 4 (2), in that it refers to rights and principles derived from the 'common principles' of the Member States' constitutions and not to rights derived from these constitutions. However, it should have been made clear that the Convention and the Charter are to be regarded only as a source of principles and that they are not binding on the Union as agreements.

In the first paragraph the reference to fundamental rights and freedoms apparently covers the whole range of human rights, but comparison with the second paragraph suggests that it in fact relates to the area dealt with in the European Convention (and thus primarily, though not exclusively, to civil and political rights). The undertaking to 'maintain and develop' economic, social, and cultural rights appears less clear-cut than the obligation to 'grant' the other fundamental rights, but the substance may be taken to be the same.

In addition to the European Convention and the European Social Charter, the draft on which Parliament's resolution of 14 September 1983 was based also mentioned the International Covenants on human rights as sources for the provisions on the protection of human rights. This reference was subsequently dropped from the resolution and from the draft Treaty. Article 4 (1) and (2) have thus not departed from the

line set out in the case law of the Court of Justice of the European
Communities.

Finally, it is important to note that the undertaking referred to in
paragraph 2 is subject to the limits of the Union's competence which
supports the notion that there should be no interference with national
provisions on economic, social, and cultural rights. This should also
apply to the rights covered by paragraph 1, which, however, merely
indicates those persons to whom the rights in question are to be granted
(persons coming within the jurisdiction of the Union). In the final
analysis, paragraphs 1 and 2 leave unanswered several textual questions
which, in view of the importance of the subject, should have been
resolved.

5. Under paragraph 3, the possibility of the Union acceding to the
European Convention on Human Rights, the European Social Charter,
and the two Covenants established by the United Nations in 1966, is
left open for a period of five years, within which a decision (for or
against) must be taken. Although the possible accession of the Communities to the European Convention has been fully discussed (and
firmly supported in resolutions of similar content adopted by the European Parliament and the Assembly of the Council of Europe), the possibility of its accession to the European Social Charter or the Covenants
has not so far been considered in depth.[2] Moreover, in order to give
effect to its desire to accede to these international agreements, the Union
will have to open negotiations with the existing parties to them and
discuss the changes needed to facilitate participation by an entity other
than a State.

The deadline of five years is also set for the adoption of a declaration
by the Union on fundamental rights. The wording suggests that the
'declaration' *must* be drawn up and since the procedure for revision
laid down in Article 84 must be followed, it therefore seems logical to
assume that the Commission will have to submit to the legislative authority a draft organic law if this has not been done previously by one
representation within the Council of the Union or by one-third of the
Members of Parliament. However, the draft will then have to be approved by the two arms of the legislative authority and ratified by all
the Member States (see Article 84) and there is no guarantee that either

---

[2] See, however, in connection with the 'integration' into Community law of the Cov-
enant on Civil and Political Rights, the European Parliament resolution of 16 November
1977, OJ C 299 of 12 December 1977, pp. 26-7.

of these two procedures would have a favourable outcome. On the other hand, the use of the word 'declaration' clearly does not imply that the document to be drawn up is to have no binding effect. On the contrary, the use of the revision procedure indicates that the aim is to introduce provisions modifying the Treaty and in particular Article 4.

6.   The obligation on each Member State to comply with the principles of democracy and to respect fundamental rights on its territory, that is, in relation to its inhabitants, is implied in paragraph 4, which provides for sanctions. Logically, any sanction presupposes an obligation, and in that sense the implicit function of Article 4 is as important as its wording. On the other hand, as mentioned above, the preamble affirms the Contracting Parties' commitment to the principles of pluralist democracy and respect for human rights. In essence, this 'commitment' must be understood as a specific obligation to behave in a manner consistent with these principles, an interpretation which becomes clear in the light of Article 4 (4).

This point having been clarified, it must be said that the sanction provided for in this paragraph simply results from the more general principle set out in Article 44, whereby any case of serious and persistent violation by a Member State of the provisions of the Treaty sets in motion the procedure leading to the adoption of the suspension measures described in that Article. The concept of 'serious violation' echoes the wording used by the United Nations to designate this category of offences ('flagrant and systematic violations of human rights') which, on a proposal from the Subcommission on the Prevention of Discrimination and the Protection of Minorities, are submitted to the Commission on Human Rights in the context of the procedure for examining individual statements, on the basis of Council Resolutions 728 F/xxviii and 1503/xlviii. Article 12 of the draft articles on the responsibility of states, adopted in part by the United Nations International Law Commission, contains a list of international crimes that includes *serious violations* of obligations of vital importance in safeguarding the fundamental interests of the international community.

Article 5

Territory of the Union

The territory of the Union shall consist of all the territories of the Member States as specified by the Treaty establishing the European Economic Community and by the treaties of accession, account being taken of obligations arising out of international law.

Preparatory documents:

Doc. 1/575/83/C, De Gucht working document, paragraphs 72-4.
Resolution of 14 September 1983, paragraph 5.

Provisions in force:

ECSC Treaty, Article 79.
EEC Treaty, Article 227.
EAEC Treaty, Article 198.
1972 and 1979 Treaties of Accession.

1. Article 5 defines the territory of the Union. The Treaty thus introduces a new term (German *Hoheitsgebiet*, French *territoire*). The Community treaties contain provisions specifying the geographical area of their application. This difference in terminology does not represent any qualitative strengthening of the law of the Union by comparison with Community law. The Union does not have its own territory in the sense that a State does. The 'territory' still refers to the area over which the Union has authority and within which the law of the Union is valid and must be applied. The identity of the Union as a subject of international law is, however, underlined in Article 5, and in Articles 3 (Citizenship) and 6 (Legal personality), since its own territory is attributed to it and the field of application of the Treaty is not simply defined by reference to the territories of the Member States.

   In the Federal German Constitutions of 1871 (Article 1) and 1919 (Article 2) the 'Federal area' or 'Reich area' is defined, as in this case, as the total area of all the German Länder, whereas Article 23 of the Basic Law of 1949 simply defines its area of validity but does not speak of a distinct federal area. The distinction is not important in the present case.[1]

The change in terminology by comparison with Article 227 of the EEC Treaty is not, however, intended to give the Union a pre-federal character. The decisive element here is the nature of the power of the Union.

In a federal state the federation has the power to alter its external frontiers. This is not true of the European Union under the present Treaty. The Member States continue to have the exclusive power to determine or alter the frontiers of their territories. In this respect also, Article 5 does not bring about any change in the existing legal situation. The extent of the territory of the Union depends on the extent of the territories of the Member States. If the Member States alter their frontiers, the territory of the Union is altered accordingly. The *'principle of moveable treaty limits'* which follows from Article 29 of the Vienna Convention on the Law of Treaties[2] thus applies in theory. It will remain a matter of controversy whether the Member States are entitled to alter their frontiers as they wish and at what point such alterations may affect their membership of the Community or the Union.[3] In short, Article 5 does not specify that the Union will assume the authority of a State; it does, however, emphasize the independence of its sovereign power under international law.

2.   Article 5 contains a twofold definition of the territory of the Union. It first refers to the territories of the Member States but then limits these to those territories 'specified' by the EEC Treaty and the treaties of accession.

Article 227 of the EEC Treaty specifies that the Treaty applies to the Member States. The Treaty lays down special rules concerning the overseas departments and specifically mentions overseas countries and territories (Annex IV). The accession treaties, which in any case extend the territory by the territories of the acceding States, also contain special territorial provisions. Reference to Article 198 of the EAEC Treaty and

---

[1] It relates to the recognition in the Basic Law of the special situation regarding the unresolved German question; see Maunz in Maunz-Durig, *Grundgesetz* (1962 ed.), Article 23.

[2] 'Unless a different intention appears from the treaty or is otherwise established, a treaty is binding upon each party in respect of its entire territory.'

[3] See, with regard in particular to the withdrawal of Greenland, the commentaries on Article 227 of the EEC Treaty, e.g., J. Thiesing in H. von der Groeben *et al.*, *Kommentar zum EWG-Vertrag*, 3rd ed. (1983), Article 227, points 66 ff.

Article 79 of the ECSC Treaty is unnecessary since they are the same in content as Article 227 of the EEC Treaty. They refer to the territories of the Member States, whereas Article 227 of the EEC Treaty is addressed to each of the Member States as a subject of international law. Article 227 of the EEC Treaty thus states more clearly that the Treaty applies at all times to all existing territories of the Member States, independently of any changes that may be made in their frontiers.[4]

While Article 5 adopts the definition contained in Article 227 of the EEC Treaty by its reference to that Treaty, it also makes explicit mention of 'all the territories ... specified' in the treaties in question. This provision should not, however, be interpreted as referring only to the status quo existing at the time of the entry into force of the Treaty; as shown above, it refers, like the previous Community treaties, to the entire territories of the Member States at any given time.

This interpretation is confirmed by the addition of the phrase 'account being taken of obligations arising out of international law'. This addition was not intended to suggest that Member States could consider making territorial changes which would run counter to their obligations under international law and that such changes should therefore be excluded. As was made clear during the preparatory work, the phrase relates to the maritime and air space included in the territories of the Member States. Paragraph 5 of the resolution of 14 September 1983 gives explicit clarification of this point. Such clarification, however, seemed unnecessary in the text of the Treaty. There is no longer any doubt that existing Community law applies to all the territories and maritime and air space over which the Member States exercise sovereignty under the provisions of international law. This principle will also apply to the law of the Union.

[4] With regard to the principle of moveable treaty limits, see J. Thiesing, op. cit., Article 227, point 23.

Article 6

Legal personality of the Union

The Union shall have legal personality. In each of the Member States, the Union shall enjoy the most extensive legal capacity accorded to legal persons under national legislation. It may, in particular, acquire or dispose of movable and immovable property and may be a party to legal proceedings. In international relations, the Union shall enjoy the legal capacity it requires to perform its functions and attain its objectives.

Preparatory documents:

None.

Provisions in force:

ECSC Treaty, Article 6.
EEC Treaty, Articles 210 and 211.
EAEC Treaty, Articles 184 and 185.

1. Article 6 sets out, in Title 1—the introductory Title—of the Treaty, an essential characteristic of the Union: the Union shall possess its own legal personality. It is to be an independent legal entity. The Union will therefore take over the legal position of the previous three Communities, on each of which the Treaties conferred a separate legal personality. The foundation of the Union will lead to a fusion of the three previous Communities. The Treaty hereby achieves the declared aim of the Member States, set down in the April 1965 Merger Treaty, to effect the unification of the three Communities. The institutions provided for in the Treaty will therefore act on behalf of a legal entity—the European Union.

The Union's legal personality is distinct from that of the Member States. The Union is to exist as an independent legal personality alongside the Member States. Like the Member States, it may have its own rights and obligations. As has been the case hitherto, the legal personality of the Union will be limited as to its functions: it may operate only in the limited framework allotted to it by the Member States. A distinction should be made here between three separate legal spheres of operation for the Union's legal personality: international relations, the legal order created by the Union, and the legal orders of Member States.

It may be argued that, logically, the acknowledgement of a separate legal personality and the definition of the legal nature of the Union should have been placed at the beginning of the Treaty. However, Article 6 is largely of a technical legal nature, and the basic provisions concerning Members of the Union, the rights of its citizens, and its sovereign territory were therefore placed at the beginning on the model of the previous Treaties.

2.   The opening sentence of Article 6 refers not only to the legal personality of the Union in respect of international law, as Article 210 of the EEC Treaty is frequently represented as doing;[1] rather, the Union is comprehensively accorded legal capacity to act as an independent legal entity in any legislation provided for, explicitly or implicitly, in the Treaty. It is clear from the Treaty that the sphere of competence of this legal personality is limited compared with that of individual Member States; but this is the case with all international organizations.

The second and third sentences define more closely the legal capacity attached to the Union's legal personality with regard to the legal orders of Member States.

The fourth sentence defines the legal capacity of the Union in international relations. The Union can also act as a separate legal personality in the legislation it itself creates, i.e. it can establish rights and obligations with regard to its employees or other legal entities of the Union.[2]

3.   The second and third sentences are similar in content to Article 6 (3) of the ECSC Treaty, Article 211 of the EEC Treaty, and Article 185 of the EAEC Treaty. The differences in the wording are insignificant. Parliament considered it appropriate that the text of the Treaty should state clearly that the Union should enjoy legal capacity in the national legal orders, even if this meant some repetition of the Community patrimony.

4.   The fourth sentence is new and is found neither in the EEC Treaty nor in the EAEC Treaty. However, it is similar in substance to the second paragraph of Article 6 of the ECSC Treaty. (The term *inter-*

---

[1] See J. Schwarze in H. von der Groeben *et al.*, *Kommentar zum EWG-Vertrag*, 3rd edn. (1983) vol. 2, Article 210, point 5.
[2] See Article 33 of the Treaty.

nationale Beziehungen' (international relations) is more comprehensive than the term *'zwischenstaatliche Beziehungen'* (relations between States) which appears in the German text of the ECSC Treaty.) It is designed to promote the recognition and effectiveness of the Union's legal capacity in international relations.

5.   Article 6 does not refer to the question of the representation of the Union, hitherto dealt with both in the fourth paragraph of Article 6 of the ECSC Treaty and the second sentence of Article 211 of the EEC Treaty. Under the former, the Community as a whole is to be represented by all its institutions, 'each within the limits of its powers'; the two other Community Treaties refer solely to Community representation by the Commission. However, the context indicates that this representation by the Commission applies only to action by the Communities in the national legal systems of the Member States and not in other legal systems. The notion of exclusive representation by the Commission is belied by Community budgetary practice, whereby the other institutions are entitled to implement their own individual sections of the budget;[3] there are differences also as regards staff regulations and liability,[4] with the result that these three Community Treaties do not differ significantly on this matter despite the fact that they contain differing provisions regarding powers of representation.

The Treaty of Union does not define the powers of representation of the institutions. It is not possible to draw a meaningful conclusion from a comparison between the Community Treaties and Article 6. The legal situation which has prevailed so far will remain in force by virtue of Article 7 until the institutions of the Union introduce regulations establishing a standard procedure for representation (see Article 7 (3)).

---

[3] See Article 18 (2) of the Financial Regulation of 21 December 1977, OJ L 356 of 31 December 1977, p. 1.

[4] See J. Grunwald in H. von der Groeben *et al.*, *Kommentar zum EWG-Vertrag*, 3rd edn. (1983) vol. 2, Article 211, points 26 ff.

Article 7

The Community patrimony

1. The Union shall take over the Community patrimony.

2. The provisions of the treaties establishing the European Communities and of the conventions and protocols relating thereto which concern their objectives and scope and which are not explicitly or implicitly amended by this Treaty, shall constitute part of the law of the Union. They may only be amended in accordance with the procedure for revision laid down in Article 84 of this Treaty.

3. The other provisions of the treaties, conventions and protocols referred to above shall also constitute part of the law of the Union, in so far as they are not incompatible with this Treaty. They may only be amended by the procedure for organic laws laid down in Article 38 of this Treaty.

4. The acts of the European Communities, together with the measures adopted within the context of the European Monetary System and European Political Co-operation, shall continue to be effective, in so far as they are not incompatible with this Treaty, until such time as they have been replaced by acts or measures adopted by the institutions of the Union in accordance with their respective competences.

5. The Union shall respect all the commitments of the European Communities, in particular the agreements or conventions concluded with one or more non-member States or with an international organization.

Preparatory documents:

Resolution of 14 September 1983, paragraph 21.

1. Article 7 (1) provides that the Union shall inherit the 'Community patrimony' ('*acquis communautaire*'). This term has been used to indicate the entire corpus of Community law and practice; certain aspects of the Community patrimony, both within and beyond the limits of the

Community Treaties, are spelt out in subsequent paragraphs of Article 7.

The notion of *'acquis communautaire'* was central to the successive enlargements of the Communities: it denoted the acceptance by the acceding States not only of the formal obligations of the Community treaties and Community legislation, but also 'in a more general way, of all matters which under different headings embrace the work of the Communities since their inception'.[1]

Although the term *'acquis communautaire'* was not used in the successive accession treaties, the idea it denotes is embodied in them: see, for example, Part One of the Act of Accession annexed to the Treaty of 22 January 1972.

2.   Article 7 (1), which provides in broad terms that the Union shall take over the Community patrimony, is a fundamental provision of the Treaty. While paragraphs 2, 3, and 4 of Article 7 correspond to paragraph 21 of the Resolution of 14 September 1983, paragraph 1 of Article 7 is new. In the Resolution, a general introductory paragraph in the section on the economy (paragraph 29) and individual paragraphs dealing with the Policy for Society (paragraphs 58–65) envisaged that the Union would proceed 'starting from the Community patrimony'. The same idea is found in Article 45 (1) of the Treaty, which deals generally with all of the policies of the Union. Article 45 is the first Article of Part Four of the Treaty ('The Policies of the Union'). But Article 7 makes it clear that the Community patrimony underlies the entire Treaty.

Various components of the Community patrimony are dealt with in paragraphs 2–5 of Article 7. Paragraphs 2 and 3 deal with the treaties establishing the Communities and the conventions and protocols relating thereto. Paragraph 4 deals with the legislation and other measures adopted by the Community institutions, and also with the measures adopted within the context of the European Monetary System and European Political Co-operation. Paragraph 5 deals with the Community's commitments, including commitments to third States.

3.   Article 7 (2) and (3) must be understood as covering the basic constitutional texts of the European Communities. These include, as well as the Treaties establishing the three Communities and the Protocols

[1] See J.-P. Puissochet, *The Enlargement of the European Communities* (1975), pp. 28 ff.

annexed to them, the treaties amending those Treaties (the Merger Treaty of 8 April 1965, the Budgetary Treaties of 22 April 1970 and 22 July 1975, and the Accession Treaties of 22 January 1972 and 28 May 1979). The term 'conventions' in Article 7 (2) and (3) certainly includes the convention on certain Institutions common to the European Communities (25 March 1957); but it is not entirely clear whether it covers the conventions concluded among Member States pursuant to Article 220 of the EEC Treaty, notably the Brussels Convention of 27 September 1968 on Jurisdiction and Enforcement of Judgments in Civil and Commercial Matters as amended by the Convention of Accession of 9 October 1978. Probably, however, the latter Conventions could be amended by the Contracting States, without the use of the procedure for revision of the Treaty or the procedure for organic laws prescribed by Article 7 (2) and (3) respectively.

A fundamental distinction is made in paragraphs 2 and 3 of Article 7 between those provisions of the Community treaties which concern their objectives and scope (Article 7 (2)) and the other provisions of those treaties (Article 7 (3)). The former can be amended only in accordance with the revision procedure laid down in Article 84; the latter can be amended by the procedure for organic laws laid down in Article 38. Thus the former provisions are 'entrenched' and have the same status as the present Treaty; the latter provisions can be more easily amended.

It may not always, however, be readily apparent which provisions of the Community treaties fall into each category. A clear example of a provision concerning the objectives of the Communities is Article 2 of the EEC Treaty: but that Article is replaced by Article 9 of the present Treaty. Provisions which concern the scope of the Community Treaties are those delimiting their scope *ratione loci*, *ratione temporis*, and *ratione materiae*. However, Article 227 of the EEC Treaty, which appears to delimit the scope of that Treaty *ratione loci*, is replaced by Article 5; and Article 240 of the EEC Treaty (scope *ratione temporis*) is repeated by Article 87.[2] As for the material scope of the Community treaties, the question is not free from difficulties. By way of example, Article 48 (4) of the EEC Treaty provides that that Article shall not apply to employment in the public service. It does not seem to follow, however, that employment in the public service is outside the scope of that Treaty and could be brought within the present Treaty only by the revision

[2] See the commentaries on Articles 5 and 87.

procedure. Article 48 (4) merely recognizes that a Member State may restrict access to its public service by nationals of other States. It does not preclude, for example, measures to achieve equality of access for men and women. (Compare Article 55, paragraph 1 and Article 222 of the EEC Treaty; in each case, different considerations will be relevant, but with similar results.) It is not easy to see which are the provisions concerning the material scope of the Treaties which can be amended only by the revision procedure.

Any dispute over the status of a particular provision of the Community patrimony is likely to fall within the jurisdiction of the Court of Justice: see Article 30 (1) and Article 43 of the Treaty. A proposal within the Institutional Committee to make express provision for the jurisdiction of the court in such a case was rejected on the ground that it was superfluous: such jurisdiction was necessarily implied. However, it may be desirable for the Court to rule in advance on the question whether a provision of a Community Treaty falls under Article 7 (2) or under Article 7 (3) so that the appropriate amendment procedure can be used: possibly the necessary jurisdiction could be conferred on the Court pursuant to Article 43.

4.   Article 7 (4) preserves all 'acts' of the European Communities, a term which embraces both acts of the institutions (e.g. acts falling within Article 189 of the EEC Treaty and acts *sui generis*) and acts of a political character of the Community itself (declarations, resolutions, etc.), again insofar as they are not incompatible with the draft Treaty, but envisages their eventual replacement by acts of the institutions of the Union.

The same applies to measures adopted within the context of the European Monetary System and European Political Co-operation: both those systems, which have been developed by the Member States of the European Communities outside the framework of the Community Treaties, are fully integrated within the Union, and the competences of the Union institutions extended to adopt or amend them as necessary.

The incorporation of the European Monetary System and European Political Co-operation within the framework of the Union is one of the principal features of the Treaty. The Treaty thus removes the somewhat arbitrary distinctions affecting the Community system between those matters which fall within the competence of the Community institutions under the Community Treaties and those matters for which the Member States retain their competence but exercise their competences jointly.

The European Monetary System is specifically provided for by Article 52: see the commentary on that Article. European Political Co-operation falls within Part Four, Title III, 'International Relations of the Union'. The experience of the Community has shown that the attempt to distinguish between international relations generally, which have been handled on the intergovernmental level, and economic and commercial relations between the Community and third States, dealt with by the Community institutions, leads to artificial and impractical distinctions. Within the Union an integrated and coherent system should be possible.

5. Article 7 (5) provides for the Union to respect, *inter alia*, the network of agreements concluded by the Communities with third States. The text does not envisage that the Union will formally succeed to the rights and obligations of the Communities under those agreements, but the eventual replacement of the Communities by the Union will have that result by operation of law, without any express provision being required. However, the question was not dealt with expressly because of the possibility that the Treaty will enter into force among some of the Member States, which would not entail *ipso facto* the disappearance of the Community (see Article 82).

Consequently Article 7 (5) does not involve the controversial doctrine of State succession to treaties (as to which see the 1978 Vienna Convention on Succession of States in Respect of Treaties), a doctrine which it is even more difficult to apply to international organizations, if the Union can be so regarded. In many cases, however, it will probably be correct to treat the Union as having taken over the functions of the Community, just as the Community has taken over the functions of Member States in some areas, e.g. the GATT. In Cases 21-4/72 *International Fruit Company* [1972] ECR 1219, the Court held that the provisions of the GATT were binding on the Community, since the Community had assumed the powers previously exercised by the Member States: a doctrine of substitution rather than succession. The doctrine of substitution will apply equally to the Union insofar as it takes over the functions of the Community.

Article 7 (5) refers to 'all the commitments of the European Communities, in particular the agreements concluded with one or more non-member States or with an international organization'. Other commitments which devolve on the Union include:

(i) agreements which have not been concluded by the Community

Article 8

Institutions of the Union

The fulfilment of the tasks conferred on the Union shall be the responsibility of its institutions and its organs. The institutions of the Union shall be:

— The European Parliament,
— The Council of the Union,
— The Commission,
— The Court of Justice,
— The European Council.

Preparatory documents:

Resolution of 14 September 1984, paragraph 16.

Previous texts:

ECSC Treaty, Article 7.
EEC Treaty, Article 4.
EAEC Treaty, Article 3.

1. In the first, introductory part of the Treaty, Article 8 summarizes the organizational structure of the Union and specifies that the institutions and organs of the Union are responsible for fulfilling the tasks conferred on the Union. The inclusion of the European Council is a new feature. The structure and responsibilities of the individual institutions are described in more detail in the third part of the Treaty (Articles 14 ff.). The choice of the term 'institutions' is consistent with the terminology used in the previous treaties, except in the case of the German text ('*Organe*' in Article 4 of the EEC Treaty). The adjustment of the German text will avoid the previous possibility of confusion with secondary organs and bodies.[1]

2. The first sentence of Article 8 did not appear in the European Parliament's resolution of 14 September 1983 (paragraph 16). This sentence refers to the specific allocation of tasks and corresponds to the

[1] See the commentary on Article 33 below.

first sentence of Article 4 of the EEC Treaty. The wording in German differs only in respect of the term *Übertragung* (transfer). It would have been more appropriate to refer, as in the past, to the *Zuweisung* (conferment) of tasks, which excludes the possible interpretation that these tasks were originally tasks of the Member States. The correct term should therefore be *Zuweisung* rather than *Übertragung*.

3.   Article 8 differs in a number of respects from the corresponding provisions of the three Community Treaties. Article 8 lacks the final sentence of Article 4 (1) of the EEC Treaty which specifies that each institution shall act 'within the limits of the powers conferred on it by this Treaty'. This rider seemed unnecessary since the powers of each of the institutions are defined by the provisions contained in Articles 14 ff. Nor is the principle of specific competence, which was inferred, *inter alia*, from the wording of Article 4 (1) of the EEC Treaty, called into question by this shorter text. Only the tasks provided for in the Treaty may be carried out by the institutions of the Union. The adoption of the Community patrimony, provided for in Article 7 (1), also safeguards the general legal principles which have already been established, including the principle that the institutions may not act outside the limits of the tasks conferred upon them.

The other organs of the Union referred to in Article 8 are described individually in Article 33. (In the German texts, the term *'Einrichtungen'* is used, rather than *'Organ'*, since some of the bodies have their own legal personality.) The specific mention of the Economic and Social Committee and the Court of Auditors in Article 4 (2) and (3) of the EEC Treaty seemed unnecessary.

4.   The legal significance of Article 8 is limited, but it provides more than just an overall summary.

First, the separation of the institutions from the other organs (Article 33) is important. The distinguishing features of the *institutions* are their participation in the external affairs of the Union, their independence, autonomy, and leading position, and the scope of their responsibilities, which encompass almost all the tasks of the Union. This combination of distinguishing features is not shared by any of the organs listed in Article 33 or yet to be created.

The European Parliament appears first on the list of institutions. This reflects the fact that Parliament occupies a prominent position as the only institution with direct democratic legitimation. Because of its democratic basis it should represent the identity of the Union. In paragraph 137 of the resolution of 14 September 1983 this particular feature was attributed to the European Council (see Article 31 of the Treaty).

The inclusion of the European Council in the list of institutions means that in principle it is subject to all the provisions of the Union relating to the institutions. It remains to be seen whether the provisions concerning the seat, staff, budget, and financial control, *inter alia*, are applied to the European Council in practice. This need not automatically be the case.

Article 8 indicates that the power of the Union is shared among a number of institutions. Their relative importance in the decision-making process can be determined only by reference to Articles 14 ff. concerning the allocation of tasks and responsibilities. The order in which they are listed reveals nothing in this respect. Underlying this distribution of the Union's power among several institutions is the unwritten requirement of fair co-operation. It would not be possible to exercise the Union's power satisfactorily if the individual institutions did not take into account, when carrying out their tasks, the responsibilities of the other institutions. Their internal autonomy and separate responsibilities do not free them from the obligation to do everything in their power to contribute to the joint working of all the institutions. Inter-institutional agreements are still possible and necessary in certain cases for as long as the relative powers of the institutions laid down in Articles 14 ff. are not altered.

The allocation of the Union's tasks to the institutions could also imply that responsibilities may not be delegated, either to the Member States or to other organizational units of the Union. Only the institutions and organs are authorized to carry out the tasks. Under this provision it is possible to transfer power, where necessary, to organs or other subsidiary organizational units only if measures are taken to ensure that responsibility for carrying out the tasks and for supervision remains with the institutions concerned.

PART TWO

THE OBJECTIVES, METHODS OF ACTION, AND COMPETENCES OF THE UNION

Article 9

Objectives

The objectives of the Union shall be:

— the attainment of a humane and harmonious development of society based principally on endeavours to attain full employment, the progressive elimination of the existing imbalances between its regions, protection and improvement in the quality of the environment, scientific progress, and the cultural development of its peoples,

— the economic development of its peoples with a free internal market and stable currency, equilibrium in external trade, and constant economic growth, without discrimination between nationals or undertakings of the Member States by strengthening the capacity of the States, their citizens, and their undertakings to act together to adjust their organization and activities to economic changes,

— the promotion in international relations of security, peace, co-operation, détente, disarmament and the free movement of persons and ideas, together with the improvement of international commercial and monetary relations,

— the harmonious and equitable development of all the peoples of the world to enable them to escape from under-development and hunger and exercise their full political, economic, and social rights.

Preparatory documents:

Resolution of 6 July 1982, paragraph 4.
Resolution of 14 September 1983, paragraphs 13, 76, and 77.

Provisions in force:

ECSC Treaty, Articles 2 and 3.
EEC Treaty, Articles 2 and 3.
EAEC Treaty, Article 2.

1. By contrast with the equivalent articles in the EEC and EAEC Treaties, Article 9 confines itself to defining the objectives of the Union,

without going on to list the policies intended to enable those objectives to be achieved. The latter course of action was envisaged but was rejected, since it would have led to overlapping with Part Four, which is devoted to the policies of the Union. For the same reason, this article sets out the objectives of the Union in the area of international relations, even though the resolution defined them in a specific paragraph in the part devoted to international relations. However, Parliament felt it necessary to reiterate and develop further the Union's objectives in the field of international relations in Article 63 (1).

Article 9 is intended to incorporate the substance of the resolution, but efforts were made to phrase it much more succinctly. Drafting the article was not easy since paragraphs 12, 76, and 77 of the resolution reflect a balance between the differing political positions and the definitive wording of Article 9 had to retain that balance.

2.   The first indent places particular emphasis on the achievement of a European society which would be concerned with human beings and their harmonious development. The list of the means of attaining that objective reflects the specific preoccupations of the time (full employment and the protection of the environment), the particular concerns of certain States (elimination of imbalances between regions), and the will to implement a policy for education, research, and culture (scientific progress and the cultural development of peoples). The insistence with which certain members of the Committee on Institutional Affairs stressed the need to eliminate imbalances between regions should be noted. The Committee rejected a draft amendment by Mr Adonnino seeking to insert in the article on sectoral policies the following words: 'Prevention and reduction of imbalances between regions are among the priority objectives of the sectoral policies of the Union.'

Parliament rejected amendments of the same kind, which made the reduction and prevention of imbalances between regions one of the priority objectives of all the common policies. Their rejection was justified by the fact that inclusion of the reduction of imbalances between regions in the objectives of the Treaty provided an adequate guarantee of future action by the Union in that area and that to accord specific importance to that objective would imply that the other objectives were secondary, which is not the case.

3.   The second indent places emphasis on economic development. Its wording is the result of the adoption by the Parliament of amendment

No. 31 by the Christian Democrats. Their essential objective was to emphasize the requirement of a free internal market, stable currency, economic growth, and equilibrium in external economic relations. The other matters (non-discrimination and strengthening of the capacity to adapt to economic initiatives) were already included in the text submitted to Parliament on 14 February 1984.

4.   The third indent summarizes the objectives of the Union in the area of international relations. Its wording was considered very carefully. While the reference to disarmament is not accompanied by the requirement that it be multilateral, it appears only after references to the need for security, peace, co-operation, and *détente*, which in the view of the majority means that disarmament is to be the culmination of a process based above all on security and *détente*. The reference to the free movement of persons and ideas will also be noted.

5.   Finally, the fourth indent deals with the action of the Union in the area of development. The Union's contribution is not limited to economic aspects, but is intended also to ensure the observance of human rights (political, economic, and social rights). One of the constant preoccupations of the Parliament is thus included in the objectives of the Union.

6.   Article 9 should not be read in isolation. Article 7 of the Treaty incorporates the Community's objectives into the law of the Union, with the same status as the Treaties, provided they are not incompatible with those of the Union. In interpreting Article 9, account must be taken of the text not only of that article but also of the corresponding article of each of the Community Treaties.

Article 10

Methods of action

1. To attain these objectives, the Union shall act either by common action or by co-operation between the Member States; the fields within which each method applies shall be determined by this Treaty.

2. Common action means all normative, administrative, financial and judicial acts, internal or international, and the programmes and recommendations, issued by the Union itself, originating in its institutions and addressed to those institutions, or to States, or to individuals.

3. Co-operation means all the commitments which the Member States undertake within the European Council.

The measures resulting from co-operation shall be implemented by the Member States or by the institutions of the Union in accordance with the procedures laid down by the European Council.

Preparatory documents:
Doc. 1-575/83/B, De Gucht Report, paragraphs 24-7.
Resolution of 14 September 1983, paragraphs 14, 17, and 18.

1. The purpose of Article 10 is to define the methods by which the Union is to pursue its objectives under Article 9. For that purpose it draws a distinction between common action and co-operation.

2. While the use of the term co-operation gave rise to no difficulties, there was much hesitation on the other hand regarding the words *common action*. Certain Members would have preferred to retain the term *common policy* used in the EEC Treaty, but the desire was to avoid the conclusion that use of the same term in connection with both the Communities and the Union meant that it had the same scope. The term 'common action' was chosen, and should be interpreted in the widest possible sense, since it applies to any action carried out by the institutions of the Union within the fields of competence of the Union.[1]

[1] Articles 41 and 111 (1) of the French text of the EEC Treaty refer to common action in contrast to co-ordination.

3. The Treaty defines the areas reserved for co-operation and those for common action. This means that there is a borderline between the two areas, which may be crossed only to the extent allowed by the Treaty, that is, in the cases referred to in Article 11.

The field of common action coincides with the fields of competence of the Union and can be extended only if these competences are extended. The coextensiveness of the area of common action and the fields of competence of the Union derives from the similarity of the definitions of common action (Article 10(2)) and of the Union's competence.

As regards the extent of the field of co-operation, the question arises as to the limits placed on it. The authors of the Treaty wished co-operation to apply to all fields not covered by common action, but there is some doubt as to whether the text as adopted faithfully reflects this intention. Article 10(1) lays down that the fields of common action and of co-operation are to be determined by the Treaty. This suggests that each field is strictly defined, but only common action is limited in this way, since co-operation may extend to all sectors not covered by common action. A reading of the whole Treaty reveals that, in the field of the Union's internal competences, two articles refer to co-operation, Article 46 (homogeneous judicial area) and Article 54 (industrial co-operation). Article 46 provides for co-ordination of national laws with a view to constituting a homogeneous judicial area, a vast but not unlimited field of activity. As regards international relations, Article 66 defines the field of co-operation by reference to the subsidiarity principle. Article 68 provides that the European Council may extend the field of co-operation. A priori, this would imply that the field of co-operation is subject to limits, since otherwise it would be unnecessary to provide for its extension. However, the European Council decision is not required to take a particular form, which means that the field of co-operation may be extended without difficulty. An analysis of the text of the Treaty could lead to the conclusion that the field of co-operation is limited, but in the case of international relations these limits are theoretical.

4. Article 10(2) defines common action as all measures emanating from the institutions of the Union. The list is intended to be exhaustive, so that all measures, whether normative or otherwise, are covered, regardless of their addressees, whether institutions of the Union, States, or individuals. It has been pointed out that if, as regards the addressees, third countries could be considered to be covered by the general term

'state' in the case of international acts, international organizations ought also to have been mentioned.

5.   Defining co-operation was a delicate task, although all that was required was to codify existing practices. The resolution of 14 September 1983 adopted a simple, but incorrect, wording: 'Where the Union acts within the context of co-operation, decisions shall be taken by the European Council; they shall be implemented by the Member States.'

The wording is incorrect since, the European Council having become an institution of the Union, its decisions, like those of the other institutions, may come within the sphere of common action. Moreover, co-operation is not confined to decisions, but may take other forms. Finally, both measures adopted in the context of co-operation and those resulting from common action may be implemented by the Member States.

6.   The first sentence of Article 10 (3) makes it clear that co-operation is embodied in commitments undertaken by the Member States within the European Council. Whereas common action is attributable to the Union, co-operation is attributable to the Member States. As a result, a State may not be bound without its consent, unless there has been an agreement to the contrary. For that reason, it did not seem appropriate to state, as proposed in an amendment by the British Conservatives at a plenary sitting, that the European Council would be able to determine its own decision-making procedure. The term 'commitments' is used in a very broad sense, to include both political commitments, expressed in the form of resolutions or the adoption of joint positions, and international agreements concluded within the European Council.

7.   The second sentence of Article 10 (3) states that the measures resulting from co-operation are to be implemented by the Member States, which is the normal rule, or by the institutions of the Union in accordance with the procedures laid down by the European Council. The second form of words was inspired by Mr Prag for reasons specific to the conduct of the international relations of the Union. It was considered that in certain cases the States might wish to delegate the implementation of commitments given in the context of co-operation to institutions of the Union; Article 67 specifies the tasks in that area. The European council is responsible for co-operation, the Council of the Union is to be responsible for its conduct, and the Commission may be

charged with implementing measures at the request of the European Council or of the Council of the Union. In the view of those who proposed it, this solution should enable political co-operation to be more closely integrated into the institutional structures of the Union by making those structures available for political co-operation. This essentially pragmatic approach is not without difficulties, in so far as it entrusts to the institutions of the Union, which should normally act within the framework of common action, tasks in the area of co-operation. Is this blurring of the distinction between the tasks of the institutions not liable to raise difficulties in the future because of the different conditions which will apply to the conduct of co-operation on one hand, and of common action on the other, by the same institutions? Furthermore, is there not a risk that the Member States may take advantage of that situation in order to meddle in the conduct of common action?

If the objective pursued by the authors of the Treaty was to integrate two different methods within the same framework, namely common action, which could be described as action by the Union, and co-operation, or more particularly political co-operation, this has given rise to certain of the difficulties encountered in the wording.

Article 11

Transfer from co-operation to common action

1. In the instances laid down in Articles 54 (1) and 68 (2) of this Treaty, a matter subject to the method of co-operation between Member States may become the subject of common action. On a proposal from the Commission, or the Council of the Union, or the Parliament, or one or more Member States, the European Council may decide, after consulting the Commission and with the agreement of the Parliament, to bring those matters within the exclusive or concurrent competence of the Union.

2. In the fields subject to common action, common action may not be replaced by co-operation.

Preparatory documents:

Doc. 1-575/83/B, De Gucht Report, paragraph 29.
Resolution of 14 September 1983, paragraphs 20 and 54.

1. Article 11 is one of the manifestations of the desire to enable the Union to develop progressively as solidarity between the Member States increases. In order to describe the situation set out in Article 11, the resolution of 14 September 1983 referred to the notion of potential competence. This involved fields of competence entrusted to the Union, but exercised within the context of co-operation. They might be the subject of common action, that is to say they might be brought within the exclusive or concurrent competence of the Union, by decision of the European Council. In other words, certain sectors falling within the area of co-operation could be transferred to common action without it being necessary to revise the Treaty.

In the definitive wording, recourse to the notion of potential competence has been eliminated so as not to over-complicate the presentation of the system of competences, but the possibility of transfer remains. It is not unlimited and operates only in the cases laid down by the Treaty.

2. In the area of internal competence, the only possible transfer to common action is that provided for in Article 54 (1) which provides for the creation of industrial co-operation structures between the States,

and the conversion of those forms of co-operation into common action if the common interest justifies it. As regards international relations, Article 11 refers to Article 68 (2), which is much less restrictive, since any field of co-operation in international relations may be the subject of common action. The machinery for development of the Union by recourse to potential competences therefore operates with far-reaching effects in the field of external relations. It is true that thus, and specifically in this sector, the conditions for action are very special, since the veto provided for in Article 23 (3) may operate without limitation as to time.[1]

From the procedural point of view, the mechanism whereby the transfer takes place is triggered on the initiative of an institution of the Union (other than the European Council or the Court of Justice) or of one or more Member States. The decision is taken by the European Council, which consults the Commission. It requires the consent of the Parliament. It was not considered appropriate to provide for action by the Council of the Union, since the States which are represented therein must give their approval within the European Council. The procedures according to which the European Council is to express its views are not described, since it was considered preferable to leave the European Council to determine its own decision-making procedures (Article 32 (2)). Moreover, the question may be asked whether it might not be unanimously agreed to dispense with the requirement of unanimity in certain cases. The procedure instituted by Article 11 refers only to the implementation of the transfer as far as the Union is concerned. There is a possibility that in cases where the Heads of State or Government may not, under their national constitutions, firmly commit their country without parliamentary authorization, the implementation of the decision may be made subject to such authorization.

3.   The effect of a transfer is to bring the area transferred either into the sphere of exclusive competence or into the sphere of concurrent competence. The repercussions of choosing one or the other are not inconsiderable. Transfer into the area of concurrent competence does not allow the Union immediately to undertake common action, since the implementation of such action is subject to the adoption of an organic law.[2] By virtue of Article 11 (2), transfers are one-way and it is impossible to substitute co-operation for common action in those areas

---

[1] See commentary on Article 68.
[2] See commentary on Article 12.

which the Treaty, or a decision of the European Council adopted pursuant to Article 11 (1), has assigned to common action. The intention here was to avoid a progressive return to inter-Statism. However, this rule loses some of its significance in the light of Article 68 (3) which, *lex specialis*, allows the European Council alone, without Parliament's consent, to reverse the process where the transfer took place in the field of international relations of the Union. The reverse process goes even beyond the *status quo ante*, since it is possible to assign a matter which was the subject of co-operation to the competence of the Member States.[3] This mobility, inspired by the United Kingdom Conservatives, may indeed be illusory since, if the consent of the States within the European Council (and the consent of Parliament) is required for a question to be transferred from co-operation to common action, a decision of the European Council is required to move in the reverse direction. If the European Council acts unanimously, the opposition of one State can prevent a move backwards just as it can paralyse any movement forward.

[3] See commentary on Article 68 (3).

Article 12

Competences

1.   Where this Treaty confers exclusive competence on the Union, the institutions of the Union shall have sole power to act; national authorities may only legislate to the extent laid down by the law of the Union. Until the Union has legislated, national legislation shall remain in force.

2.   Where this Treaty confers concurrent competence on the Union, the Member States shall continue to act so long as the Union has not legislated. The Union shall only act to carry out those tasks which may be undertaken more effectively in common than by the Member States acting separately, in particular those whose execution requires action by the Union because their dimension or effects extend beyond national frontiers. A law which initiates or extends common action in a field where action has not been taken hitherto by the Union or by the Communities must be adopted in accordance with the procedure for organic laws.

Preparatory documents:

Note by Mr Spinelli on certain problems of terminology in Doc. 1-575/83/C, p. 165.

Doc. 1-575/83/B, De Gucht Report, paragraph 29.

Resolution of 14 September 1983, paragraph 20.

1.   The classification of competences as exclusive, concurrent, or potential competences, is one of the fundamental aspects of Parliament's draft, since it determines the development of the Union through the gradual exercise of concurrent or potential competences. Article 11 establishes the concept of potential competence without using the term itself, while Article 12 distinguishes between exclusive and concurrent competence. This distinction is inspired both by the Basic Law of the Federal Republic of Germany (Articles 71 and 72) and by the proposals drawn up by the Commission during the preparation of the Tindemans Report.

Thus there will be a number of matters which fall exclusively within Union competence; ... Between the two there is bound to be an extensive border area in which both Union and States may have competence.

An expression which might be used to describe this border area is that of concurrent competence, which is to be seen in numerous provisions of the Treaties establishing the European Communities ... Under this arrangement, both Union and Member States are entitled to deal with the problems concerned. The Union would assert its authority only when it felt the need—for instance, by deciding to act only in respect of certain aspects of any given matter. It might also enact outline legislation to cover the whole field, specifying the areas reserved respectively for the Union itself and for the Member States. The Member States would then remain free to act on all aspects on which the Union had not taken action. ...

In such cases, the concept of potential competence might be applied ... The field in question would be placed within the competence of the Union, but a decision on the scope and nature of the Union's powers and the date on which the Union would begin to exercise them could be left to be made later by a special procedure.[1]

The distinction between exclusive and concurrent competence is not alien to Community law. With regard in particular to the common commercial policy or the common fisheries policy, the Court of Justice of the Communities has made use of the concept of exclusive competence,[2] the other competences assigned to the Communities being classified as concurrent.[3] Previous solutions are, however, given systematic form in the Treaty of Union.

2.   When the Treaty enters into force, the Union will have only those competences attributed to it exclusively or previously exercised by the European Communities (as emerges from the reference to the Communities in the final sentence of Article 12 (2)). But it will be entitled, in cases of need assessed by reference to the subsidiarity principle, to extend its field of action in the area of concurrent competences in accordance with the procedure set out in Article 12 (2). Finally, the European Council may enable it to take action regarding certain matters which are assigned to co-operation, where they are brought within the competence of the Union in accordance with the procedure provided for in Article 11.[4]

By the operation of this machinery, all the areas of competence of the Union are defined in the Treaty, and they are assigned powers

[1] *EC Bulletin*, Suppl. 5/75, paragraphs 13-17.

[2] Opinion 1/75, [1975] ECR 1355, 1365.

[3] On these points see, e.g., J. V. Louis, Le Droit de la C.E.E., vol. 10, *La Cour de Justice: les actes des institutions*, ULB 1984, pp. 550 ff.

[4] On potential competence see commentary on Article 11.

(*'compétences d'attribution'*). In certain quarters the desire was expressed that the Court of Justice of the Union should adhere to the case law of the Court of Justice of the European Communities and continue to recognize, by virtue of the rule of effectiveness (*'effet utile'*), the existence of implied fields of competence of the Union. However, it must be pointed out that the problem of limiting the competences of the Union has on several occasions been brought to the attention of the Committee on Institutional Affairs, and that the suggestion was made, without success, that it should draft an article comparable to Article 235 of the EEC Treaty. Majority opinion on the Committee was that while Article 235 was conceivable in a partial Community such as the EEC, the position was different in a Union with much wider fields of competence, where it might be dangerous to temper the rule of assigned powers by a course of action enabling the field of common action to be extended considerably further than was envisaged in Article 11. It should however be noted that the policies of the Union are so defined that the terms used do not constitute an excessively rigid framework and that in several cases (conjunctural policy, credit policy, social policy, and road policy), the use of the adverbial phrase 'in particular' allows a broad interpretation of the competence of the Union.

3. The rules in the Treaty regarding exclusive competence are simple. Where the Union has exclusive competence, the Institutions of the Union are to have sole power to act and the Member States may legislate only to the extent to which the law of the Union, adopted in the exercise of that competence, so allows. The action to be taken by the States is therefore a matter of implementation (cf. Article 34, Definition of Laws).

A problem arises as to what is to happen to national laws in force when faced by an exclusive competence. This question may arise regarding the exclusive competences of the Union when the Treaty enters into force or the concurrent competences of the Union when they are exercised by the Union and the law of the Union allows certain national measures to remain in force, without making any provision as to what is to happen to them. The resolution of 14 September 1983 provided that those laws were to remain in force as laws of the Union.

The aim in view was to prevent the Member States from being able, during the period between recognition of the exclusive nature of the Union's competence and the adoption of the laws of the Union, to amend their national legislation so that the adoption of a Union law might become more difficult. By converting those laws into laws of the

Union, any unilateral modification was prevented, but disparate laws which thereafter were to rank as laws of the Union were frozen.

Provision for national laws to remain in force is designed to prevent the possible formation of a legal vacuum. If for any reason the Union delayed legislating, existing national legislation would temporarily fill the vacuum. Exceptional conditions would be required for such a situation to arise, if only because the exclusive competences assigned to the Union by the Treaty (trade between Member States, common commercial policy, competition policy) have already been exercised by the Communities and the Community patrimony would fill any vacuum. However, it was felt necessary to provide for such a situation.

During the discussions in the Committee on Institutional Affairs it was pointed out that if the Union delayed legislating, it would be impossible to amend national laws still in force, since the states would no longer have the competence to do so. It was therefore proposed that such amendments could be made subject to authorization from the Commission. This solution was rejected both by the Commission and by Parliament in plenary sitting. The conclusion that had to be drawn was that national laws still in force could no longer be amended by the Member States and a textual interpretation suggests this reading of Article 12 (1).

However, the Court of Justice of the Union could adopt, *mutatis mutandis*, the solution chosen by the Court of Justice of the Communities in the judgment of 5 May 1981, *Commission v. United Kingdom*:[5]

As this is a field reserved to the powers of the Community, within which Member States may henceforth act only as trustees of the common interest, a Member State cannot therefore, in the absence of appropriate action on the part of the Council, bring in any ... measures ... except as part of a process of collaboration with the Commission and with due regard to the general task of supervision.

4. The concept of concurrent competence, which is familiar to German lawyers, is not always understood in the other Member States.[6] It is not surprising that there have been a number of misunderstandings. The view was expressed that where there was concurrent competence,

---

[5] Case 804/79, [1981] ECR pp. 1075-6.
[6] Cf. Article 72 of the German Basic Law: '1) In matters falling to be dealt with by concurrent legislation, the Länder shall be entitled to legislate provided that, and to the extent to which, the Federation does not avail itself of its power to legislate.'

simultaneous action by the Union and the Member States was possible. That is certainly not the case.

As in the case of exclusive competence, concurrent competences are conferred upon the Union and upon the Union alone. The Union cannot share the exercise of such powers with the Member States. But while the powers defined as exclusive competences by the Treaty are to be exercised by the Union from the entry into force, the exercise of its concurrent powers is postponed and made subject to compliance with certain conditions. Until those conditions are satisfied, the Member States will retain the right to legislate, and will lose that right when the Union decides to exercise its competence in the area in question. The expression 'virtual competence' perhaps conveys the concept better than concurrent competence.

The Treaty confers concurrent competence upon the Union, but authorizes the States to act until the Union decides to exercise it. When this decision is taken, the Union's competence is the same as in those cases where it has exclusive competence and the Member States are not entitled to act except where the law of the Union grants them the right to adopt implementing measures.

The situation of the Member States in relation to exclusive and concurrent competence can be compared only by reference to a specific point in time. Where a concurrent competence is exercised by the Union, a Member State may no longer intervene, as in the case of an exclusive competence, except where the law of the Union authorizes them to adopt implementing measures.[7] Where a concurrent competence has not been exercised by the Union, the States may act freely, provided their action is not designed to make future action by the Union impossible (in accordance with the obligation to co-operate in good faith contained in Article 13).

5.   The first action taken by the Union in an area of concurrent competence is of particular importance and is therefore subject to conditions both of form and of substance.

The formal condition is that an organic law must be adopted to enable the Union to take action, that is to say a qualified majority is

---

[7] Even where an exclusive competence has not been exercised, the situation is very different from that which arises where a concurrent competence has not been exercised. In the former case, even supposing that the States may still act, which is not certain, they would do so as 'trustees of the common interest' under Commission supervision. In the second case, the States have an independent right to act.

required in the Parliament and the Council.[8] This law may be limited to stating the principle that the Union is to take action or it may also lay down detailed procedures. Thus it is only the principle of the exercise of a concurrent competence which is governed by the organic law, since Article 12 (2) stipulates that 'a law which initiates ... common action ... must be adopted in accordance with the procedure for organic laws.' The detailed procedures for Union action may be laid down in an ordinary law. This means that if the organic law includes provisions concerning the content of the common action, these provisions may be amended by an ordinary law, provided the field of common action is not extended. This gives rise to the paradoxical situation in which the organic law can be amended by an ordinary law.

The question has been asked whether the adoption of an organic law in an area of concurrent competence is sufficient for the whole field in question to become an exclusive competence of the Union. While the resolution may not have been clear on this point, the Treaty is an improvement in so far as it states that in the case of concurrent competence 'the Member States shall continue to act *so long as* the Union has not legislated.' As a result, the organic law must specify the scope of the action to be taken by the Union, and matters falling outside that scope will continue to be governed by national law. The expression 'so long as' has a restrictive effect.

The question has also arisen whether by including within the areas of concurrent competence certain areas which were a matter of Community competence and in which the Communities legislated, there was not a risk of a step backwards, enabling the States temporarily to exercise once more powers which had ceased to be available to them. The wording of the Treaty removes that danger in so far as it requires recourse to organic laws only in those areas in which neither the Union nor the Communities have yet taken action, which means that in the areas where the Communities have already taken action, the Community patrimony is expressly preserved and the competence of the Union is exclusive.

6.   But the possibility of common action in an area of concurrent competence is not subject only to the adoption of an organic law but also to a substantive condition, namely respect of the principle of subsidiarity. The Union may only act 'to carry out those tasks which may

---

[8] See comments on Article 38 regarding the procedure for the adoption of an organic law.

be undertaken more effectively in common than by the Member States acting separately'.

This is based directly on the German Constitution. Certain doubts have been expressed regarding the appropriateness of a reference in Article 12 to the principle of subsidiarity already mentioned in the preamble. It was pointed out that since that principle applies fully to the division of fields of competence, it was irrelevant to mention it here. Moreover, since German experience showed that it was not really a principle enforceable at law, was it in fact appropriate to reiterate it in Article 12? Discussions on this point have not resolved the ambiguity.

A majority of the Committee on Institutional Affairs felt that the principle can indeed be enforced and that it would be possible to refer to the Court an organic law which authorized common action, on the ground that the principle of subsidiarity had not been respected. However, can an assessment by the Court rather than the Union legislator be carried out without evaluating the advisability of the law, which would go beyond the Court's legal role? If the qualified majority required for the legislative body to adopt an organic law is obtained, surely it must be presumed that the condition of subsidiarity has been fully met.

An interim solution could perhaps be found by requiring the legislature to examine the need for the action with reference to the subsidiarity principle, and by exercising a minimum level of control which could in particular sanction manifest errors.

It would be for the Court to decide on the enforceability of the principle at law and, where appropriate, on the extent of the control to be exercised.

The question arises as to whether, where the subsidiarity principle no longer justifies Union intervention, the legislature may decide no longer to exercise the relevant competence. This is a theoretical question which was not considered during the preparatory work. A negative answer is prompted by Article 11, which states that common action may not be replaced by co-operation and by the exceptional character of Article 68 (3) which authorizes a transfer from common action to the competence of the Member States. If the reverse process had been possible, it would have been unnecessary to introduce a special rule providing for it in the cases referred to in Article 68. However, there is nothing to prevent the Union legislature from confining itself to provisions of a very general nature and leaving the Member States an extremely wide secondary field of action.

7.   The detailed procedures for Union action in the area of concurrent competences depend on the specific provisions relating to each competence. Part Four of the Treaty, concerning the policies of the Union, indicates for each policy the objectives to be pursued by the Union and the instruments it may use. Depending on the policy, the Union may take all the measures needed to achieve the objectives assigned to it or may be restricted to drawing up strategies (e.g. Article 53 (f)) or defining objectives (e.g. Article 60).

Article 13

Implementation of the law of the Union

The Union and the Member States shall co-operate in good faith in the implementation of the law of the Union. Member States shall take all appropriate measures, whether general or particular, to ensure fulfilment of the obligations arising out of this Treaty or resulting from action taken by the institutions of the Union. They shall facilitate the achievement of the Union's tasks. They shall abstain from any measure which could jeopardize the attainment of the objectives of the Union.

Preparatory documents:

Resolution of 14 September 1983, paragraph 25.

Provisions in force:

EEC Treaty, Article 5.

Paragraph 25 of the resolution of 14 September 1983 referred to the need for good faith between the Union and the Member States: 'The Union and the Member States shall co-operate in good faith in the implementation of the law of the Union and its administrative execution.'

This principle appears in the first sentence of Article 13, which then reproduces the text of Article 5 of the EEC Treaty. Unlike that article, Article 13 explicitly lays down the principle of co-operation in good faith between the Union and the Member States which was asserted by the Court in its judgment on Parliament's places of work, to be derived implicitly from Article 5:[1]

It must nevertheless be emphasized that when the Governments of the Member States make provisional decisions they must in accordance with the rule imposing on Member States and the Community institutions mutual duties of sincere co-operation, as embodied in particular in Article 5 of the EEC Treaty, have regard to the power of the Parliament to determine its internal organization.

[1] Case 230/81 *Grand Duchy of Luxembourg v. European Parliament* [1983] ECR 255, paragraph 37.

It was considered essential to incorporate into the Treaty the provisions of Article 5 of the EEC Treaty, in view principally of the place occupied by that article in the Court's case law with regard both to the competences of the Community[2] and to the supremacy of Community law.[3]

[2] Case 61/77 *Commission v. Ireland* [1978] ECR 417.
[3] Case 30/72 *Commission v. Italy* [1973] ECR 72.

PART THREE

INSTITUTIONAL PROVISIONS

Article 14

The European Parliament

The European Parliament shall be elected by direct universal suffrage in a free and secret vote by the citizens of the Union. The term of each Parliament shall be five years.

An organic law shall lay down a uniform electoral procedure; until such a law comes into force, the procedure applicable shall be that for the election of the Parliament of the European Communities.

Preparatory documents:

Resolution of 14 September 1983, paragraphs 121 and 122.
Doc. 1-575/83/C, Zecchino working document, p. 150.
Doc. 1-575/83/B, Zecchino Report, p. 39.

Provisions in force:

EEC Treaty, Article 138.
EAEC Treaty, Article 108.
Act concerning the election of the representatives of the Assembly by direct universal suffrage.[1]

As a whole, the provisions on the Parliament did not give rise to much discussion since, in essence, all that was done was to take over the Community patrimony. As Mr Zecchino noted in his working document: 'In fact, the present Community Parliament presents no problems or difficulties, and the constitution, composition and period of office of the Union's Parliament could be based entirely on those of the existing model.'[2]

Thus, the first paragraph of Article 14 repeats the provisions of the Act concerning the election of the representatives of the Assembly by

[1] OJ L 278 of 8 October 1976.
[2] Op. cit., p. 150.

direct universal suffrage. Added to it is a reference to the free and secret nature of the vote; those principles did not appear in the Act, but it may be considered that the authors of the Act regarded them as automatically included since they are common to the voting systems of all the Member States. The term of each Parliament is unaltered and thus remains fixed at five years (see Article 3 of the Act).

As regards the electoral system to be applied, the second paragraph of Article 14 refers, as a temporary measure, to the system in force in the European Communities, until the Union adopts an organic law providing for a uniform electoral procedure. The objective of Article 138 of the EEC Treaty is thus reaffirmed, although it does not imply total unity of the voting system. This objective will presumably be more easily attainable through an organic law than through the procedure set out in Article 138 and in Article 7 of the Act, which has not been fully implemented.

The mention of the 'citizens of the Union' in Article 14 refers back to Article 3.

From the technical point of view, part of the second paragraph could have been included in an article specially reserved for the transitional provisions, but for reasons of clarity that course was not followed by Parliament.

Article 15

Members of the Parliament

The members of the Parliament shall act and vote in an individual and personal capacity. They may not be bound by any instructions nor receive a binding mandate.

Preparatory documents:

Doc. 1-575/83/B, Zecchino Report, p. 39.
Resolution of 14 September 1983, paragraph 121.

Provisions in force:

Article 4 of the Act of 20 September 1976.

Article 15 reproduces paragraph 1 of Article 4 of the Act of 20 September 1976. In view of the difficulties caused by the tourniquet system which obliged representatives elected from the French DIFE list (Gaullists) to resign after one year in office, and the hold of groups on elected representatives, it was considered appropriate to reproduce the wording of the Act, which sets out one of the fundamental principles of any representative system.

Article 16

Functions of the Parliament

The Parliament shall:

— participate, in accordance with this Treaty, in the legislative and budgetary procedures and in the conclusions of international agreements,

— enable the Commission to take office by approving its political programme,

— exercise political supervision over the Commission,

— have the power to adopt by a qualified majority a motion of censure requiring the members of the Commission to resign as a body,

— have the power to conduct inquiries and receive petitions addressed to it by citizens of the Union,

— exercise the other powers attributed to it by this Treaty.

Preparatory documents:

None.

In a concern for uniformity and clarity, it was considered appropriate to recapitulate all the functions entrusted to the Parliament. A similar approach was adopted for the other Institutions. As a matter of caution, it was nevertheless made clear that that list was not exhaustive (see the last indent of the Article).

1. On participation in the legislative process the draft refers to Articles 36, 37, and 38 regarding legislative authority, to Articles 70 *et seq.* regarding the budgetary authority and to Article 65 (3) and (4) regarding the Parliament's participation in the conclusion of international agreements.

2. On the investiture of the Commission the draft refers to Article 25. The wording adopted, following an amendment by Madame Veil, confirmed that the investiture of the Commission and the approval of its programme are the result of one and the same vote.

3. On political control of the Commission the draft lays down the principle whereby the Parliament has a general power of control over the Commission, which is not limited to censure, but involves the Parliament's right to be informed of the activities of the Commission and therefore to question the Commission about them and to impart its views to the commission (cf. Article 29 (1) and (2)).

4. On motions of censure the text refers by implication to Article 29 (3). It should be noted that the Parliament rejected an amendment by Mr Eisma (No. 71) creating the possibility of individual responsibility attaching to the Commissioners.

5. The power to conduct inquiries and the right of petition are included in Article 18 of the draft.

Article 17

Majorities in the Parliament

1. The Parliament shall vote by a simple majority, i.e. a majority of votes cast, abstentions not counted.

2. Where expressly specified by this Treaty, the Parliament shall vote:

(a) either by an absolute majority, i.e. a majority of its members;

(b) or by a qualified majority, i.e. a majority of its members and of two-thirds of votes cast, abstentions not counted. On the second reading of the budget, the qualified majority required shall be a majority of the members of Parliament and three-fifths of votes cast, abstentions not counted.

Preparatory documents:

Resolution of 14 September 1983, paragraph 123.

Provisions in force:

EEC Treaty, Article 141.
EAEC Treaty, Article 111.

To facilitate the reading of the Treaty, the details of the various types of majority referred to in the Treaty are grouped together in specific articles. Article 17, which relates to the Parliament, is the counterpart of Article 23, which relates to the Council.

1. Article 17 (1) provides in principle for voting by a simple majority, that is to say the majority of the votes cast. This rule reproduces the content of Article 141 of the EEC Treaty. For greater clarity it is stated that, for that purpose, abstentions are not to be regarded as votes cast.

2. Article 17 (2) defines an absolute majority as the majority of the members of the Parliament, that is to say of the members making up the Parliament. The calculation is based on the number of seats actually filled as at the date of the vote.

It establishes two kinds of qualified majority: one for budgetary matters, being a majority of the members of Parliament and three-fifths of the votes cast, which is the majority prescribed at present by Article 203 of the EEC Treaty for the Parliament's exercise of its right of final decision on budgetary matters, and another majority for other areas, namely a majority of the members of Parliament and two-thirds of the votes cast, which is the majority at present required by Article 144 of the EEC Treaty for a motion of censure to be carried. It is stated— which was not absolutely necessary—that abstentions are not to be taken into account in calculating the votes cast.

The distinction between the two types of qualified majority is based on political rather than technical grounds. A qualified majority is required for measures involving a degree of solemnity (censure motions, the adoption of organic laws, and the rejection on a second reading of the budget of amendments adopted by the Council).

The Parliament's right of final decision on budgetary matters is already recognized, provided that it acts by a majority of its members and of three-fifths of the votes cast. There was therefore no reason to place greater difficulties in the way of the right of final decision regarding adoption of the Union budget. On the other hand, it was sought, by continuing to require a majority of two-thirds of the votes cast for a censure motion, to affirm the need to preserve the stability of the Commission or at least not to give the impression that, by reducing the majority required for a censure motion, the Treaty engendered the risk of instability.

In those circumstances, logic dictated that the adoption of organic laws, which are the most important legal measures which can be adopted by the institutions of the Union and take precedence over ordinary laws, should require the more important qualified majority.

3. Cases where an absolute majority is required:
    — adoption of the Parliament's rules of procedure (Article 19)
    — amendment of a draft organic law on a first reading (Article 38 (1))
    — approval of a law after an agreement reached by the Conciliation Committee (Article 38 (4))
    — the adoption of a law where the Conciliation Committee fails to reach agreement (Article 38 (4))
    — approval of international agreements (Article 65 (4))
    — modification on a first reading of amendments to the draft budget adopted by the Council (Article 76 (2)(b))
    — adoption of the budget (Article 76 (2)(f)).

4.   Cases where a qualified majority is required:

(a) A majority of two-thirds of the votes cast and a majority of the members of Parliament:

— motion of censure (Article 29 (3))
— approval of an organic law on a first reading (Article 38 (1))
— approval of an organic law on a second reading (Article 38 (4)).

(b) A majority of three-fifths of the votes cast and a majority of the members of the Parliament:

— retention of a budgetary amendment on a second reading despite opposition by the commission (Article 76 (c))
— rejection on a second reading of amendments to the budget adopted by the Council (Article 76 (f)).

5.   On the whole, the Parliament has imposed strict requirements upon itself, since the draft requires large majorities for the exercise of its legislative powers. They are particularly large where the Parliament wishes to prevail over the Council or the Commission. In general, the system is coherent. It is to be regretted, however, that in the case of organic laws, the requirement, applicable as from the first reading, of the larger majority may partly undermine the value of the conciliation procedure provided for in the Treaty, since if conciliation fails, Parliament will be able to decide in the final instance against the Council's opinion by the same majority as that required for a decision at the first reading. Admittedly it will have to give its decision on the text emanating from the Council and can adopt amendments only with the Commission's consent.[1]

[1] See commentary on Article 38.

Article 18

Power to conduct inquiries and right of petition

The procedures for the exercise of the power of the Parliament to conduct inquiries and of the right of citizens to address petitions to the Parliament shall be laid down by organic laws.

Preparatory documents:

Resolution of 14 September 1983, paragraph 129.

Under the Community Treaties, the rights of inquiry and of petition are based on the rules of the European Parliament. As a result, the other institutions and the Member States are not obliged to respond to requests for information from Commissions of Inquiry appointed by the Parliament (or to act upon the conclusions of inquiries instigated by Parliament).

By expressly recognizing the rights of petition and of inquiry, Article 18 provides them with a legal basis which can be invoked against the States and the institutions, and the same applies to the procedures for the exercise thereof laid down in the organic laws.

No action was taken on the proposal to create a Union ombudsman.

Article 19

Rules of procedure of the Parliament

The Parliament shall adopt its rules of procedure by an absolute majority.

Preparatory documents:

Resolution of 14 September 1983, paragraph 123.

Provisions in force:

ECSC Treaty, Article 25.
EEC Treaty, Article 142.
EAEC Treaty, Article 112.

Article 19 reproduces the first paragraph of Article 142 of the EEC Treaty. The importance of this power of the Parliament is well known and the Court of Justice of the Communities perceives in it a power for the Parliament to determine its internal organization, on the basis of which the Parliament is entitled to take all appropriate measures to ensure the due functioning and conduct of its proceedings:[1]

the Parliament is authorized, pursuant to the power to determine its own internal organization given to it by Article 25 of the ECSC Treaty, Article 142 of the EEC Treaty and Article 112 of the EAEC Treaty, to adopt appropriate measures to ensure the due functioning and conduct of its proceedings.[2]

The rules regarding majorities are contained in Article 17. It was not considered appropriate to state expressly in Article 19 that the rules of procedure would contain provisions regarding the quorum and publication of the proceedings of the Assembly, but that does not release the Parliament from the obligation to include in its rules of procedure provisions regarding those matters.

[1] Case 208/80 *Lord Bruce of Donington* [1981] ECR 2219; Case 230/81 *Grand Duchy of Luxembourg* v. *European Parliament* [1983] ECR 255.
[2] *Grand Duchy of Luxembourg* v. *European Parliament*, paragraph 38.

Article 20

The Council of the Union

The Council of the Union shall consist of representations of the Member States appointed by their respective governments; each representation shall be led by a minister who is permanently and specifically responsible for Union affairs.

Preparatory documents:

Doc. 1-575/83/C, Zecchino working document, paragraphs 16–30.
Resolution of 14 September 1983, paragraph 124.

Provisions in force:

EEC Treaty, Article 146.
Merger Treaty, Article 2.

1. The Council of the Union is so called to distinguish it from the European Council (Article 31).

2. The Council of the Union consists of represent*ations* of the Member States appointed by their respective governments (compare Article 146 of the EEC Treaty, as amended by Article 2 of the Merger Treaty: 'The Council shall consist of represent*atives* of the Member States. Each Government shall delegate to it one of its members.' The Council of the European Communities has a dual function, being at the same time a Community institution and (at least de facto) an intergovernmental organ, a duality which has limited its effectiveness.[1]

Article 20 of the Treaty seeks to emphasize the Council of the Union's quality as a Union institution, rather than an intergovernmental organ, by providing that each representation shall be led by a minister permanently and specifically responsible for Union affairs. Such a minister will also be able to co-ordinate the attitudes of different ministries more effectively than under the Community system. However, while consideration was given to other possible methods of appointing the

---

[1] See the remarks of Advocate General Dutheillet de Lamothe in Case 22/70 *Commission v. Council* [1971] ECR 263 at 287-8, and see also P. H. J. M. Houben, 'Le Conseil des Communautés européennes', in *Aspects européens*, Leiden 1964; P. Chandernagor, 'La difficulté d'être du Conseil', *Revue Administrative* No. 17, September 1982.

members of the Council,[2] members are to be appointed by governments in accordance with their own methods. The possibility remains open of regulating the method of appointment at the level of the Union, subject always to the terms of Article 20, by an organic law: see Article 34 (2).

While the members of the Council continue to be appointed by governments, Article 20 envisages that the minister 'permanently and specifically responsible for Union affairs' will be appointed by a formal act which will have effect until it is formally revoked, thus achieving an element of continuity in the composition of the Council.

However, Article 20 requires governments to appoint a 'minister', rather than a 'member' of the government as in the Community system, where, in the absence of any further precision in the Treaties or in the rules of procedure, practice shows that governments often delegate persons who do not have final political responsibility.

The creation of representations, led by a minister permanently responsible for Union affairs, is also designed to put an end to the nomination of representatives *ad hoc* for specific subjects. In the Community the practice has developed of 'specialized' Councils meeting to deal with specific subjects such as agriculture, social affairs, or the environment. Such specialized Councils will be unnecessary in the Union, whose Council will be permanently responsible for all Union affairs, although the Minister for Union Affairs will no doubt be assisted, as the occasion requires, by the appropriate specialist minister.

3.　Similarly, the permanency of the Council will render unnecessary the Committee of Permanent Representatives of the Member States (COREPER) (Article 4 of the Merger Treaty). It has been a recurrent criticism of the Community system that too much of the work of the Council has been taken over by COREPER and by officials from the Member States.

4.　In contrast with Article 146 of the EEC Treaty, Article 20 of the Treaty contains no provision for the presidency of the Council; this will be regulated, together with other procedural questions, by the Council itself under Article 24. Certain duties devolve on the President of the Council; for example, the President may be called upon to act as spokesman of the Union in international affairs (see Article 67 (5)), or to establish that the legislative procedure has been completed (Article 39).

[2] See the Zecchino report, paragraph 23–6.

Article 21

Functions of the Council of the Union

The Council shall:

— participate, in accordance with this Treaty, in the legislative and budgetary procedures and in the conclusion of international agreements,

— exercise the powers attributed to it in the field of international relations, and answer written and oral questions tabled by members of the Parliament in this field,

— exercise the other powers attributed to it by this Treaty.

Preparatory documents:

Doc. 1-575/83/C, Zecchino working document, paragraphs 31-7.
Resolution of 14 September 1983, paragraphs 130-1.

Provisions in force:

EEC Treaty, Article 145.
Merger Treaty, Article 1.

1. The council constitutes, together with the Parliament, both the legislative authority (Article 36) and the budgetary authority (Article 70 (1)).[1] Moreover, the Council has, with regard to legislation, the power of 'legislative initiative'. In contrast to the EEC Treaty, which reserves the right of initiative in almost all sectors to the Commission, Article 37 (2) of the present Treaty gives the Council, in certain circumstances, the right to propose legislation.

2. The Council retains a leading role in the conclusion of international agreements, a role which, however, it shares with the European Parliament: such agreements, in accordance with Article 65 (4), require the approval of the Council and the Parliament, each acting by an absolute majority.

The Council has broad powers in the field of international relations generally: in particular it issues guidelines for the conduct of the Union's

---

[1] For the role of the Council in the legislative and budgetary procedures, see the commentary on Articles 38 and 76 respectively.

international relations under Part Four Title III of the Treaty, where those relations are the subject of *common action* under Article 64 (see Article 65 (2)); while in those areas where relations are the subject of *co-operation* under Article 66, the Council is responsible for the conduct of such co-operation (see Article 67 (1)). It is also responsible for approving the establishment of respresentations of the Union in non-member States and in international organizations (Article 69 (1)).

3.   Article 21 specifically requires the Council to answer questions in the Parliament in the field of international relations. That provision is intended to give the Parliament a degree of political control over the Council's activities in that field. Such control is formally lacking in the Community system, although in practice the Council has accepted, for example, that the Parliament should receive reports on the progress of European political co-operation.

A *contrario* the Council is not called upon under the present Treaty to answer questions in the Parliament in fields other than that of international relations. The issue was discussed at length in the Institutional Committee, which concluded that an extension of the Council's answerability to other fields would be incompatible with the relations between the two legislative chambers.

Article 22

Weighting of votes in the Council of the Union

The votes of the representations shall be weighted in accordance with the provisions of Article 148 (2) of the Treaty establishing the European Economic Community.

In the event of the accession of new member states, the weighting of their votes shall be laid down in the treaty of accession.

Preparatory documents:

Doc. 1-575/83/C, Zecchino working document, paragraphs 27-9.
Resolution of 14 September 1983, paragraph 125.

Provisions in force:

EEC Treaty, Article 148.

1. Article 22 provides for the weighting to be given to the vote of each Member State within the Council.

Weighted voting is rare in international organizations of a general character but is frequently encountered in organizations of a technical character, such as financial and commodity organizations. In those organizations the weighting is commonly linked to the scale of the member States' financial contribution to the budget, or to their share in the operating capital, or to some other appropriate technical criterion. In the ECSC Treaty, Article 28 gives special weight to Member States which individually account for at least one eighth of the total value of the coal and steel output of the Community.

Article 22 of the present Treaty preserves the weighting provided for by the EEC Treaty (Article 148), in which votes are weighted on the basis of more general demographic, political, and economic criteria.[1]

If all the Member States of the Communities join the Union, their votes will accordingly be weighted as follows: Germany, France, Italy, United Kingdom: 10 votes; Belgium, Greece, Netherlands: 5 votes; Denmark, Ireland: 3 votes; Luxembourg: 2 votes.

[1] G. Isaac, *Droit communautaire général* (1983), p. 55.

2. However, under the EEC Treaty weighted voting operates only where the Council is required to act by a qualified majority, while in the draft Treaty the votes are also weighted in the calculation of a simple majority: see Article 23 (1). It will therefore be possible to attain a simple majority in the Council without the votes of a majority of the Member States.

3. The second paragraph of Article 22 obviates the need for a revision of the Treaty on the accession of new member States.[2]

[2] See the commentary on Article 2.

Article 23

Majorities in the Council of the Union

1. The Council shall vote by a simple majority, i.e. a majority of the weighted votes cast, abstentions not counted.

2. Where expressly specified by this Treaty, the Council shall vote:

(a) either by an absolute majority, i.e. by a majority of the weighted votes cast, abstentions not counted, comprising at least half of the representations;

(b) or by a qualified majority, i.e. by a majority of two-thirds of the weighted votes cast, abstentions not counted, comprising a majority of the representations. On the second reading of the budget, the qualified majority required shall be a majority of three-fifths of the weighted votes cast, abstentions not counted, comprising a majority of the representations;

(c) or by unanimity of representations, abstentions not counted.

3. During a transitional period of ten years, where a representation invokes a vital national interest which is jeopardized by the decision to be taken and recognized as such by the Commission, the vote shall be postponed so that the matter may be re-examined. The grounds for requesting a postponement shall be published.

Preparatory documents:

Resolution of 14 September 1983, paragraphs 126-7.

Provisions in force:

EEC Treaty, Article 148.

1. Article 23 provides for five separate majorities:

  (i) a simple majority (Article 23 (1))

 (ii) an absolute majority (Article 23 (2)(a))

(iii) a qualified (two-thirds) majority (Article 23 (2)(b))

 (iv) a special qualified (three-fifths) majority for the vote on the second reading of the budget (Article 23 (2)(b): see also Article 76 (2)(e) below)

  (v) unanimity (Article 23 (2)(c)).

In all cases abstentions are not counted: Article 28 thus differs from the EEC Treaty, except in the case of unanimity (Article 148 (3)). The result is to facilitate the attainment of the required majority. By way of illustration, if there were ten Member States whose weighted votes collectively amounted to 63, then a majority would be 32 votes, and a two-thirds majority 42. But if abstentions are not counted, then if, for example, two Members States whose votes were each weighted as ten were to abstain, then the relevant total would be only 43 instead of 63 and it would be correspondingly easier to attain a majority of the weighted votes cast (22 instead of 32), or a two-thirds majority (29 instead of 42).

2.   The simple majority is the general rule; the other rules apply only where the Treaty so provides.

3.   It is noteworthy that not only a simple majority, but also an absolute majority, can be attained without the votes of a majority of the representations; for an absolute majority, the votes of only half of the representations are required.

An absolute majority is required in the Council for the adoption of its rules of procedure (Article 24) and for the approval of international agreements (Article 65 (4)). In addition, where the Council approves a draft law, other than an organic law, by an absolute majority, and the draft law has previously been approved by the Parliament, then the Council's vote is sufficient to complete the legislative procedure.[1]

4.   A qualified (two-thirds) majority is sufficient to complete the legislative procedure on a draft organic law, or on a draft law on which the Commission has expressed an unfavourable opinion: see Article 38 (3). Where the conciliation procedure has been used, the text adopted by the Parliament can be rejected by the Council only by a qualified majority: see Article 38 (4).

5.   Under the budgetary procedure, the Council may, on the second reading of the budget, either refer the whole budget, as amended by the Parliament, back to the Commission, or further amend the amendments approved by the Parliament: in either case, a qualified majority is re-

[1] See Article 38 and commentary thereon.

quired; but for these purposes Article 23 (2)(b) prescribes a three-fifths rather than a two-thirds majority of the weighted votes cast. The three-fifths majority is the same as that prescribed for the Parliament on the second reading of the budget (Article 17 (2)(b)), and is also prescribed for the Parliament (but not for the Council) in the Community budgetary procedure: see EEC Treaty, Articles 203 and 204.

In general, it will be slightly easier to attain a qualified majority in the Council, whether a two-thirds or a three-fifths majority is prescribed, than under the EEC Treaty (Article 148), where 45 votes out of 63 are required for a qualified majority.

6.   The Treaty nowhere provides expressly for a unanimous vote in the Council. In that respect it differs markedly from the EEC Treaty, which lays down a requirement of unanimity not infrequently (Article 54 (1), Article 100, Article 235, etc.).

In at least one case, however, a requirement of unanimity may arise under the present Treaty. In certain fields of international relations, the Union will act by the method of co-operation (Article 66) and the European Council will be responsible for such co-operation. It can be supposed that in such cases the European Council will act unanimously. It is natural to suppose that the Council of the Union, to which institution the conduct of co-operation is entrusted under Article 67 (1), may also be required to act unanimously.

Article 23 (3) deals with the vexed question of the 'national veto' resulting from the Luxembourg Accords of January 1966: a subject which has been considered in a number of recent documents on European Union, notably the Report of the 'Three Wise Men' of October 1979, the draft European Act (the Genscher–Colombo proposal) of 6 November 1981, and the Solemn Declaration on European Union signed by the Heads of State and Government on 19 June 1983.[2]

The draft European Act envisaged that a Member State invoking 'vital interests' should have to justify its attitude concretely and in writing; the Council would then adjourn a decision to its next meeting, when a decision would be blocked only if the Member State concerned again invoked vital interests.

The Solemn Declaration on European Union recognizes[3] that 'The application of the decision-making procedures laid down in the Treaties

---

[2] See above, pp. 8–9.
[3] Point 2.2.2.

of Paris and Rome is of vital importance in order to improve the European Communities' capacity to act,' and that 'Within the Council every possible means of facilitating the decision-making process will be used, including, in cases where unanimity is required, the possibility of abstaining from voting.'

Article 23 (3) goes further than previous proposals in providing for the elimination of the 'national veto' after a period of ten years. The text reflects a compromise reached after considerable debate in the Institutional Committee: some wished the veto to be eliminated immediately or within a shorter period, while others considered that it should be retained for a longer period, if not indefinitely.

However, in one case the ten-year time limit, which is one of the very few transitional periods in the Treaty, does not apply, and the veto may continue to operate without any time limit. This is the case where, in the field of external relations, the European Council decides to transfer a particular matter from co-operation to common action. In that event, the provisions of Article 23 (2) apply without any time limit.[4]

In comparison with the Community arrangements under the Luxembourg Accords of January 1966, Article 23 (3) also incorporates three safeguards against possible abuse. The 'vital national interest' must be recognized as such by the Commission; the grounds invoked by a Member State must be made public; and the effect of the exercise of the veto is merely to postpone the vote so that the matter may be re-examined. The matter may then be brought before the Council again at a later date, when the conditions for the exercise of the veto may no longer obtain.

The Treaty does not expressly require that the date at which the matter is to be re-examined in the Council should be fixed at the time of the postponement. Since the grounds invoked by a representation for requesting the postponement are to be published, the need to fix the date is of less importance. It will be possible to see whether with the passage of time, the grounds invoked remain valid, and for other representations to judge when the matter should be brought back before the Council. It may also be possible for the Commission to take the view that, with the passage of time, the grounds invoked are no longer sufficient and to withdraw the recognition it had initially given.

Article 23 (3) embodies a compromise solution of a highly controversial problem and did not escape criticism in the plenary debate

---

[4] See Article 68 (2) and the commentary thereon.

preceding the adoption by the European Parliament of the Treaty. It was suggested that it was illogical that the existence of a vital national interest should be subjected to assessment by the Commission. Nevertheless it may be thought that a reasonable balance is achieved between the individual interests of the Member States and the collective interest of the Union.

Article 24

Rules of procedure of the Council of the Union

The Council shall adopt its rules of procedure by an absolute majority. These rules shall lay down that meetings in which the Council is acting as a legislative or budgetary authority shall be open to the public.

Preparatory documents:

Resolution of 14 September 1983, paragraph 124.

Provisions in force:

Merger Treaty, Article 5.

1. The first sentence of Article 24 provides for the adoption by the Council of its rules of procedure. Their adoption requires an absolute majority, i.e. a majority of the weighted votes cast, abstentions not counted: see Article 23 (2)(a). Article 5 of the Merger Treaty does not lay down any voting rule for the adoption by the Council of the European Communities of its rules of procedure; accordingly that Council acts by a majority of its members (EEC Treaty, Article 148 (1)).

Undoubtedly the Council has the competence, acting under the first sentence of Article 24, to set up subordinate bodies to which tasks of a subsidiary character can be delegated. However the creation of a body such as COREPER (Committee of the Permanent Representatives of the Member States), which was initially set up by the Council of the European Communities but was subsequently institutionalized by the Merger Treaty (Article 4), would not be compatible with the present Treaty. Article 20 clearly envisages that the representations making up the Council of the Union should themselves have the permanent responsibility for the conduct of the Council's business.[1]

2. The second sentence provides for a major change and is designed to meet a long-standing criticism of the secrecy of meetings of the Council of the European Communities.

[1] See the commentary on Article 20.

Publicity is, however, limited to meetings of a legislative or budgetary character: it would be inappropriate for the Council to meet in public when exercising its other powers, especially its powers in the field of international relations.

Article 25

The Commission

The Commission shall take office within a period of six months following the election of the Parliament.

At the beginning of each parliamentary term, the European Council shall designate the President of the Commission. The President shall constitute the Commission after consulting the European Council.

The Commission shall submit its programme to the Parliament. It shall take office after its investiture by the Parliament. It shall remain in office until the investiture of a new Commission.

Preparatory documents:

Resolution of 6 July 1982, paragraphs 7, 8(b) and (d).
Doc. 1-575/83/B, Zecchino Report, pp. 41 ff.
Doc. 1-575/83/C, Zecchino working document, pp. 139 ff.
Resolution of 14 September 1983, paragraphs 128 and 132 f.

Provisions in force:

Merger Treaty, Article 11.
Solemn Declaration on European Union of 19 June 1983, paragraph 2.3.5.

1.   Article 25 determines the manner in which the Commission is to be appointed and invested and thus establishes an essential political principle of the Treaty. The commonly agreed reason for change was stated clearly in the resolution of 6 July 1982: in future the European Parliament should participate in the constitution of the Commission. With regard to the extent of this participation, an alternative to Article 25 was discussed which provided for the Commission to be appointed jointly by the Parliament and the Council of the Union for a fixed period.[1] This method would ensure that the Commission was not always dependent on the political majorities in Parliament, would take equal account of the intergovernmental aspect and would, lastly, guarantee a stable period of office. Despite the possible lack of cohesion of

[1] Cf. Working document of Mr Zecchino, paragraphs 45 ff.

the political forces represented in Parliament, which was recognized in the working document of Mr Zecchino (paragraph 53), the Parliament decided in Article 25 in favour of parliamentary approval of the Commission, but ensured the continued influence of the Member States through the participation of the European Council. This influence excludes the possibility of a constructive non-confidence vote by Parliament alone, i.e. a solution whereby Parliament, by adopting a motion of censure, could always invest a new Commission at the same time. Such a procedure would deprive the Council of any part in the designation of the Commission.

The European Council is henceforth to appoint only the President of the Commission, who in turn has influence on the choice of Members. The decision to 'invest' the Commission as a whole is taken by a simple majority in Parliament. However, a qualified majority is required for the adoption by Parliament of a motion of censure obliging the Commission to resign. These different decision-making procedures for investiture, on one hand, and dismissal, on the other, are the essential aspects of the solution adopted in Article 25, a solution which may not always promote stability. Parliament is able to pass a motion of censure on the Commission but may not be in a position to invest a new Commission on its own initiative. No provision is made for the early dissolution of Parliament in the event of a political stalemate.

2. Paragraph 1 specifies that the Commission shall take office within a period of six months following the election of the Parliament. No mention is made of any sanctions in the event of this deadline not being respected. It is clearly not the intention, however, that a deadline should be set only for the first investiture after the entry into force of the Union Treaty. The Parliament must also invest a new Commission within a period of six months following the beginning of every subsequent parliamentary term (Article 14). This six-month period should allow the new Commission sufficient time to draw up and submit a programme and obtain Parliament's approval. If the deadline is not met, the previous Commission remains in office until the investiture of a new Commission (see paragraph 3, third sentence). This will also apply at the time of transition from the Community Treaties to the present Treaty and will have to be covered by the appropriate transitional provisions.

3. The second paragraph concerns the 'constitution' of the Commission. The Member States exercise considerable influence over the

constitution of the Commission; the European Council appoints the President of the Commission, who in turn constitutes the new Commission after consulting the European Council. The 'constitution' of the Commission must be distinguished from its 'investiture' (paragraph 3) by the Parliament. The constitution of the new Commission involves the exercise by the European Council of its exclusive right to designate the President, and the provisional appointment of the members of the Commission by the designated President. The sole task of the Commission is to draw up the programme which it must submit to the Parliament before its formal investiture (paragraph 3). Until the investiture, the newly constituted Commission and the existing Commission therefore exist side by side (paragraph 3, second sentence).

There are thus two new elements in the procedure for appointing the Commission. Whereas in the past the Governments of the Member States appointed all the members of the Commission by common accord (Article 11, Merger Treaty), it is now the right of the European Council, as an institution of the Union, to appoint the President. The existing President of the Commission, who takes part in the work of the European Council, may not participate in the European Council's discussions on the designation of his successor (see Article 31). The newly appointed President of the Commission is entitled to appoint the remaining members of the Commission himself. The organic law to be issued pursuant to Article 26 will contain more detailed provisions relating to the number and the expertise and personal qualities required of members of the Commission. The only way in which the Member States can exercise any influence at this stage is through the non-binding consultation of the European Council. It is hoped that this limitation will allow the newly appointed President of the Commission to assemble a team who are compatible in terms of both expertise and personal qualities and should, from the political point of view, be suitable for investiture by the European Parliament. At the same time it is intended to ensure that the Commission cannot be subject to the determining influence of the Member States and is dependent only on the Parliament in respect of its final investiture and dismissal.

4.   The third paragraph of Article 25 specifies that the Commission must submit its programme before the final investiture by the Parliament. Article 25 as a whole goes much further than the Solemn Declaration on European Union of 19 June 1983,[2] which provides for a vote

---

[2] Point 2.3.5.

on the Commission's programme only and not on the appointment of the Commission. Reservations on this point were, moreover, expressed by Denmark.

According to the first indent of Article 28, the programme must include 'the guidelines for action by the Union' and is thus to be distinguished from the annual general reports which the Commission is at present required to submit to Parliament, pursuant to Article 143 of the EEC Treaty. The programme is therefore a political statement of the line of action which the Commission, as the vehicle of legislative initiative (Article 37 (1)), intends to follow during its period of office. The phrase 'guidelines for action by the Union' used in Article 28 is therefore too broad, since Union policies can be influenced by other institutions, such as the European Council, for example, which can address communications to the other institutions of the Union (Article 32, fourth indent).

Unless otherwise specified, the investiture by Parliament is by a simple majority vote (Article 17 (1)). This is not a vote of confidence in an administration which is already in office but an investiture establishing the new Commission. The investiture marks the end of the activities of the previous Commission. The second indent of Article 16 states more clearly the connection between approval of the Commission's programme and its investiture ('The Parliament shall enable the Commission to take office by approving its political programme'). The Parliament cannot, therefore, express itself on the nomination of each member of the Commission, it can only accept or refuse to invest the entire Commission. This method of investiture reflects the nature of the Commission's responsibility to the Parliament. Under Article 29 (3) Parliament can only oblige the Commission to resign as a body, through the adoption of a motion of censure by a qualified majority.

The third sentence of paragraph 3 ensures the continuity of the Commission's work by requiring the existing Commission to remain in office until the investiture of the new Commission. The existing Commission is responsible not merely for dealing with day-to-day business, pursuant to the second sentence of Article 29 (4), after the adoption of a motion of censure by Parliament, but for continuing to carry out all the work of the Commission. This difference is justified by the fact that the Commission had the confidence of Parliament during the previous parliamentary term.

Article 26

Membership of the Commission

The structure and operation of the Commission and the Statute of its members shall be determined by an organic law. Until such a law comes into force, the rules governing the structure and operation of the Commission of the European Communities and the Statute of its members shall apply to the Commission of the Union.

Preparatory documents:

Resolution of 6 July 1982, paragraph 8(b).
Doc. 1-575/83/C, Zecchino working document, paragraphs 63 ff.
Resolution of 14 September 1983, paragraph 133, first subparagraph.

Provisions in force:

Merger Treaty, Articles 10-15, 17-18.

1. Articles 25 and 28 of the Treaty alter the method of appointment and the powers of the Commission. The influence of the Member States is reduced and a decisive part is played by the European Parliament. These alterations may mean that the structure of the Commission and its internal division of responsibilities will have to be reviewed. Article 26 allows for this possibility without itself specifying any changes. There are similar provisions in Article 30 (3) relating to the Court of Justice and in the second subparagraph of Article 33 (1) relating to the other organs.

2. The first sentence specifies that the structure and operation of the Commission and the Statute of its members are to be determined by an organic law. This provision accords with Article 7 (3), which also specifies that any subsequent alterations to the institutional structure of the Union may be made simply by organic law rather than any formal amendment of the Treaty. The same principle is stated once more in Article 34 (2), which would, in fact, have been sufficient to cover all the cases in question.

With regard to the structure of the Commission, the question of whether the President should retain the status of *primus inter pares* or be given genuine powers of leadership was discussed in the Zecchino report. Under the appointment procedure specified in Article 25, the President has a special status insofar as he alone is designated by the European Council. He could also occupy a special position within the Commission for this reason, but need not automatically do so. The organic law will also determine the number of members of the Commission. It can therefore be decided later whether the Commission will in future be composed of only one member from each Member State or whether it will still be possible to have two Commission members from one Member State (see Merger Treaty, Article 10(1)). The organic law will have to adapt all the relevant provisions contained in Articles 10 to 18 of the Merger Treaty in the light of the new status of the Commission under the Union Treaty.

The method of operation of the Commission will be determined principally by the rules of procedure provided for in Article 27. Essential questions, such as the extent of the responsibility of individual members of the Commission, and matters previously covered by the Merger Treaty, must be dealt with in the organic law provided for in Article 26.

The same will apply to the Statute of the members.

3.   The second sentence of Article 26 adds a typical transitional provision which would have been better included among the final and transitional provisions. The rules to which the second sentence refers are those contained in Articles 10 to 15, 17, and 18 of the Merger Treaty.

Article 27

Rules of procedure of the Commission

The Commission shall adopt its rules of procedure

Preparatory documents:

None

Provisions in force:

Merger Treaty, Article 16.

1. Article 27 allows the Commission independence in the matter of its rules of procedure. It does not bring about any change in the existing legal situation. Article 16 of the Merger Treaty simply adds that the rules of procedure must be published. Similar provisions are found in Articles 19 (Parliament), 24, first sentence (Council of the Union), 30 (4) (Court of Justice) and 33 (3).

Article 27 and the content of the rules of procedure must be distinguished from the organic law referred to in Article 26[1] which determines the structure and operation of the Commission and the Statute of its members. The organic law is to contain only the essential provisions governing operation. The existing legal situation may be taken as a guide in making this distinction. Rules previously contained in the three Community Treaties or the Merger Treaty will in future be included in the organic law. The rules of procedure will, as in the past, deal primarily with the administrative aspects of the organization of work.

2. Article 27 was included in the text purely for reasons of consistency. Without it the existing legal situation would automatically have been maintained as a result of the adoption of the Community patrimony (Article 7 (1)).

The existing rules of procedure of the Commission of the European Communities continue to apply until the entry into force of the new rules of procedure. This is a logical consequence of Article 26 (2).

[1] See commentary on Article 26, paragraph 2.

Article 28

Functions of the Commission

The Commission shall:

— define the guidelines for action by the Union in the programme which it submits to the Parliament for its approval,

— introduce the measures required to initiate that action,

— have the right to propose draft laws and participate in the legislative procedure,

— issue the regulations needed to implement the laws and take the requisite implementing decisions,

— submit the draft budget,

— implement the budget,

— represent the Union in external relations in the instances laid down by this Treaty,

— ensure that this Treaty and the laws of the Union are applied,

— exercise the other powers attributed to it by this Treaty.

Preparatory documents:

Resolution of 6 July 1982, paragraph 8(b).
Doc. 1-575/83/C, Zecchino working document, paragraph 64.
Resolution of 14 September 1983, paragraph 133, second subparagraph.

Provisions in force:

ECSC Treaty, Article 8.
EEC Treaty, Article 155.
EAEC Treaty, Article 124.

1. Article 28 lists the functions of the Commission and thus follows the principle of specific individual authorization. Corresponding provisions for the other institutions are found in Articles 16, 21, 32, and 43. The reference to other powers in the last indent indicates that the list is not exhaustive. Almost all the functions and powers are described in more detail elsewhere in the Treaty.

There was scarcely any disagreement in the Committee on Institutional Affairs over the list of functions. The new features to be noted are the Commission's independent powers in the matter of implementation and its right to represent the Union in external relations.

2. In its programme the Commission is to define the guidelines for action by the Union. Under Article 25, submission of the programme is a prerequisite for investiture by the Parliament. The general reports referred to in Article 143 of the EEC Treaty and Article 18 of the Merger Treaty, which in practice are accompanied only by a programme statement, are not comparable with the Commission's 'administrative programme'. The 'guidelines for action by the Union' do not contain provisions which are binding in any way on the activities of the other institutions. The European Council in any case has the possibility of making fundamental statements on the policy of the Union by addressing 'communications to the other institutions' (Article 32 (1), fourth indent). The guidelines referred to here concern only the future activities of the Commission, whose initiatives will play an important part in determining the activities of the Union as a whole. This restrictive interpretation can be explained by reference to the following indent.

3. The Commission is to introduce the measures required to implement the programme. The introduction of legislative measures is naturally the most important element here.[1] The term 'measures' also covers all general political statements of opinion, recommendations (see Article 155, second indent, EEC Treaty) and action which need not necessarily lead to the adoption of legislation. Measures in the field of external policy are also possible.

4. The proposal of draft laws and participation in the legislative procedure, in accordance with Articles 37 and 38, are still key functions of the Commission. They are described in further detail in Article 37 (1). The discussions in the Committee on Institutional Affairs and the Commission's opinion on the Treaty repeatedly drew attention to the importance of the exclusive power of initiative as a means of ensuring the Commission's independence and defending Community interests in the legislative procedure. If this power of initiative were shared by Members

---

[1] See point 4 below.

of the Council, for example, it could lead to the 'renationalization' of initiatives.[2]

Article 37 (1) leaves the power of initiative with the Commission as a general rule. However, Article 37 (2) grants the power of initiative, in certain cases, to the Parliament or to the Council. While the Treaty deprives the Commission of its exclusive power of initiative, it does so only in exceptional circumstances and taking account of the Commission's increased role in the legislative process (see Articles 37 and 38).

5.   The fourth indent empowers the Commission to issue the regulations needed to implement the laws and take the requisite implementing decisions. This power is regulated in Article 40. It represents a considerable extension of the Commission's powers by comparison with Article 155 of the EEC Treaty. Whereas the fourth indent of Article 155 of the EEC Treaty allowed the Commission to exercise powers in the matter of implementation only when they were expressly conferred upon it by the Council, the Union Treaty gives the Commission direct and independent responsibility for legislative and administrative provisions implementing the laws of the Union. However, under Article 40, the Council and Parliament as the legislative authority will still be able to include in the laws specific requirements relating to the content and procedural details of the implementing measures. They must, however, restrict themselves as far as possible to determining fundamental principles (see Article 34 (1)).

6.   The fifth indent, concerning the submission of the draft budget, relates to Article 76 (1).

7.   The sixth indent specifies the Commission's responsibility for implementing the budget and also relates to the financial part of the Treaty. Like Article 205 (1) of the EEC Treaty, Article 78 emphasizes that the Commission implements the budget on its own responsibility.

8.   The Commission is to be empowered to represent the Union in its external relations. There is no such clear reference to this right of representation either in Article 155 of the EEC Treaty or elsewhere in the Community Treaties. The second sentence of Article 211 of the EEC

---

[2] See Mr Thorn's statement, sitting of 13 September 1983, OJ European Parliament *Debates* No. 1–303, p. 48.

Treaty concerns only the representation of the Community in matters relating to national law. The first sentence of Article 65 (1) of the Union Treaty specifies that this right of representation applies to the Community's external relations in the field of common action. Article 65 (4) empowers the President of the Commission to deposit the instruments of ratification of agreements concluded by the Union. In the area of co-operation, however, Article 67 leaves open the question of which individual institution is to represent the Union. Paragraph 5 states that the European Council may call on its President, on the President of the Council of the Union or on the Commission to act as the 'spokesman of the Union'.

9. The Commission's responsibility for ensuring that the Treaty and the laws of the Union are applied is provided for under existing Community Law (Article 155, first indent, EEC Treaty). The fourth sentence of Article 42 provides for an organic law laying down in detail the procedures to be followed by the Commission to ensure the implementation of the law of the Union.

10. The ninth and final indent concludes this article with a reference to the 'other powers' attributed by the Treaty. Similar blanket provisions are included at the end of the articles listing the functions of the other institutions (see Articles 16, 21, and 32). Article 155 of the EEC Treaty did not contain a provision of this sort. It was clear, however, that it was not intended to provide an exhaustive list of the Commission's functions. Under the EEC Treaty the Commission has independent powers in many areas not mentioned in Article 155 but provided for in the Treaty.

Article 29

Responsibility of the Commission to the Parliament

1. The Commission shall be responsible to the Parliament.

2. It shall answer written and oral questions tabled by members of the Parliament.

3. The members of the Commission shall resign as a body in the event of Parliament's adopting a motion of censure by a qualified majority. The vote on a motion of censure shall be by public ballot and not be held until at least three days after the motion has been tabled.

4. On the adoption of a motion of censure, a new Commission shall be constituted in accordance with the procedure laid down in Article 25 of this Treaty. Pending the investiture of the Commission, the Commission which has been censured shall be responsible for day-to-day business.

Preparatory documents:

Resolution of 6 July 1982, paragraphs 7, 8(b) and (d).
Doc. 1-575/83/C, Zecchino working document, paragraphs 42 ff. and 61.
Resolution of 14 September 1983, paragraph 12.

Provisions in force:

ECSC Treaty, Articles 23 (3) and 24.
EEC Treaty, Articles 140 (3) and 144.
EAEC Treaty, Articles 110 (3) and 114.

1. Article 29 specifies the Commission's political responsibility to the Parliament and thereby establishes a connection with Article 25 concerning the investiture of the Commission by the Parliament. While the previous Community Treaties required the Commission to answer questions and provided for motions of censure, they contained no express mention of the Commission's political responsibility to Parliament.

2. Paragraph 1 specifies that the Commission is responsible to Parliament. The members of the Commission do not therefore have individual

responsibility. The political nature of Parliament's supervision is made clear in the third indent of Article 16. This responsibility is designed to reinforce the democratic authority of the Commission by means of democratically approved supervision.

3.   The right of Members of Parliament to put questions to the Commission, provided for in paragraph 2, is recognized in the existing Treaties. By institutional agreement it has been extended to include questions to the Council. This was expressly confirmed in the Solemn Declaration on European Union signed in Stuttgart on 19 June 1983.[1] Since the relationship between the Parliament and the Council is altered by the Treaty in that they are to share legislative authority, the right to put questions to the Council has become redundant. It is not specified, however, whether the Parliament still has the right to put questions to the European Council on matters of co-operation. This is not mentioned in Articles 66 to 68 of the Treaty.

4.   The provisions governing motions of censure in Article 29 (3) are taken almost directly from the existing treaties. The alternative of a constructive no-confidence vote could not be adopted since, under Article 25, the Parliament would not be able to act alone in the designation of a new Commission. The participation of the European Council is still required in the designation of the Commission.

A motion of censure can be adopted only by a qualified majority in Parliament. In line with Article 144, second paragraph of the EEC Treaty, Article 17 (2)(b) states that this means a majority of the members and two-thirds of the votes cast.

5.   Paragraph 4 states that if a motion of censure is adopted, a new Commission must be constituted in accordance with the procedure laid down in Article 25.[2] In order to ensure the continuity of the Commission's work, the second sentence provides that the Commission which has been censured must carry out the day-to-day business until the investiture of the new Commission by the Parliament. No time limit is laid down for the investiture of the new Commission. However, it may be inferred from the first paragraph of Article 25 that, by analogy, the

---

[1] Point 2.3.3.
[2] See commentary on Article 25 (1).

investiture of the Commission must take place within a period of six months following the adoption of the motion of censure.

When carrying out the day-to-day business, the Commission is restricted in its activities and cannot take decisions on fundamental political matters. The delay between the dismissal and investiture procedures may therefore lead to a degree of political paralysis.

Article 30

The Court of Justice

1. The Court of Justice shall ensure that in the interpretation and application of this Treaty, and of any act adopted pursuant thereto, the law is observed.

2. Half the members of the Court shall be appointed by the Parliament and half by the Council of the Union. Where there is an odd number of members, the Parliament shall appoint one more than the Council.

3. The organization of the Court, the number and Statute of its members, and the duration of their term of office shall be governed by an organic law which shall also lay down the procedure and majorities required for their appointment. Until such a law comes into force, the relevant provisions laid down in the Community Treaties and their implementing measures shall apply to the Court of Justice of the Union.

4. The Court shall adopt its rules of procedure.

Preparatory documents:

Doc. 1-575/83/B, Zecchino Report, p. 33.
Resolution of 14 September 1983, paragraphs 134-5.

Provisions in force:

ECSC Treaty, Articles 31-2(c) and 45.
EEC Treaty, Articles 164-8 and 188.
EAEC Treaty, Articles 136-40 and 160.

1. This article establishes two characteristics of the Union's judicial institution: its function and the way in which its members are to be appointed. All other aspects are left to a future organic law, except for the Procedure, which will be governed by rules of procedure adopted by the Court itself. Until the organic law is issued and enters into force, the legal system based on community law—the Treaties and Protocols relating to the Statute of the Court—will continue to apply.

It is important to bear in mind the close link between Article 30 and Article 43, which concerns judicial review. In the resolution of 14 September 1983, paragraphs 134, 135, and 136, which correspond to the two articles in question, were grouped under the same heading (The Court of Justice) but it was subsequently felt preferable to include judicial review among the provisions concerning acts of the Union. It is the existence of Article 43 which explains why Article 30 does not refer to a matter of supreme importance, i.e. the Court's powers.

2. The first paragraph of Article 30 is worded in a similar manner to Articles 164 of the EEC Treaty, 136 of the EAEC Treaty, and 31 of the ECSC Treaty, but in particular the latter, since Article 30(1) refers to the interpretation and application both of the Treaty and 'of any act adopted pursuant thereto' (Article 31 ECSC referred to the Treaty and the implementing rules). The function of the new Court is thus to act as a judicial guarantor of compliance with all the laws in the Union's legal system. Under Article 7, Community law forms part of this system, in that the legal patrimony representing the Community's achievements is taken over by the Union. There is thus continuity between the Court of Justice of the Community and the Court of Justice of the Union, which is intended to continue the work of the former without reducing its importance or scope, and to extend it to include all the areas governed by Union law.

3. As regards the system of appointing the members of the Court, paragraph 2 states categorically that both the Parliament and the Council of the Union are to be involved in selecting the individuals to be appointed to this high judicial office. In its resolution of 6 July 1982 the European Parliament asserted that it must be involved in the appointment of the members of the Court and this explains the opposition of the majority of Members to amendments tabled at the final plenary sitting, which sought to establish that the members of the Court should be appointed by the Council of the Union alone, or appointed by the Council subject to ratification by Parliament (a solution similar to that adopted in the United States, where the Senate is empowered to grant or withhold approval of the appointment by the President of Supreme Court judges). The system of having half the members appointed by each of the political institutions was preferred to that of having each member appointed jointly by the two institutions.

The organic law referred to in the subsequent paragraph will establish, among other things, the total number of members (at present nineteen: thirteen judges and six advocates-general), their statute, the duration of their term of office, and the detailed arrangements for their appointment (procedure and majorities required). This inevitably means that the application of paragraph 2 will be subject to the entry into force of the organic law.

A comparison between these articles and those in the Community Treaties relating to the appointment of the members of the Court of Justice (Articles 167 EEC Treaty, 139 EAEC Treaty and 32(b) ECSC Treaty) clearly shows that the point of the new system is to increase Parliament's role at the expense of the Member States, as is the case with many provisions in this Treaty. Parliament is indeed given distinct precedence, since, if there is an odd number of members, it is entitled to appoint one more than the Council. At present it is the Governments of the Member States who appoint the members of the Court of Justice of the Community 'by common accord', so that the act of appointment does not even involve a decision by the Council. The existing system has in practice led to a kind of sharing out of the seats in the Court (at least one for each of the nationalities corresponding to the Member States and more than one for the 'large' Member States), and has resulted in a situation where the appointment made by each government for the seat considered to be set aside for one of its citizens is generally regarded as being uncensurable by the other governments. It has been suggested that, even with the system envisaged in Article 30 (2), the risk of the seats being shared out on the basis of nationality would be as great and would indeed be increased by empowering Parliament to appoint half the members and the Council the other half. However, it is to be hoped that the new system will succeed in correcting the existing tendency. In this connection it should be pointed out that, during the debate on the preliminary draft Treaty, Parliament rejected a draft amendment providing that the Court should in any event include at least one citizen from each Member State.

A further point to be noted is that the term 'member of the Court' could include both judges and advocates-general, categories which are specifically referred to in the Community Treaties. However, the question as to whether the second category is retained or not is left open: the organic law might even prefer all members of the Court to hold the office of judge in order to deal with the increased work-load.

4.   The matters to be dealt with in the future organic law have already been mentioned. 'The organization of the Court' certainly includes not only the composition of the Court itself, but also the distinction between

the plenary and the Chambers, the President's powers and those of the registrar. It could also include those procedural aspects which it is felt should not be left to the rules of procedure. However, other aspects, both procedural and organizational, will be dealt with in the rules of procedure, just as in the existing Community system the provisions laid down in the rules of procedure complete those set out in the Treaties and in the Statutes of the Court of Justice.

As regards the continued application of Community law until the entry into force of the organic law (for the adoption of which no deadline is set), the expression 'the relevant provisions laid down in the Community Treaties and their implementing measures' in effect refers to all Community rules applicable to the Court of Justice and to its procedure including the Statutes of the Court and the existing Rules of Procedure, as well as, for example, the provisions of the Staff Regulations governing legal proceedings brought by officials.

5. The power of the Court to adopt its rules of procedure corresponds to the power granted to the other institutions independently to adopt their internal procedural rules. The requirement to obtain the Council's approval, laid down in the Community system in Articles 188 of the EEC Treaty, 160 of the EAEC Treaty, and 44 of the Statute of the Court annexed to the ECSC Treaty, has been removed.

Article 31

The European Council

The European Council shall consist of the Heads of State or Government of the Member States of the Union and the President of the Commission who shall participate in the work of the European Council, except for the debate on the designation of his successor and the drafting of communications and recommendations to the Commission.

Preparatory documents:

Doc. 1-575/83/B, Zecchino Report, p. 33.
Doc. 1-575/83/C, Zecchino working document, p. 155.
Resolution of 14 September 1983, paragraph 137.

1. The list of the institutions of the Union set out in Article 8 includes (in fifth place) the European Council; the innovatory aspect of its inclusion as compared with the Community Treaties has already been pointed out. It will suffice here to note that the European Council was set up in its present form in 1974 by decision of the Paris Summit and that it remains outside the Community structures, although the Heads of Government meeting in Paris conferred on the new body the extremely important task of 'ensuring progress and overall consistency in the activities of the Communities and in the work on political co-operation'. The inclusion of the European Council in the institutional structure of the Union is thus a major innovation. It is backed up by the recognition of co-operation as one of the Union's methods of action (see Article 10), although the European Council has additional functions which also fall within the domain of common action (see Article 32).

2. Article 31 lays down the composition of the European Council. The first point to be made in this connection is that, whereas point 3 of the communiqué issued following the 1974 Paris Summit provided for regular meetings of the Heads of Government (of the Community Member States) accompanied by the foreign ministers, this new provision does not refer at all to the ministers but to 'the Heads of States or Government of the Member States of the Union'. This is to take account of the

practice whereby the President of the French Republic has taken part in Summit and Council meetings. In general, the participation of Heads of State must depend on the nature of their constitutional powers in the field of foreign policy, and does not preclude the simultaneous presence of the Heads of Government of all the Member States.

As regards the position of the President of the Commission, he is indubitably a member of the European Council (and thus entitled to take part in its meetings), but he should not be involved in the formation of joint positions of the States. Current practice in the Council shows that unanimity (or sometimes a consensus) is achieved only among the Heads of Government present. A voting system is clearly not appropriate for a body intended to operate as an instrument of intergovernmental co-operation.

The President of the Commission is explicitly excluded from taking part in the work of the Council when it is discussing two matters, in relation to which his interests might conflict with those of the other members of the Council: the designation of his successor and the drafting of communications and recommendations to the Commission.

Article 32

Functions of the European Council

1. The European Council shall:
   — formulate recommendations and undertake commitments in the field of co-operation,
   — take decisions in the cases laid down by this Treaty and in accordance with the provisions of Article 11 thereof on the extension of the competences of the Union,
   — designate the President of the Commission,
   — address communications to the other institutions of the Union,
   — periodically inform the Parliament of the activities of the Union in the fields in which it is competent to act,
   — answer written and oral questions tabled by Members of the Parliament,
   — exercise the other powers attributed to it by this Treaty.

2. The European Council shall determine its own decision-making procedures.

Preparatory texts:

Doc. 1-575/83/B, Zecchino Report, p. 33.
Doc. 1-575/83/C, Zecchino working document, pp. 155–6.
Resolution of 14 September 1983, paragraph 138.

1. Under Article 32 (1) the first task of the European Council is to formulate recommendations and undertake commitments in the field of co-operation. For a proper understanding of this expression, it is necessary to refer to the definition of co-operation in Article 10 (3) ('all the commitments which the Member States undertake within the European Council') and to take account of the distinction between common action and co-operation and between their respective domains (Article 10). Co-operation takes place outside the fields subject to common action (Article 46).

In the light of these preliminary remarks, it is possible to assess the difference between the European Council's current role and that assigned to it by the Union Treaty. At present, the European Council is the highest body concerned with the drafting and implementation of Community policies and is also the body in which the Member States discuss the development of policies lying outside the Community's competence (above all, foreign policy). The Treaty, however, attributes responsibility for common action principally to the European Parliament, the Council, and the Commission, apart from certain specific and limited powers granted to the European Council. As a general rule the European Council must not interfere in the area which could be referred to as integration and which corresponds to the range of exclusive or concurrent competences exercised by the Union (Articles 47 to 62, 64, 65, and 70 to 81).

The reference to recommendations and commitments contained in Article 32 (1), first indent, is linked to Article 10 (3), second subparagraph ('The measures resulting from co-operation shall be implemented by the Member States or by the institutions of the Union in accordance with the procedures laid down by the European Council'). This implies that, in the field of co-operation, that is, in sectors of activity in which the Treaty does not provide for common action, the European Council requests the Member States or institutions to act in a certain manner or promotes informal agreements between the Member States to ensure co-ordination of their policies, or uses the institutions as a means of action.

2. The power to decide 'on the extension of the competences of the Union', the second item in the list contained in Article 32 (1), means in effect the power to transfer certain questions from the field of co-operation, in which they have been placed by the Treaty, to that of common action, thus extending the Union's exclusive or concurrent competences. The procedure for this is set out in Article 11, which is explicitly referred to in the Article now under consideration. This transfer is possible with regard to the whole field of foreign policy (Article 68 (2)) but is restricted, within the Union, to one very specific area: industrial co-operation structures established by Member States outside the scope of the Treaty (Article 54 (1)).

A question that arises is whether a European Council decision to extend competences, which clearly constitutes an agreement between states, should be submitted to those states for ratification through the national parliaments. The importance of the subject suggests that this should be the case.

The procedure which precedes the decision is governed by Article 11 and involves intervention, as has been seen, by the Commission, the Parliament, and sometimes also the Council of the Union. In addition, without deciding to increase the Union's competence as described above, the European Council may extend the field of co-operation on foreign policy (see Article 68 (1)). The exercise of this power is not subject to any particular procedure. This is explained by the fact that the definition of the restrictions on co-operation is primarily a negative one (see, with regard to international relations, Article 66), so that, in the final analysis, co-operation can be extended only in areas hitherto excluded from the scope of the European Council's political activities (defence, armaments, sales of arms, and disarmament).

3. The function of the European Council which has the greatest influence on the structure of the Union and hence, although indirectly, on the field of common action, is the designation of the President of the Commission. Under the Community Treaties, all the Members of the Commission are appointed by common accord of the Governments of the Member States (Article 11 of the Merger Treaty), so that the procedure for appointing the President laid down in the Union is, as it were, what remains of this prerogative of the Member States' Governments. However, although it is the President, appointed by the European Council, who constitutes the Commission of the Union, he must first consult the European Council (Article 25 (2)).

The European Council is required to keep in constant contact with Parliament, by informing it periodically of its activities (defined as 'the activities of the Union in the field in which it is competent to act') and by answering questions tabled by Members of Parliament. This represents a form of political control by Parliament over co-operation, for which there is an important precedent in the rules of procedure of the European Parliament, where it states that Members may also put questions to the Foreign Ministers meeting in political co-operation.

The European Council's power to address communications to the other institutions echoes the idea that certain powers of the Council are comparable to those of a Head of State in a parliamentary system.[1] Although these communications are of course political and not legal documents, the power to address them to the institutions does attenuate the sense of the European Council's isolation from the field of common action. Indeed, in exercising this power the European Council may also

[1] See Doc. 1-575/83/B, p. 33.

in future provide political guidance for the process of integration. In any event, these communications will be of value in co-ordinating direct action and co-operation.[2]

The Treaty confers other powers on the European Council, which are referred to in the final indent of Article 32 (1). One such power, to which attention should be drawn, is that of determining the seat of the institutions (Article 85). Even more important is the right to impose sanctions on Member States which seriously and persistently violate the Treaty, although here the exercise of this power is the preliminary to a complex inter-institutional procedure (see Article 44).

4.   Under Article 32 (2) the European Council independently determines its decision-making procedures. This power is comparable with the power granted to all the other Institutions to adopt their rules of procedure (Articles 19, 24, 27, and 30 (4)). However, the wording here is broader, since it allows both for permanent and standard rules in the proper sense of the term, or for a flexible system on the basis of which the European Council would select the appropriate decision-making procedures for each case. Either arrangement would have to be introduced unanimously but the procedures thereby established could provide for decisions to be taken unanimously or by consensus or by a majority. There is likely, however, to be a tendency not to alter the practice whereby European Council decisions have always been taken unanimously, or rather unopposed (that is, by consensus, without a vote). It should also be said that, in this context, the word 'decision' refers not only to cases in which the Council undertakes commitments or imposes obligations but to all cases in which it exercises its functions.

[2] See the working document by Mr Zecchino: Doc. 1-575/83/C, p. 155.

Article 33

Organs of the Union

1. The Union shall have the following organs:
   — the Court of Auditors,
   — the Economic and Social Committee,
   — the European Investment Bank,
   — the European Monetary Fund.

Organic laws shall lay down the rules governing the competences and powers of these organs, their organization and their membership.

2. Half the members of the Court of Auditors shall be appointed by the Parliament and half by the Council of the Union.

3. The Economic and Social Committee shall be an organ which advises the Commission, the Parliament, the Council of the Union, and the European Council; it may address to them opinions drawn up on its own initiative. The Committee shall be consulted on every proposal which has a determining influence on the drawing up and implementation of economic policy and policy for society. The Committee shall adopt its rules of procedure. The membership of the Committee shall ensure adequate representation of the various categories of economic and social activity.

4. The European Monetary Fund shall have the autonomy required to guarantee monetary stability.

5. Each of the organs referred to above shall be governed by the provisions applicable to the corresponding Community organs at the moment when this Treaty enters into force.

The Union may create other organs necessary for its operation by means of an organic law.

Preparatory documents:

Resolution of 6 July 1982, paragraph 8(i).
Doc. 1-575/83/C, Zecchino working document, paragraphs 71-5 and 77.
Resolution of 14 September 1983, paragraphs 22 (3) and 139-46.

Provisions in force:

EEC Treaty, Articles 129-30, 193-8, 206.

Protocol on the Statute of the European Investment Bank.

1. Article 33 appears at the end of the title dealing with the institutions and aims to give a concise description of the other organs. The different points made in various preparatory texts are brought together in Article 33. However, additional mention is made in Articles 51 (European Capital Market Committee and European Bank Supervisory Authority), 54 (specialized European agencies), and 61 (European University Institute and European Foundation) of certain organs which, in view of their specialized nature, should be dealt with in the provisions relating to the subject areas concerned. Provisions relating to the Union's own research establishments and its own revenue-collecting authorities are contained in Article 53 (2)(d) and Article 71 (3), third sentence.

The Union Treaty makes specific provision for the organs named in paragraph 1. Unlike the other organs of the European Community, their existence is guaranteed. The competences, powers, organization, and membership of these organs are regulated by an organic law (see Article 38).

2. The organizational structure which has developed around the Community institutions has many levels. It is almost impossible to calculate the total number of organizational units. In terms of importance they range from legally independent bodies with legal personality and considerable power, such as the European Investment Bank, to completely subsidiary and dependent auxiliary bodies of the institutions. Article 33 contains a selection intended to cover those organs which are most important to the Union. This is true in the case of the Court of Auditors, the Economic and Social Committee, and the European Investment Bank, referred to in Article 4 (2) and (3) and Article 129 (f) of the EEC Treaty, although the European Monetary Fund was previously dealt with, as the European Monetary Co-operation Fund, only in legislation based on Article 235 of the EEC Treaty.[1] The Monetary Fund, like the German Federal Bank (Article 88 of the Basic Law), thus becomes a body with constitutional status. All the organs which are not specifically named in Article 33, such as the Consultative Committee referred to in the ECSC Treaty, the Supply Agency referred to in the EURATOM Treaty, and Community bodies with legal personality set up on the

[1] OJ L 89 of 5 April 1973, p. 2.

basis of Article 235 of the EEC Treaty (European Centre for the Development of Vocational Training, European Foundation for the Improvement of Living and Working Conditions, and the European Agency for Co-operation) are included in the Community patrimony, which, pursuant to Article 7, is to be adopted by the Union. Mention of these organs in the Union Treaty was unnecessary since there was no reason to alter their role or structure or underline their importance.

3.   The term 'organ' (*'Einrichtung'* in German, *'organe'* in French) does not carry any specific meaning. It can therefore be used as a generic term for organizational units, covering those which have legal personality (European Investment Bank and Monetary Fund) and those which are organically related to the institutions (Court of Auditors and Economic and Social Committee). The Court of Auditors and Economic and Social Committee are secondary organs to the institutions; they are not subject to the influence of the institutions to any great extent, but they do not have a legally independent status.

4.   The appointment of the members of the Court of Auditors was considered so important by Parliament that it was felt that the Treaty should provide, in paragraph 2, for the method of appointment, rather than that it should be determined by an organic law. Whereas the previous Treaties provided for the members to be appointed by the Council 'after consulting the Assembly', the Council and Parliament are now each to appoint half of the members. This method is also adopted for the appointment of the members of the Court of Justice (Article 30 (2)), by analogy also with the German Constitutional Court, one half of whose members are appointed by the *Bundestag* and the other half by the *Bundesrat*.

5.   Paragraph 3 lays down the principal duties, powers, and structural features of the Economic and Social Committee. Whereas Article 33 essentially leaves the details of the other three organs to the subsequent organic laws, the Economic and Social Committee is given particular attention. This can perhaps be explained by the particular interest which the Economic and Social Committee has shown in the discussions of Parliament's Committee on Institutional Affairs.

The first sentence extends the institutional relations of the committee, previously confined to the Council and the Commission, to include

Parliament and the European Council. As a result, the previously pronounced association with the Council is diminished. This is also reflected in the third sentence, giving it independence in the matter of its rules of procedure, since these rules no longer have to be approved by the Council as in the past (Article 196 (2) of the EEC Treaty). The right of initiative of the Economic and Social Committee, which was for a long time a subject of controversy, is now firmly established by the first sentence of this paragraph. Hitherto, the Committee could invoke it only on the basis of its rules of procedure.[2] The Committee's consultative powers are also extended; it is no longer consulted simply in isolated cases 'where the Treaty so provides' (Article 198 (1) of the EEC Treaty), but must be consulted on every proposal which has a determining influence on the drawing up and implementation of economic policy and policy for society. If the expression 'determining influence' were narrowly interpreted, this would scarcely widen the scope of the consultation provided for in the present Treaties. Optional consultation by the Council and the Commission (Article 198 (1), second sentence, of the EEC Treaty) is still possible, but henceforth the Committee may also be consulted by Parliament and the European Council. It remains to be seen which institution will normally initiate this consultation. The fourth sentence is basically superfluous since this provision relating to membership is almost identical to Article 193 (2) of the EEC Treaty. The only addition is the specification that there should be 'adequate' representation of the various categories of economic and social activity, but this criterion is already applied under the present regime.

In conclusion, the Economic and Social Committee will continue in the role of a secondary organ but will break away from its particular institutional dependence on the Council, particularly if the relevant organic law takes up the process begun in the Treaty and applies it to such areas as staffing and budgetary matters. The possibility of giving the Economic and Social Committee equal status as an institution, at one time a repeated demand of the Committee, was not discussed in Parliament.

6. Paragraph 4 gives the European Monetary Fund the autonomy required to guarantee monetary stability. This ensures that it is not dependent on instructions from other institutions. This provision should

---

[2] Article 20 (4) of the Rules of Procedure of 13 June 1974, OJ L 2284 of 19 August 1974, p. 1.

logically have been included in Article 52, which describes in detail the
European Monetary System and also deals with the Statute and operation of the European Monetary Fund in the first indent of paragraph 3,
albeit with a reference to Article 33. The relationships of the central
banks to the governments and parliaments take different forms in different Member States. The need to provide clear guidance in the Treaty
on this question made it appropriate to provide for the fundamental
principle of the autonomy of the Fund, but only to the extent to which
autonomy was required to guarantee monetary stability. The autonomy
of the European Monetary Fund will develop in accordance with Article
52 (2), which provides for the progressive achievement of full monetary
union.

7.   The first sentence of paragraph 5 is a transitional provision which,
given the structure of the Treaty, seems superfluous at this point. It
reproduces a provision which follows of necessity from Article 7. Parliament did not, moreover, include any general transitional measures
for the institutions in Part 6 of the Treaty (see Articles 82 ff.).

The second sentence, on the other hand, is of far-reaching importance, since it will allow the Union to create other organs necessary for
its operation by means of organic laws. This provision gives a clear
legal basis for the further institutional development of the Union by
making qualified provision for the creation of other organs. The Community Treaties contain no provision specifying this possibility. Under
the EEC Treaty, organs with separate legal personality have been
created on the basis of Article 235. There was particular disagreement
over whether it was possible to create organs on the basis of the individual provisions allocating responsibilities, which the Court of Justice
mentioned in the case of the Laying-Up Fund for Rhine Shipping by
reference to Article 75 of the EEC Treaty.[3]

The extent of the powers granted to the Union in this respect will
remain a matter of controversy since the term 'organ' is imprecise and
is not clearly defined in legal terminology. It is clearly not intended that
all new organizational units of a secondary nature (e.g. committees)
should be subject to an organic law. The second sentence of Article
33 (5) will have to be interpreted as meaning that an organic law is
necessary for the creation of any organ which, in terms of its impor-

[3] Opinion 1/76 of 26 April 1977, 1977 [ECR], 741; the agreement did not enter into
force.

tance, the significance of its work, and its institutional independence is comparable to the organs listed in paragraph 1. This will mean that the creation of a new organ with legal personality will normally be subject to an organic law. An organic law will also be required if, pursuant to Article 51, the establishment of a European Bank Supervisory Authority is planned. A further limitation of the requirement for an organic law is contained in Article 54 (2) of the Union Treaty, which specifies that specialized agencies may be created by an ordinary law.

Article 61 (2) states that the European University Institute and the European Foundation 'shall become establishments of the Union'. Although they existed before the Union, their creation as establishments of the Union follows directly from the Treaty. If it is accepted that they fall within the category of organs, an organic law will be necessary to amend their organization, competences, and powers (Article 33 (1)).

Article 33 (5) can also serve as a basis for setting up the Union's own research establishments (see Article 53, second paragraph, (d)). However, these will normally be specialized agencies (see Article 54 (2)) or internal organizational units of the Commission.

8. Article 33 leaves unanswered a number of questions concerning the future development of the organizational structure of the Union. It does, however, provide the Union with clearer and more definite possibilities than those granted to the Communities for adapting organizational structure to the progress of integration. The scope of organic laws will remain a problem since Article 54 (2) specifies that specialized agencies may be set up by ordinary laws and each of the institutions must be allowed a certain amount of independent leeway with regard to its own internal organizational units. As a whole, Article 33 provides an important basis for the future organizational development of the Union, without resolving all the questions that may arise.

Article 34
Definition of Laws

1.   Laws shall lay down the rules governing common action. As far as possible, they shall restrict themselves to determining the fundamental principles governing common action and entrust the responsible authorities in the Union or the Member States with setting out in detail the procedures for their implementation.

2.   The organization and operation of the institutions and other matters expressly provided for in this Treaty shall be governed by organic laws adopted in accordance with the specific procedures laid down in Article 38 of this Treaty.

3.   Budgetary laws shall be adopted pursuant to the provisions of Article 76 of this Treaty.

Preparatory documents:

Doc. 1-575/83/B, De Gucht Report, p. 9.
Doc. 1-575/83/C, De Gucht working document, p. 12.
Resolution of 14 September 1983, paragraph 22.

1.   In the hierarchy of the sources of Union law, laws come immediately after the Treaty and are the principal instrument of common action. They are binding and of general application, but each law will establish whether it imposes obligations on the Member States, on institutions, or on individuals, or on more than one of these categories (see Article 10 (2)).

Under the Community system, the judicial act which has this effect is the regulation (Articles 189 of the EEC Treaty and 161 of the EAEC Treaty) or decision (Article 14 of the ECSC Treaty). In the Union, however, the term 'regulation' applies to the acts implementing laws (see Article 28), although it is extended in the French and Italian versions of the Treaty to each institution's internal rules of procedure (Articles 19, 24, 27, 30 (4), and 32 (2)). There is a further important difference between the sources of Community and Union law: the directive, a familiar feature of Community law, does not appear in the Union's legal system, where it is replaced by laws determining fundamental principles, whose implementation is entrusted to the national authorities.

The reasons for this innovation should be explained. Under Community law, the increasingly detailed content of directives and their interpretation in accordance with the principle of direct effect have gradually blurred the distinction between directives and regulations. Moreover, the provisions of many regulations are not immediately applicable, being drafted in the form of principles which the Commission or the national authorities are required to supplement with secondary legislation. The difficulties raised by certain national judges concerning the principle of direct effect and the misunderstandings that have arisen over the conditions accompanying it have on occasion jeopardized the uniform implementation of directives. It was therefore considered preferable to establish laws as the sole source of Union legislation and to replace the distinction between regulations and directives by that between detailed laws and laws laying down principles. The difference between these two types of law lies in their degree of detail which may or may not imply the existence of implementing regulations in order for them to be fully effective.

2. Article 34 provides for three types of law: ordinary laws (paragraph 1), organic laws (paragraph 2), and budgetary laws (paragraph 3).

3. With regard to ordinary laws, a further distinction may be drawn between those which are complete in themselves and those which require supplementary provisions to complete them. In general, ordinary laws should be of the second kind, to which could be applied the term 'framework legislation' used in paragraph 22 of the European Parliament resolution of 14 September 1983. In accordance with Article 34 (1), the laws promulgated by the European legislative authority should, as far as possible, govern only the fundamental principles of common action, the procedures for their implementation being set out in detail in acts adopted either by other Union authorities (principally Commission regulations) or by the Member States (national laws or regulations).

However, there is no absolute distinction between 'fundamental principles' and 'the procedure for their implementation'. In practice, either the law will contain not only the principles but also additions to and developments of them, in which case the only task remaining will in fact be to determine the detailed arrangements, or the law will confine itself to introducing genuine principles, in which case the subsequent legislation, while described as implementing procedures, will involve major choices on the part of the Commission or the national authorities. In other words, it will involve the process of decentralized legislation explicitly referred to in paragraph 22 of the resolution of 14 September 1983. The Treaty does not prejudge either possibility and it also allows for the adoption of laws which are complete in themselves. It will be for the Union legislator to determine the structure of legislation and one can only hope that there will be no repetition of the situation in which Community directives have become excessively detailed and prolix.

4.   Organic laws are distinguished from ordinary laws by the fact that, at certain stages of the voting procedure, qualified and hence larger parliamentary majorities are required for their adoption than for ordinary laws (see Article 38). On the other hand it is difficult to draw a distinction in terms of the subject-matter of the laws since, in addition to the organization and operation of the institutions (see for example Articles 14, second paragraph, 18, 26, 30 (3), 42, and (43) and organs (Article 33 (1) and (5)), a wide range of matters are governed by organic laws: for example, monetary questions (Article 52 (3)), financial affairs (Articles 71 (2), 73, and 75 (4)) and the selection of the seat of the institutions if the European Council fails to decide within two years (Article 85). An organic law is also required to amend provisions of the Community Treaties other than those concerning the Community's objectives and scope (Article 7 (3)), and whenever a decision is taken to introduce common action in a field where action has not hitherto been taken by the Union or by the Communities (Article 12 (2)). Finally, for laws amending the Treaties, the procedure applicable to organic laws is followed but their entry into force depends on subsequent ratification by the Member States (Article 84).

5.   Budgetary laws are characterized both by their specific function and by the procedure for their adoption (governed by Article 76). The constitutional law of many States also draws attention to the special nature

and function of budgetary laws as formal acts granting authorization. In Union law, this special nature is indicated in Article 75 (1) of the Treaty, which states that 'the budget shall *lay down* and *authorize* all the revenue and expenditure of the Union in respect of each calendar year.'

Article 35

Differentiated application of laws

A law may subject to time limits, or link to transitional measures, which may vary according to the addressee, the implementation of its provisions, where uniform application thereof would encounter specific difficulties caused by the particular situation of some of its addressees. However, such time limits and measures must be designed to facilitate the subsequent application of all the provisions of the law to all its addressees.

Preparatory text:

Doc 1-575/83/C, De Gucht working document, paragraph 44.
Resolution of 14 September 1983, paragraph 25.

1. In connection with the definition of laws, Article 35 allows for the possibility of deferring immediate and uniform implementation of a law by all the addressees if specific problems make this necessary. The law itself can therefore provide for different transitional periods and measures for individual addressees, with the ultimate aim, however, of ensuring uniform application by all the addressees. Article 35 therefore allows for temporary exemption from the uniform and general application of laws.

2. The European Parliament is here taking up an idea which was expressed in the 1975 Tindemans Report to the European Council on European union. According to that report, progress in economic and monetary policy should be achieved by means of 'graduated integration': while all Member States should decide on a goal to be achieved, some should be permitted by Council decision, on the basis of objective criteria, not to take part immediately in the proposed developments. The report adds two conditions: the States which move ahead should provide special assistance to ensure that a uniform degree of integration can be reached, and all the Member States should continue to take part 'in assessing the results obtained in the fields in question'.[1] As in the present Article 35, this does not mean a '*Europe à la carte*' but simply a difference

---

[1] See *EC Bulletin* Supplement 1/76, p. 21.

in time scales for the implementation of jointly agreed measures. The 'partial agreements' associated with the Council of Europe should not, therefore, be taken as models, since their application is in some cases limited in the long term to only certain Member States.

3. The idea of graduated integration is also taken up in Article 68 (2) and Article 82 of the Treaty. Article 68 (2) concerns decisions to transfer a field of co-operation in external policy to common action, from which the Council may exempt individual Member States. Article 82 authorizes the entry into force of the Treaty establishing European Union once it has been ratified by a majority of the Member States, whose population represents two-thirds of the total population of the Communities. In neither case is there any specific requirement that the resulting differences in the extent of integration are to be corrected within a given time limit.[2]

4. Article 35 is based on the consideration that joint decisions on laws relating to common action may be facilitated if allowances are made for the particular situations and difficulties of individual addressees as regards the subsequent application and implementation of these laws. As pointed out in paragraph 25 of the Resolution mentioned above, the 'addressees' may be Member States, regions, or individuals. The larger the geographical area, the number of Member States, and the differences in the structure of their economies, the greater the need to take account of the specific situation of individual addressees and their particular difficulties when it comes to the implementation of a measure. It is therefore the law itself which provides for the differences in application. The same law must also provide for the subsequent achievement of uniform implementation by all the addressees. Article 35 specifies only this objective and does not expressly mention the duty of the more advanced Member States to assist the progress of those addressees initially remaining behind. However, the second sentence of Article 35 conveys the same meaning, since it refers to measures designed to facilitate the subsequent application of all the provisions of the law to all its addressees.

Article 35 thus temporarily sacrifices the idea of a uniform legal area within the Union in order to make possible the further development of the Union, and envisages the future restoration of legal unity. In addi-

[2] For more details see the commentary on Articles 68 and 82.

tion, the implication is that it applies only to new legal measures and does not affect the existing uniform Community patrimony, although the terms óf the Article do not exclude this possibility. The temporary differentiation permitted by the Article will not, in any case, be allowed to conflict with the basic aims of the Union and can therefore have only limited significance.

Article 35 does not contradict the principle of non-discrimination and the application of uniform law throughout the Union. If material reasons make differentiation necessary, the different measures adopted do not involve the application of Article 35. There are thus already many measures which are not applied to all potential addressees within the Communities because of material differences or particularities (e.g. measures relating to rivers, mountain regions, olive producers, safeguard clauses, and frontier regions).[3]

5. In the discussions on the Treaty there was some criticism of the content of Article 35 and it was suggested that it should be deleted. In view of its limited scope, however, this alternative was disregarded in the final debate. The report of the Committee set up by the European Council of Fontainebleau, the Dooge Committee, adapted the idea of the differentiated application of Community rules provided that such differentiation was limited in time, was based solely on social and economic considerations, and respected the principle of budgetary unity.

[3] See C. D. Ehlermann, 'How flexible is Community law? An unusual approach to the concept of "two speeds"', 82 *Michigan Law Review* 1984, p. 1274.

Article 36

Legislative authority

The Parliament and the Council of the Union shall jointly exercise legislative authority with the active participation of the Commission.

Preparatory documents:

Resolution of 6 July 1982, paragraph 8(b).
Doc. 1-575/83/B, Zecchino Report, pp. 40-1.
Resolution of 14 September 1983, paragraph 130.

The purpose of Article 36 is solely to draw attention to the basic principles governing the exercise of legislative authority in the Union, that is to say division of the power to legislate between the Parliament and the Council of the Union, and also the active participation of the Commission in the legislative process. Those principles are illustrated in Articles 37 and 38 of the Treaty. From the technical point of view, Article 36 was not indispensable, but it provides, in essence, a synthesis in so far as the intended balance of powers is not immediately apparent from Articles 36 and 37, by reason of their complexity.

From the substantive point of view, the Parliament acquires the power of joint decision which it has been claiming for a considerable period and which the Vedel Report[1] proposed should be conferred upon it. While discussions within the Committee on Institutional Affairs focused on the procedures for the exercise of that power of joint decision, in particular on the basis of the counter-proposals from Mr Hansch,[2] the actual principle of joint decision was never challenged. The *ad hoc* Committee set up by the European Council of Fontainebleau also accepted the principle of joint decision in recommending that the Parliament should have an effective participation in the legislative power whose sphere would be expressly defined in the form of a joint decision with the Council.

[1] *EC Bulletin*, Suppl. 4/1972, point 4.
[2] See commentary on Article 38.

Article 37

Right to propose draft laws and amendments thereto

1.   The Commission shall have the right to propose draft laws. It may withdraw a draft law it has submitted at any time until the Parliament or the Council of the Union have expressly adopted it on first reading.

2.   On a reasoned request from the Parliament or the Council, the Commission shall submit a draft law conforming to such a request. If the Commission declines to do so, the Parliament or the Council may, in accordance with procedures laid down in their rules of procedure, introduce a draft law conforming to their original request. The Commission must express its opinion on the draft.

3.   Under the conditions laid down in Article 38 of this Treaty:

— the Commission may put forward amendments to any draft law. Such amendments must be put to the vote as a matter of priority,

— Members of the Parliament and national representations within the Council may similarly put forward amendments during the debates within their respective institutions.

Preparatory documents:

Resolution of 13 June 1982, paragraph 8(b).
Doc. 1-575/83/B, Zecchino Report, pp. 40-1.
Resolution of 14 September 1983, paragraph 130, subparagraphs 1-3.

Provisions in force:

EEC Treaty, Article 149.
EAEC Treaty, Article 119.

1.   Article 37 contains all the provisions on the right to propose both draft laws and amendments thereto. This right to propose legislation is one of the principal functions attributed by the Community Treaties to the Commission of the European Communities. Since it has been elected by direct universal suffrage, the Parliament has sought to have such a right conferred upon it as well. Admittedly, in so far as such a right

might have appeared contrary to the Treaties, there could be no question of a direct right attaching to Parliament, but the demand for 'prior
consultation' before the Commission makes any formal proposal, the
adoption of Parliamentary own-initiative resolutions intended to encourage the Commission to make proposals in a particular area, and
the exercise of an indirect right of proposal in connection with the
budget are the manifestations of that desire. For its part, the Commission has always sought to preserve the independence of its right to
propose legislation, in the full awareness that if it accepted that it was
bound by the Parliament, the Commission's authority, which depends
upon its autonomy, would be reduced.

Since a strong Commission was considered desirable, it was appropriate to retain its right to propose legislation, but in order to be
consistent with its claims the Parliament had to ensure that it would
have an opportunity to put forward its own proposals. The solution
adopted in Article 37 achieves a satisfactory compromise. It recognizes
that the Commission has priority regarding the right to propose legislation, while according the Parliament and the Council a residual right
in that respect.

2.   Article 37 (1) establishes, in principle, the Commission's right to
propose legislation. That principle has not given rise to any difficulties.
The members of the Parliament were fully aware of current developments in national legislative systems, by virtue of which there is a
tendency for the initiative regarding legislation to be reserved to the
executive. They also knew that the Commission was better equipped,
from the technical point of view, than the Parliament or the Council
for the preparation of draft laws. Exercise of the right to propose
legislation entails the right to withdraw drafts submitted to the legislative authority. The resolution grants the Commission that power, which
was available to it at all stages of the procedure. When the Treaty was
being prepared, it appeared difficult to allow the Commission the right
to withdraw a draft when it had been adopted by one of the arms of
the legislative authority. In fact, to do so would have been to give it a
right of absolute veto, which it could use if any of its drafts was
amended in a manner which did not suit it. The 'right to object' granted
to it by Article 38 (3), which would enable it to deliver an unfavourable
opinion on the text adopted by Parliament, seems sufficient. The right of
withdrawal should be operative where it seems to the Commission, in
view of the reactions to its draft, that an unfavourable vote is inevitable

and where the Commission considers it preferable to re-examine its draft rather than risk a failure which would entail outright condemnation of its proposal. In view of the possibility of implicit adoption of a draft as a result of silence on the part of one of the arms of the legislative authority, the right of withdrawal is available until express adoption of the draft either by the Parliament or by the Council. In other words, if the draft is adopted, with or without amendment by the Parliament on a first reading, withdrawal becomes impossible. If, on the other hand, the Parliament does not give a decision within the prescribed time limit, withdrawal is possible until the council votes.

3. Article 37 (2) enables the Parliament and the Council to initiate legislation. For that purpose, either of those institutions addresses a reasoned request to the Commission, which then has the task of putting the proposal into an appropriate form, that is to say of preparing a draft law. This gives the Commission some discretionary margin for manœuvre and enables it to place its experience at the disposal of the other two institutions. Since no condition is laid down regarding a majority, the request is adopted by a simple majority in either of the two institutions. The idea was considered of granting the right to propose legislation to a national representation within the Council or to a specified number of Members of the Parliament, but, both in order to avoid an excessive number of proposals and to endow proposals with greater authority, it was considered preferable to require a majority in the Parliament or the Council. Three amendments seeking to grant the right to propose legislation to every Member of the Parliament (amendments Nos. 1, 85, and 91) were rejected by the Parliament when voted upon at a plenary sitting.[1] Of course, it will be for the rules of procedure of each of the institutions to specify the conditions applicable to initiatives for a reasoned request. In any event, an indirect right to propose legislation is recognized here in favour of each of the arms of the legislative authority.

Having received such a request, the Commission is not obliged to act upon it. In order to prevent the Commission having a right of veto, in the event of its refusal to act, the Parliament and the Council are entitled to exercise a direct right to initiate legislation by introducing a draft law. In order to avoid abuse of procedure, it is prescribed that the draft

[1] In fact, amendment No. 91 concerned only the right to submit a reasoned request. That request had then to be adopted by the Parliament or the Council.

must conform to the original request, a matter which will not always be easy to assess. Draft laws introduced in these circumstances will be accompanied by an opinion from the Commission, enabling the Commission to state the reasons for its reticence and, possibly, to persuade the arm of the legislative authority which did not initiate the draft to vote against it. The Resolution required the Commission to state the reasons for its refusal to act upon a request from the Parliament or the Council. It became apparent that such a requirement was self-evident, since it was difficult to imagine a Commission responsible to the Parliament refusing to explain its decision. It is true that the Commission is not answerable to the Council of the Union, but it is still unlikely that it would refuse to state the reasons for its refusal.

4. The right of amendment is shared by the Commission, the Members of the Parliament and the national representations within the Council. But the Commission is in a privileged position since its amendments must be considered as a matter of priority. This means that the Institution to which they are submitted must put them to a vote, since it will not be possible to cause them to lapse by adopting an amendment emanating from a member of the Institution which moves further away from the original text. In certain cases, the Commission even has a monopoly on the tabling of amendments (cf. Article 38 (4) regarding cases where conciliation is unsuccessful). However, like other amendments, the Commission's amendments will have to be tabled within the time limits laid down for that purpose in the rules of procedure of the Parliament and the Council.

The conditions for the exercise of the right of amendment within the Parliament and the Council will also have to be specifically laid down in the rules of procedure of those institutions. The draft leaves open the question whether each Member of the Parliament or of the Council will be entitled to propose amendments. It might be considered that if it had been intended that that right should be available to each Member personally, it would have been easy to say so in the text. However, the wording chosen 'Members of the Parliament and national representations within the Council' does not imply that each Member is not entitled to propose amendments. At present, Parliament's rules of procedure give each Member the right to propose amendments, except in relation to the budget, amendments to which must be signed by at least five Members. The existing text thus raises the problem of the exercise by individuals of the right to propose amendments. Does it create a right for each Member or is the matter left to the rules of procedure of each institution? In our view and with reference to Article 15, this right should be accorded to each Member of Parliament and to each representation.

5. The text of Article 37 appears to be particularly apposite as regards the role which it reserves to the Commission. The Parliament has been able to increase its rights in a very moderate fashion while at the same time essentially maintaining the privileges of the Commission. This bears witness to the realistic approach of the members of the Parliament and of their desire to preserve the authority of the Union's executive. The Treaty is more complete than the text of the Resolution, in so far as it grants the right to propose amendments to the Members of the Parliament and the national representations within the Council.

The provisions of Article 37 apply only to the adoption of laws which are subject to Article 38 (ordinary laws and organic laws). Moreover, Article 37 (3) refers expresssly to Article 38. The adoption of budgetary laws is governed by special provisions. As a result, the Commission has no right to propose amendments on budgetary matters, since Article 76, which applies to such matters, does not lay down any such right.

Article 38

Voting procedure for draft laws

1. All draft laws shall be submitted to the Parliament. Within a period of six months, it may approve the draft with or without amendment. In the case of draft organic laws, the Parliament may amend them by an absolute majority; their approval shall require a qualified majority.

Where the majority required for approval of the draft is not secured, the Commission shall have the right to amend it and to submit it to the Parliament again.

2. The draft law approved by the Parliament, with or without amendment, shall be forwarded to the Council of the Union. Within a period of one month following approval by the Parliament, the Commission may deliver an opinion which shall also be forwarded to the Council.

3. The Council shall take a decision within a period of six months. Where it approves the draft by an absolute majority without amending it, or where it rejects it unanimously, the legislative procedure is terminated.

Where the Commission has expressly delivered an unfavourable opinion of the draft, or in the case of a draft organic law, the Council shall by a qualified majority approve the draft without amending it or reject it, in which cases the legislative procedure is terminated.

Where the draft has been put to the vote but has not secured the majorities referred to above, or where the draft has been amended by a simple majority or, in the case of organic laws, by an absolute majority, the conciliation procedure laid down in paragraph 4 below shall be opened.

4. In the cases provided for in the final subparagraph of paragraph 3 above, the Conciliation Committee shall be convened. The Committee shall consist of a delegation from the Council of the Union and a delegation from the Parliament. The Commission shall participate in the work of the Committee.

Where, within a period of three months, the Committee reaches agreement on a joint text, that text shall be submitted for approval to the Parliament and the Council; they shall take a decision by an absolute majority or, in the case of organic laws, by a qualified majority within a period of three months. No amendments shall be admissible.

Where, within the period referred to above, the Committee fails to reach agreement, the text forwarded by the Council shall be submitted for approval to the Parliament which shall, within a period of three months, take a decision by an absolute majority or, in the case of organic laws, by a qualified majority. Only amendments tabled by the Commission shall be admissible. Within a period of three months, the Council may reject by a qualified majority the text adopted by the Parliament. No amendments shall then be admissible.

5.   Without prejudice to Article 23 (3) of this Treaty, where the Parliament or the Council fails to submit the draft to a vote within the time limits laid down, the draft shall be deemed to have been adopted by the institution which has not taken a decision. However, a law may not be regarded as having been adopted unless it has been expressly approved either by the Parliament or by the Council.

6.   Where a particular situation so requires, the Parliament and the Council may, by common accord, extend the time limits laid down in this Article.

Preparatory documents:

Resolution of 6 July 1982, paragraph 8(c).
Doc. 1-575/83/B, Zecchino Report, pp. 40-1.
Resolution of 14 September 1983, paragraphs 130 (5) ff.

1.   Article 38 is one of the provisions of the Treaty whose drafting required the greatest care. The structure of the legislative process had to reflect preoccupations which it was not easy to reconcile. The process had to be made democratic by increasing the Parliament's role, while at the same time safeguarding the rights of the Council of the Union. The aim was to achieve a balance between the Parliament and the Council, that is to say between the representatives of the peoples and of the

States, while at the same time facilitating effective co-operation between the two Institutions in the event of disagreement. It was necessary to take due account of the need for a strong executive which can participate authoritatively in the legislative process. The rights of the Commission were studied very closely. A final objective was to prevent the hold-ups which now occur from recurring within the Union and, for that purpose, to find a means of compelling an Institution which wishes to paralyse the legislative process to give a decision for or against the draft law. In order to achieve those results, the present procedure was taken as a basis and changes were made to reflect the need for Parliament to be given a power of joint decision; and certain courses of action were adopted which have proved their worth in relation to the budgetary procedure, such as the rules whereby an Institution is deemed tacitly to have given its acceptance upon the expiry of prescribed periods. Of course, certain features of national systems regarding relations between the two chambers of national parliaments were also taken into account. On the basis of all this information, the Parliament considered it appropriate to adopt the very elaborate legislative procedure which is described in great detail in the Resolution of 14 September 1983. When the draft Treaty was being prepared, it was not possible to depart from the principles thus laid down, since they reflected a considerable degree of political agreement. However, the Resolution was imprecise in certain areas and contained certain imperfections which would have made the procedure unworkable if the text of the Treaty had merely followed that of the Resolution.

That is why on many points differences are to be seen between the Resolution and the draft Treaty. The text of the draft was also improved at the plenary sitting by amendments by Madame Veil (Amendment No. 47) and by Mr Spinelli (Amendment No. 124). The wording of Article 38 may appear to be complex, but it must be agreed that that complexity, which is more apparent than real, is due to the multiplicity of the interests which it was sought to safeguard.

2.   Each reading of draft laws before each of the arms of the legislative authority is subject to particular time limits (Article 38 (5)). As noted earlier, endeavours were made to ensure that silence on the part of an Institution would not paralyse the legislative process. The Resolution provided that if an Institution did not give a decision within the prescribed period, it would be deemed to have approved the draft. Paragraph 5 embodies that rule.

In the first place, it is wholly without prejudice to the provisions of Article 23 (4), which provides for postponement of voting in the Council where a representation claims that a vital national interest is jeopardized by the decision to be taken and the interest is recognized as vital by the Commission. To provide otherwise would have entirely negated Article 23 (3). Does that exception render the provision regarding time limits meaningless? In addition to the fact that Article 23 (3) is applicable only for a transitional period of ten years, it should be noted that it does not entail rejection of the draft law, but merely postponement of the vote, and the logical purpose of that must be to cause time to start running for a further period of six months. However, this question is closely linked to the interpretation of Article 23 (3). If it is held that application of that article cannot result in the vote being postponed indefinitely but only in a new date being fixed, the six-month period recommences from the date fixed. If, however, the vote may be postponed indefinitely, the Commission must decide whether the vital interest invoked does exist and the six-month period will recommence from the date on which the Commission establishes that the vital interest can no longer be upheld. This is the only interpretation which does not render Article 23 (3) or Article 38 (5) entirely meaningless.

3. The rule on time limits operates if there is no vote. In order to avoid tacit acceptance, it is not sufficient for an Institution to consider the draft—it must also have put it to the vote.

However, automatic application of the time limits would have enabled legislation to enter into force after implicit acceptance by both arms of the legislative authority. That was not the intention of the Parliament, which merely wished to ensure the possibility of bypassing an obstruction created by either of the Institutions; it did not wish to act against their interests, and that is why it is provided that no law is to be adopted unless it has been expressly approved by at least one of the arms of the legislative authority. Two sets of circumstances may arise. If the Parliament, which is always the first to have draft legislation placed before it, does not give a decision within a period of six months, the text must, in order to be adopted, be expressly approved by the Council without amendment. If the Parliament adopts the text on a first reading, with or without amendments, it will be definitely adopted if the Council fails to vote on it within a period of six months, when given notice to that effect. The same rule operates *mutatis mutandis* on a second reading before the Parliament or the Council, although there are specific problems which will be considered when Article 38 (4) is reviewed.[1]

These time limits may be extended by agreement between the Parliament and the Council. When the draft Treaty was approved in the Parliament, it was made clear that such an extension could take place only 'where a particular situation so requires', which means that no general rule may be established and that extensions must be decided upon case by case. The decision is to be adopted by a simple majority in each Institution.

4. The Parliament will give its decision in all cases on a first reading, having a period of six months as from submission of the draft law to it in which to do so. Four situations may arise.

(i) The text is approved without amendment, by a simple majority for an ordinary law (because no special condition regarding majorities is laid down in Article 38) or by a qualified majority for an organic law. It will then be passed immediately to the Council.

(ii) The text is approved with amendments by a simple majority in the case of an ordinary law and a qualified majority in the case of an organic law (although the adoption of amendments requires only an absolute majority). It is then passed immediately to the Council. It was sought to facilitate amendments to organic laws by requiring only an absolute majority. But is it not possible that such a difference between the majorities required might be used to frustrate the passage of a draft law by adopting, by an absolute majority, an amendment which makes adoption of the text by a qualified majority impossible?

(iii) On being put to the vote, the text is not approved. The legislative process comes to an end when the draft is rejected. The Resolution provided that when a draft law was rejected the Commission should be invited either to amend or to withdraw the draft. In fact, non-approval causes the draft law to lapse and it is therefore unnecessary to withdraw it. Under Article 38 it is possible for the Commission to amend the draft and to re-submit it to Parliament. Recourse to that possibility entails a right of re-submission, but the Commission has that right in any case by virtue of its right to propose legislation. The second subparagraph of

[1] In our opinion, implied approval takes place only if no decision is given on a text having the same wording as that which was adopted in the other Institution or if the text expressly adopted is identical to that in respect of which no decision was adopted.

Article 38 (1) appears superfluous because it is covered by Article 37 (1), but the Parliament considered that it might be politically important to make clear that the failure of a draft to secure approval did not mean that it was irretrievably rejected.

However, the Commission can use its right to submit amendments in order to modify its draft, taking account of the views expressed in Parliament's debates, so as to make its text acceptable to Parliament.

(iv) The draft law is not put to the vote within a period of six months after being submitted. It is deemed to have been adopted and is forwarded to the Council.

5.   All draft laws approved by implication or expressly by the Parliament are forwarded to the Council for a first reading. It has a period of six months in which to give a decision. The Commission is entitled to issue an opinion on the text and has a period of one month in which to do so. The Resolution provided that the opinion was to be compulsory, but it seemed difficult to give effect to such a proposal. In fact, would it have been useful to require the Commission to express its opinion if that opinion was favourable? Moreover, unless the Commission was to be given a right to block the progress of legislation, it was necessary to make that obligation to express an opinion subject to a time limit and to provide that silence during that period was tantamount to a favourable opinion. In those circumstances, the obligation to give an opinion in all cases did not make much sense. It was converted into a right on the understanding that in all probability the Commission would express an opinion only if it wished to convince the Council of the need to amend the text or to give an unfavourable opinion—the opinion relates to the text as adopted by the Parliament; it is similar to the right of the President of the United States to address communications to Congress. When the President of the United States expresses his disagreement with a bill or certain amendments, Congress knows that if it does not comply with the President's opinion it will ultimately be confronted with a Presidential veto, but as such the communication itself has no legal consequences. By contrast, where the Commission's opinion is unfavourable, its effect is to make adoption of the draft more difficult and rejection of it easier. From the formal point of view, in order to produce such a result the opinion must be wholly unfavourable. The Commission must therefore reach an all-embracing judgement; it may of course oppose the adoption of certain provisions and recommend a vote in

favour of others, but its examination of the draft must ultimately lead to an overall judgement which is favourable or unfavourable. While this procedure displays certain features of the Presidential communication, it also bears similarities to a suspensive veto, in so far as it makes progress to the further stages of the procedure more difficult.

Article 38 does not indicate whether the period of one month granted to the Commission to give its opinion forms part of the period of six months available to the Council to give its decision or whether it is to be added thereto. The latter is the logical solution. As regards submission of the text, the time limit for the Commission's opinion is laid down in Article 38 (2) and the time limit for the Council in Article 38 (3), which implies that the second period can run only after the first has expired. Moreover, the most important point is that if the two periods were not quite separate, the Council would be able to give a decision before receiving the Commission's opinion, which would make the opinion devoid of any purpose. The period granted to the Council is therefore to be calculated only as from expiry of the period granted to the Commission to give its opinion or as from the date on which the opinion is forwarded to the Council, if it is forwarded in less than a month.

6.   The first reading in the Council may give rise to five different situations.

(i) In the absence of an opinion from the Commission or if the opinion is unfavourable, the Council approves the draft by an absolute majority without amendment. The legislative process is complete and the text is definitively adopted. While only a simple majority is required on a first reading in the Parliament, an absolute majority is required in the Council, which means that at least half the delegations representing a majority of the weighted votes (abstentions not counted) must approve the draft. The aim was that, in order to enter into force, the draft should be approved by a sufficient number of Member States. In the case of an organic law a qualified majority (two-thirds of the weighted votes, abstentions not counted) is required.

(ii) If the Commission gives an unfavourable opinion, the Council may approve the draft without amendment only by a qualified majority. In order to overcome the problem of an unfavourable opinion from the Commission, the Council must therefore secure a majority greater than that required for an organic law. However, if the unfavourable opinion relates to an organic law, that fact does not in any way change the majority required, which continues to be a qualified majority in any case.

(iii) The draft is definitively rejected if the Council is unanimously against it. It is therefore extremely difficult for the Council to terminate the procedure. However, here also an unfavourable opinion from the Commission alters the majority and makes rejection by the Council easier, since rejection then requires a qualified majority. In other words, if the Parliament and the Commission are in favour of a draft, only unanimous opposition by the Member States is effective. On the other hand, if the Council and the Commission are opposed to a draft, only two-thirds of the weighted votes and a majority of the Member States are needed to terminate the procedure—that does not however mean that it is easy to arrive at such a result, since in a Union of ten States the approval of two large States and one small State is sufficient to prevent the draft from being definitively rejected.

(iv) If the draft has been amended by a simple majority, in the case of ordinary laws, or an absolute majority, in the case of organic laws, conciliation becomes appropriate. The same applies where the draft is put to the vote, without the Council's achieving a sufficient majority either to approve or to reject the draft, and this is not a far-fetched hypothesis, as has been shown by Community experience regarding the budget. If the Council adopts amendments, must it proceed to a vote approving the draft? Article 38 (3) does not require this and overall approval of the amended draft in no way changes the course of the procedure which, in any event, leads to the conciliation process. On the other hand, a vote of rejection would terminate the procedure definitively. The rules of procedure of the Council may provide that, after the vote on amendments, it will be possible for a motion to be approved rejecting the draft as a whole at the request of a representation. In our opinion, however, a vote approving the amended draft as a whole is not entirely without benefits, in cases where the Parliament remains silent after conciliation is unsuccessful.[2]

(v) Finally, if the Council fails to give a decision within the prescribed period and, during the first reading, the Parliament has expressly approved the draft, the Council's silence is tantamount to a favourable vote and the draft is definitely adopted. On the other hand, if the Parliament's approval was merely implied, all that happens on expiry

---

[2] See below, point 10.

of a period of six months with no vote in the Council is that the draft lapses. In other words, the Council need not put to the vote a draft which has not been expressly approved by the Parliament, if it is not anxious to adopt it. On the other hand, it must at all costs give a decision if it is hostile to a draft expressly adopted by the Parliament.

The procedure is followed only in the cases where amendments to the draft forwarded by the Parliament are adopted or it is impossible to approve or reject the text forwarded by the Parliament. This then leads to the conciliation phase.

7.   The purpose of the conciliation procedure is to reach an agreement between the Parliament and the Council on a joint text. The conciliation procedure was set up by the Joint Declaration of 4 March 1975, to be followed in cases of disagreement over the drafting of 'Community acts of general application which have appreciable financial implications, and of which the adoption is not required by virtue of acts already in existence'. It is initiated when the Council intends to depart from Parliament's opinion and it takes place in a committee consisting of the Council and representatives of Parliament. Its aim is to seek an agreement, but the Council retains the right to take definitive action. The procedure has not proved very successful and the Commission has put forward a proposal for reform on which the Council has not yet commented, although it has undertaken to do so in the solemn declaration on the European Union. The institutions must therefore be encouraged, if conciliation is to serve a useful purpose, to reach an agreement. The best solution appeared to be to ensure that the consequences of disagreement would be less than desirable for the institutions concerned.

The composition of the Conciliation Committee gave rise to discussions within the Committee on Institutional Affairs. In the Resolution of 14 September 1983, the Parliament prescribed that the composition and procedure of the Conciliation Committee should be the subject of a regulation adopted by the Parliament and the Council. But such a regulation would have constituted a specific legal measure for the adoption of which provision would have had to have been made in the Treaty. It was not possible to substitute an organic law for such a regulation because if, on a first reading, that law gave rise to the conciliation procedure, there would have been an impasse. The Treaty therefore had to lay down all the necessary provisions. As regards the procedure itself, the Committee on Institutional Affairs soon realized that the Conciliation Committee could decide on its own procedure and that it would suffice to prescribe the maximum time limit to be imposed on that Committee for an agreement to be reached. As regards composition of the Committee, it was decided to create a body displaying a degree of stability. In fact, while the Resolution provided that in the event of a difference between the Parliament and the Council *a* Conciliation Committee should be invited to propose a compromise, Article 38 (4) states that '*the* Conciliation Committee shall be convened', which implies that it is a permanent body with permanent members. Each Institution should appoint a delegation to hold office for a specified period. There is nothing to prevent the representatives of the Parliament having a term of office equal to that of the President and the Bureau. The representatives of the Council would have a comparable term of office, although a change in the composition of a national representation on the Council might involve a change in the composition of the Council's delegation to the Conciliation Committee. The stable composition of the Committee would make it a kind of committee of 'Wise Men' whose members, being accustomed to conciliation, would more easily arrive at compromises. The Commission is not a member of the Conciliation Committee, but takes part in its proceedings. Its role as mediator should be essential, particularly in view of the role assigned to it under the procedure in cases where conciliation is unsuccessful.

8.   Where conciliation is successful, the joint text agreed upon is submitted to the two Institutions, which have a period of three months in which to approve it by an absolute majority or, in the case of organic laws, by a qualified majority. In such cases, the text cannot be amended further. The two Institutions give their decision only on the text agreed upon by way of compromise. This is a well-conceived rule, since the purpose of a compromise is to achieve an overall agreement which cannot be challenged. Nevertheless, a difficulty remains: Article 38 (4) provides that the Parliament and the Council are to give a decision within three months. If they fail to do so, Article 38 (5) comes into operation and silence is deemed to be acceptance. But under Article 38 (5), silence on the part of both Institutions at the same time cannot amount to acceptance and at least one of them must expressly approve the joint text. In such cases, what procedure will be followed for consideration of the text? If it were considered successively, first in the Parliament and then in the Council, the Parliament would have control over the time available to the Council and might be tempted to prevent the Council from giving a decision within the time limit by retaining

the text. Moreover, if it remained silent, the Council would never be able to receive the text to give a decision on it. Consideration of the text by the two Institutions can only be simultaneous and, moreover, the prohibition of amendments renders further consideration pointless. If after three months either of the Institutions has rejected the text submitted to it, the procedure is terminated and the draft is rejected. Furthermore, if one of the Institutions votes against the draft, it is not necessary for the other to give a decision. If either of the Institutions approves the text by the required majority, the law is adopted, despite silence on the part of the other Institution.

9.   In order to ensure that the Institutions take all necessary measures to achieve a compromise, it is desirable for the failure to reach a compromise to give rise to unfavourable consequences for them. The third paragraph of Article 38 (4) provides that if conciliation is unsuccessful, the Parliament may give a final decision within a period of three months by an absolute majority, or by a qualified majority in the case of organic laws. The Parliament apparently is granted the right to have the last word and therefore would appear to have every reason to cause the conciliation to fail. That is certainly not the case. In fact, in such circumstances, the Parliament gives its decision on the text emanating from the Council, that is to say the one which the Council amended on a first reading. That text cannot be amended by the Parliament. If it has not sought a more favourable agreement, the Parliament finds, if it wishes the law to be adopted, that the Council's text is forced upon it.[3] Is it not preferable in such cases for it to co-operate in conciliation?

However, the Commission has been given the power to propose amendments, in other words to go back on its initial draft, if it drafted the legislation in question, or to reformulate proposals which it made during the conciliation procedure. This provision is evidence of the important role which it was sought to reserve for the Commission in the legislative process. In the event of agreement between the Commission and the Council, the Parliament exercises its right of final decision only on the text emanating from the Council. On the other hand, that

---

[3] However, the text emanating from the Council may in fact be the text adopted on a first reading by the Parliament, if the Council did not succeed in either amending the Parliament's text or approving it or rejecting it. In such cases, the Parliament will win; its triumph will be the sanction of the powerlessness of the Council, which always has an interest in amending a text which it cannot reject.

text may be amended by agreement between the Commission and the Parliament.

Certain advantages also accrue to the Council from successful conciliation. In the event of failure, and of agreement between the Commission and the Parliament, the Parliament may adopt a solution which will be considerably different from that desired by the Council. However, in order to prevent a law from encountering opposition from a majority of the Member States, the Council ultimately has a right of veto. During the three months following adoption of the text by the Parliament, it may reject the text by a qualified majority, but it has been seen above that such a majority would be difficult to obtain and would therefore operate only in cases of particular importance. The Council could not therefore frustrate the conciliation process in reliance upon that right of veto, because it would be able to use that right only in circumstances which it would be difficult to create.

10.   Does the rule contained in Article 38 (5) regarding implied approval operate in the event of unsuccessful conciliation? The answer is clearly affirmative where there is silence on the part of the Council, since the text approved by the Parliament enters into force in the absence of a veto by the Council. The express approval of the Council is never required. What happens where the Parliament is silent? The Parliament is called upon to give its decision on a text emanating from the Council. If that text has been amended by the Council without being expressly approved in its entirety by it, silence on the part of the Parliament cannot be deemed to constitute acceptance because by virtue of Article 38 (5) 'a law may not be regarded as having been adopted unless it has been expressly approved either by the Parliament or by the Council.' On the other hand, if the amended text has been approved in its entirety—something which should occur only rarely—silence on the part of the Parliament will entail the entry into force of the legislation in question, unless it is vetoed by the Council. This effect of the rule regarding time limits was doubtless not perceived by the members of Parliament who prepared the draft, but it is not illogical, since in such cases the intention expressly stated by the Council prevails over the silence of the Parliament. In order to avoid this effect, it is sufficient for the Parliament to put the text to the vote. If it does not obtain the required majority, it will be rejected. In the normal course of events, it would be exceptional for the Parliament to remain silent after concilia-

tion had been unsuccessful, but if such a situation arises it will have to be a matter governed by the general law.[4]

11.   The apparent complexity of the procedure may lead to its being regarded as an inexhaustible source of disputes between Institutions and in that respect the precedent of Community budgetary procedure makes a cautious approach advisable. However, Article 38 deals simultaneously with two legislative procedures, the procedure for the adoption of ordinary laws and the procedure for the adoption of organic laws, which perhaps explains partly why it is difficult to read. Furthermore, experience of the present Community budget procedure led the authors of Article 38 to envisage as far as possible the various solutions and to indicate the practicable solutions, thereby further contributing to the complexity of the text. Thus, it was necessary for example to envisage circumstances where the Council is unable either to approve or reject the text submitted to it. The structure of the procedure would have been much simpler if it had been decided to give the last word to one of the Institutions. As a result of the desire to achieve balance between the respective powers of the Parliament and of the Council and to arrive at solutions which would compel them to move towards a compromise, and the wish to assign an important role to the Commission, the procedure is laid down in the greatest detail. Finally, the concern to avoid hold-ups by providing that tacit acceptance was to follow upon the expiry of a prescribed period could only complicate matters. The procedure may be criticized as being lengthy, since the first reading may last six months in each Institution, and in the event of disagreement a further period of six months may be added. This gives a total of nineteen months if it is considered, as we consider, that the time limit granted to the Commission to give its opinion does not form part of the period granted to the Council. However, that is the maximum period and there is nothing to prevent the Institutions from proceeding more quickly. Moreover, the period allowed for discussions within the various institutions may well result in a more favourable acceptance of laws. As regards the conflicts which may arise from the conflicting

---

[4] Where the Commission has caused amendments to be made, but the Parliament, intentionally or otherwise, has not given its decision on the text approved by an overall vote, such silence may of course in no case lead to the adoption of the text amended in accordance with the wishes of the Commission, since the text has not been previously approved by the Council and the subsequent silence of the Council cannot amount to acceptance of a text not approved by the Parliament.

interpretations of Article 38, they are inevitable. At least, the Parliament was at pains to avoid recourse to concepts as imprecise as those found in the present budgetary procedure[5] and thereby reduced the most serious risks of conflict.

Mr Hänsch (German Socialist) expounded a view of the legislative procedure which differed fundamentally from the majority view and was twice rejected within the Committee on Institutional Affairs. Mr Hänsch proposed that two different procedures should be distinguished (A and B), the choice between them depending upon whether or not agreement was reached between the Parliament and the Commission.

Under procedure A, in the event of agreement between the Parliament and the Commission, the Parliament would be entitled to the last word, acting by a qualified majority, and the Council would be able to use its veto to prevent the law from entering into force.

Under procedure B, in the event of disagreement between the Parliament and the Commission or in the cases expressly provided for in the Treaty, the Council would be entitled to the last word on a second reading, after conciliation proceedings, and the Parliament would have a right of veto to prevent the law from entering into force.

The Committee on Institutional Affairs adopted certain of the suggestions put forward, above all the particular importance accorded to the Commission's position and the Council's right of a final veto.

---

[5] For example, the concept of compulsory expenditure.

Article 39

Publication of laws

Without prejudice to Article 76 (4) of this Treaty, the President of the arm of the legislative authority which has taken the last express decision shall establish that the legislative procedure has been completed and shall cause laws to be published without delay in the *Official Journal of the Union*.

Preparatory documents:

None.

1. Although the Resolution of 14 September 1983 made no provision in that respect, it seemed essential to lay down procedures for the publication of laws. This involved reiterating the provisions of Article 191 of the EEC Treaty. However, the situation was more complex than that provided for in the EEC Treaty, in view of the interaction between the Institutions resulting from the legislative procedure and, in particular, the possibility of the tacit adoption of laws by reason of the expiry of the periods prescribed for their consideration. It seemed necessary, before publication, as in the case of the budgetary procedure, for an authority to be empowered to determine that the legislative process had been completed, and to cause the law to be published. As a rule, this task is entrusted to the Head of State. In the European Union, the European Council discharges the functions of the Head of State in certain respects, but it was pointed out that the President of the European Council would be ill-equipped to undertake that task. Bearing the burden of his national duties, would he find the time to carry out that duty, in certain respects a secondary one? It was then proposed that, since the role concerned was apparently not of any great political importance, it should be assigned to the President of the Commission, *ex officio*. The unanimous opposition to that proposal showed clearly that what was involved had greater ramifications than had been claimed. In its concern to achieve equilibrium, the Parliament did not claim to have that right conferred exclusively on its President, but likewise it did not wish it to be conferred on the President of the Council of the Union. Article 39 reflects the desire for a compromise. The duty of declaring that the legislative process has been duly completed falls to the President

of the arm of the legislative authority which expressly takes a final decision, it being assumed that that Institution has a greater interest in recording completion of the procedure than the Institution which is deemed to have approved the legislation in question as a result of the expiry of the prescribed periods. After giving an express decision, each arm of the legislative authority must therefore watch how the other arm proceeds and, in particular, keep account of the time limits so as to be able to certify completion of the procedure in appropriate cases. Such certification involves an assessment of the lawfulness of the procedure and, thereafter, the law must be presumed to be valid unless and until declared otherwise by the Court of Justice of the Union. The authority certifying completion of the process causes the law to be published in the *Official Journal of the Union*.

The procedure for publication of the budgetary law is different from the ordinary publication procedure. Article 39 therefore makes a reservation regarding the budgetary law ('without prejudice to Article 76 (4)'). That reference is not indispensable, since Article 34 (3) already refers to Article 76.

2. The differences of opinion regarding determination of the authority responsible for publication were of some importance. Experience of the budgetary procedure within the Communities has shown that the power to certify adoption of the budget constitutes a weapon in the hands of the person holding that power since it enables a budget adopted on conclusion of a procedure alleged to be irregular to be made capable of implementation. There is no need to look any further for an explanation as to why the Parliament was reluctant to grant that power to the President of the European Council or the President of the Commission, not wanting either of them to be the arbitrator in any conflict which might arise between it and the Council of the Union. The only reason for its consenting to division of the power between the President of the Parliament and the President of the Council of the Union was that the whole legislative procedure is based on a balance between the two arms of the legislative authority.

By contrast with Article 191 of the EEC Treaty, Article 39 says nothing about the entry into force of laws. The reason for this lies in the fact that the first paragraph of Article 191 refers only to regulations, whereas the concept of law in the Treaty of the Union embraces both measures comparable to regulations and those comparable to directives.

The principle laid down in Article 191, first paragraph, should therefore be retained as part of the Community patrimony, i.e. laws enter into force on the date specified in them or, in the absence thereof, on the twentieth day following their publication.

Article 40

Power to issue regulations

The Commission shall determine the regulations and decisions required for the implementation of laws in accordance with the procedures laid down by those laws. Regulations shall be published in the *Official Journal of the Union*; decisions shall be notified to the addressees. The Parliament and the Council of the Union shall be immediately informed thereof.

Preparatory documents:

Doc. 1-575/83/C, De Gucht working document, p. 16.
Resolution of 14 September 1983, paragraphs 23 and 25.

1. Article 40 constitutes one of the manifestations of the will to strengthen the Commission (cf. Article 28). While Article 155 of the Treaty merely grants the Commission a limited power of implementation, since it is to 'exercise the powers conferred on it by the Council for the implementation of the rules laid down by the latter', Article 40 of the present Treaty clearly confers upon it the power to take measures for implementation of the law. The first sentence of Article 40 leaves no room for ambiguity in that respect, 'the Commission shall determine the regulations and decisions required for the implementation of laws.' That means all the regulations and decisions *necessary*, and no legislation is required to enable it to do so. However, Article 40 must be reconciled with Article 34 which provides that laws are to entrust 'the responsible authorities in the Union or the Member States with setting out in detail the procedures for their implementation'. The Member States may also have a power of implementation and the members of the Committee on Institutional Affairs who were in favour of what they described as 'decentralized implementation' of the law placed great emphasis on that right. The power of the Commission must therefore be reconciled with the power which certain laws may grant to the Member States concerning their implementation. The solution conforming most closely to the text of the provision seems to be that, in the absence of anything to the contrary in the law, the Commission must be recognized as having a power of implementation. On the other hand, laws may well specify the role to be taken by the Member States in issuing imple-

menting measures, and may even charge them with adopting all such measures. Moreover, the Commission in its implementing regulations may leave the Member States to adopt certain implementing measures.

2. Certain members of the Parliament favoured maintaining the system of management committees and committees on rules.[1] The Parliament, which has always had very considerable reservations regarding such committees, felt unable to retain that system in the present Treaty. However, it was asserted that in the case of the Union the situation would be considerably different from that in the Community and that it might be legitimate if the legislative authority, to one of the arms of which the Commission was answerable, were entitled to make adoption of measures implementing laws conditional upon consultation, or indeed upon the favourable opinion of certain bodies. It was stated in reply that it was pointless to seek to reinforce the authority of the Commission if it was then subjected to supervision by management committees or committees on rules. The question was not resolved and Article 40 leaves it to the legislature to decide in each individual case, in so far as it provides that the 'Commission shall determine the regulations and decisions required for the implementation of laws *in accordance with the procedures laid down by those laws*'. The term 'procedures' refers to the conditions which may be imposed by the law as regards the adoption of implementing regulations. A law may therefore require the Commission to observe certain procedures for the adoption of implementing measures (consultation with committees, mandatory time limits for the adoption thereof, etc.).

3. Article 40 provides for the publication of regulations and the notification of decisions, drawing on Article 191 in that respect. However, it makes no provision as to the date of entry into force of regulations. Each regulation must therefore specify that date.

4. Certain Members of the Parliament, influenced by national systems of secondary legislation, considered that the legislative authority should have a right of veto over implementing measures. Such measures would have had to have been notified to the Parliament and the Council and would not have entered into force if those Institutions had indicated

[1] Cf. amendment No. 198 tabled by Mr Hänsch during the vote on the resolution of 14 September 1983.

their opposition within a period of forty days. During its discussions on the Resolution of 14 September 1983, the Committee on Institutional Affairs rejected that course of action as encroaching dangerously upon the authority of the Commission. In any case, the Parliament enjoys a power of supervision over the Commission which it may exercise if it considers that the Commission is not implementing the laws satisfactorily. Responsibility is the natural means provided for in the Treaty to govern relations between the executive and the legislature. It is unnecessary to add a right of veto. However, Article 40 bears the imprint of that proposal, since, like the Resolution, it provides for the legislative authority to be informed of the implementing measures adopted, so that the Parliament can exercise its supervisory authority in full knowledge of the facts.

Article 41

Hearing of persons affected

Before adopting any measure, the Institutions of the Union shall, wherever possible and useful, hear the persons thereby affected. Laws of the Union shall lay down the procedures for such hearings.

Preparatory document:

Resolution of 14 September 1983, paragraph 25.

1. Paragraph 25 of the Resolution goes into great detail regarding the hearing of persons affected by a measure adopted by the Union, in particular in administrative matters and where the Union issues binding provisions to national authorities 'for its administrative action in connection with the implementation of the law of the Union'. If that wording had been retained unchanged, the Commission would have had to undertake systematic hearings before acting. The Resolution did not, however, impose the obligation of conducting hearings but asked the Union 'to ensure that, wherever possible, the hearing of those concerned by its measures is encouraged and extended'. It was more of a recommendation than a normative rule.

2. Adhering to the Resolution, Article 41 does not impose any obligation, but provides that before adopting any measure, the Institutions of the Union are, *wherever possible and useful*, to hear the persons affected. The aim was to avoid an excessive number of hearings which would merely amount to a means of preventing any action. The fact nevertheless remains that the principle involved is one whose implementation is subject to two conditions, namely possibility and usefulness, on which the Court may be called upon to rule in the future; for the absence of a hearing could be invoked as a ground for an action for annulment. Provisions for the hearing of persons affected would be laid down by a law. Madame Veil submitted an amendment on behalf of the Liberal Group that Article 41 should be deleted. The Parliament rejected that amendment. Article 41 entitles 'the persons thereby affected' to be consulted. This vague term may apply both to associations and to natural persons. The definition of 'affected' may give rise

to legal controversy if it is felt that the principle has legal significance and can be invoked before the Court.

3. The great political interest attaching to the principle of hearing persons affected is evident here. In the context of the Union, it may play a positive role by bringing together the citizens and the Institutions of the Union. The difficulties must also be borne in mind of implementing and translating into practice the terms 'possible and useful' used in Article 41. If it considers that it has jurisdiction to consider what is useful and possible, the Court will play an essential role in ensuring the efficacy of Article 41.

Article 42

The law of the Union

The law of the Union shall be directly applicable in the Member States. It shall take precedence over national law. Without prejudice to the powers conferred on the Commission, the implementation of the law shall be the responsibility of the authorities of the Member States. An organic law shall lay down the procedures in accordance with which the Commission shall ensure the implementation of the law. National courts shall apply the law of the Union.

Preparatory documents:

Doc. 1-575/83/B, De Gucht Report, p. 13.
Doc. 1-575/83/C, De Gucht working document, pp. 12–15.
Resolution of 14 September 1983, paragraphs 19 and 24.

1. The principle of the direct application of Union law set out in Article 42 means that acts with general or specific effect forming part of the legal system (laws, regulations, and decisions—see Articles 34 and 40) take effect in the Member States without any procedure for their incorporation or transformation. Their application within the Member States suggests, in particular, that the Union's legal system confers on individuals personal rights, which they are entitled to claim before national courts.

In so far as it refers to the law of the Union and not to specific sources of the law, Article 42 unites two familiar principles of Community law: the direct application of regulations and the direct effect of certain provisions of the Community Treaties, directives, decisions addressed to the Member States, and agreements concluded by the Communities. The first of these principles is based on specific provisions of the Treaties establishing the Communities (see for example Article 189 of the EEC Treaty), while the second is derived from the case law of the Court of Justice on the basis of the famous *Van Gend en Loos* judgment of 5 February 1963.[1] The principle of direct effect will remain valid in the Union and thus be applicable both to the provisions of the

---

[1] [1963] ECR 1.

Treaty and to framework legislation for which the implementing procedures (see Article 34) have not been adopted in time and more generally to the provisions of laws or regulations, and to decisions, which in appearance are addressed only to the Member States but which comprise the necessary elements to give direct legal protection to the individuals concerned.

On the other hand, it must be pointed out that not all provisions are suitable, as regards their nature or content, for direct application. For example, the provisions of the Treaty concerning the institutions, their powers and procedures, or the provisions of laws governing certain aspects of the Member States' activities, do not have direct repercussions on individuals. Moreover, the jurisprudence on direct effect is accompanied by a number of conditions and restrictions, which must be taken into account.

2.   The supremacy of Union law over national laws has the same significance and implications as the principle of the priority of Community law, which also results from the jurisprudence of the Court of Justice.[2] One of the consequences of this principle concerns national provisions which are incompatible with existing Community rules: the Court of Justice has laid down that national provision of this kind must cease to be applied by the administrative and judicial bodies in the Member States.[3]

3.   Article 42 deals with the application of Union law with regard both to its implementation (and hence to the issuing of implementing acts) and to compliance with it. The fact that the 'implementation of the law' is the responsibility of the Commission or the national authorities confirms in part the provision of Article 34 (1) concerning the 'details for ... implementation' of the framework laws, which must be set out in detail by the authorities in the Union or in the Member States. In fact, if it were felt that, under Union law, the Treaty takes precedence over laws, the term 'without prejudice' should have referred not only to the Commission's powers but also to those of the other Institutions involved in the implementation of the Treaty (notably the Parliament and the Council of the Union). The national authorities are responsible for implementing the law of the Union to the extent that this law

---

[2] See, in addition to *Van Gend en Loos* judgment mentioned above, the *Costa* v. *ENEL* judgment of [1964] ECR 585 which was followed by many similar decisions.

[3] Case 106/77 *Simmenthal* [1978] ECR 629.

includes provisions assigning the task of implementation to these authorities (central, regional, or local authorities depending on the content of
the provisions and on the constitutional requirements of each State).

4.   All parties covered by the legal system are required to comply with
the law of the Union. However, in entrusting to the Commission responsibility for ensuring implementation of the law, the problem which
Article 42 is addressing is primarily that of monitoring the fulfilment by
the Member States of their obligations under the Treaty and laws of
the Union. In the Community system, Article 155 of the EEC Treaty
states that the Commission shall ensure that the provisions of the Treaty
and the measures taken by the institutions pursuant thereto are applied
and there is no doubt that the most important action open to the
Commission in this connection is the procedure concerning infringe-
ments provided for in Article 169. It is none the less a fact that there
are other forms of control in the context of the various Community
policies and that the control function is exercised with regard not only
to the Member States but also to individuals. In addition, it is frequently
difficult to draw the line between this function and the powers conferred
on the Commission in specific fields (e.g. competition). The procedures
governing this role which, pursuant to Article 42, are to be laid down
in an organic law, may overlap with other powers granted to the Commission which are governed by ordinary laws, on the basis of the articles
of the Treaty concerned with the policies of the Union.

5.   The final sentence of Article 42 imposes an obligation on national
courts to apply the law of the Union. This could in fact be easily
deduced from the preceding text, in particular the principle whereby
national authorities (of all kinds) are responsible for implementing
Union law. It might be thought that national courts are implicitly for-
bidden to evaluate the validity of Union law and hence not to apply it
if they consider it invalid. However, the solution to this problem lies
rather in a definition of the boundary between the powers of the Court
of Justice and those of the national courts in relation to disputes over
the validity of Union legislation.

Article 43

Judicial review

The Community rules governing judicial review shall apply to the Union. They shall be supplemented by an organic law on the basis of the following principles:

— extension of the right of action of individuals against acts of the Union adversely affecting them,

— equal right of appeal and equal treatment for all the institutions before the Court of Justice,

— jurisdiction of the Court for the protection of fundamental rights *vis-à-vis* the Union,

— jurisdiction of the Court to annul an act of the Union with the context of an application for a preliminary ruling or of a plea of illegality,

— creation of a right of appeal to the Court against the decisions of national courts of last instance where reference to the Court for a preliminary ruling is refused or where a preliminary ruling of the Court has been disregarded,

— jurisdiction of the Court to impose sanctions on a Member State failing to fulfil its obligations under the law of the Union,

— compulsory jurisdiction of the Court to rule on any dispute between Member States in connection with the objectives of the Union.

Preparatory documents:

Doc. 1-575/83/B, De Gucht Report, p. 10.
Resolution of 14 September 1983, paragraph 136.

Provisions in force:

ECSC Treaty, Articles 33-44.
EEC Treaty, Articles 169-87.
EAEC Treaty, Articles 141-59.

1. It has already been pointed out in connection with Article 30 (Court of Justice) that, although Article 43 forms a separate entity, the two articles should be read in conjunction, since their combined provisions

constitute the complete body of rules governing the judicial powers conferred upon the Union. The reason why such a complex subject can be dealt with so succinctly is that reference can be made to Community law in almost all cases.

Article 43 stipulates that all the Community rules 'governing judicial review' shall apply to the Union. This expression undoubtedly includes both the rules on which the numerous powers of the present Court of Justice of the European Communities are based and its rules of procedure. However, whereas these rules of procedure may easily be amended, if necessary, by using the power conferred on the Court of the Union by Article 30(4), the rules governing the powers of the Court may only be *supplemented* by an organic law but not replaced (unless the Treaty is amended pursuant to Article 84). This is in line with the conviction already expressed in the Spinelli Report of 21 June 1982 (which preceded the resolution of 6 July of that year), that 'the Court of Justice ... in some ways has been the most successful of the Community institutions' and that therefore it should retain 'its central position in a system based on law and the separation of powers'. In the same connection, mention should also be made of paragraph 35 of the working document on the legal structure of the Union (rapporteur Mr De Gucht), which affirms that 'judicial review of the Community's acts and activities is well developed in the system in force' and, therefore, that judicial review within the Union may be governed by the same conditions as those laid down in the Community Treaties, with the details and amendments subsequently introduced by Article 43.

2. With regard to these 'details and amendments', it is clear that the text of the article is mainly concerned with laying down the principles which must be taken into account by a future organic law when the existing rules on the powers of the Court come to be 'supplemented'. It is evident that, although they confirm the nature of the Court's powers—i.e. the types of action which may be brought—the principles also imply the need for an extensive review of the limits placed on these powers at present. It should be noted that some of the amendments envisaged appeared in the reports of the Commission and the Court when the Tindemans Report was being prepared.[1]

3. The effect of the first of the seven principles listed is that, in all cases in which individuals currently enjoy a right of action against

---

[1] *EC Bulletin*, Supplements 5/75 and 9/75.

Community acts adversely affecting them, this right may be extended so that the acts of the Union are more widely subject to appeal on the initiative of private individuals. For the most part this will concern proceedings for the annulment of acts (Article 173, second paragraph, of the EEC Treaty) and for damages (Article 178 of the EEC Treaty).

It will probably also include actions for failure to act (Article 175 of the EEC Treaty) and actions brought by servants of the Union (Article 179 of the EEC Treaty), although the first case involves proceedings for a failure to act rather than an act and the second raises the problem of amending the Staff Regulations.

The idea of extending this right of action suggests in particular that the aim is to remove the disparity, with regard to proceedings for annulment or failure to act, which currently exists between the position of the Member States, the Council, and the Commission on one hand, and that of natural or legal persons on the other (who may only bring proceedings against a decision which is addressed to them or at least of direct and individual concern to them). However, there is no reason why greater protection of the interests of individuals should not also be introduced into the rules governing other types of proceedings, for example, by making it easier to take action in respect of responsibilities arising from legislative acts, a measure which the Court has recognized in its case law, though within very strict limits.

The idea of extending the legal protection afforded to natural and legal persons seems more justifiable under the Community system, which is characterized by a non-democratic procedure for creating laws, than under the Union system, in which the new role assigned to Parliament may reasonably be expected to give greater political protection to the rights of individuals. Nevertheless, any improvement in the situation of individuals and private bodies, which are in a weaker position than the States, must be welcomed.

4. The second principle—equal treatment for all the institutions before the Court of Justice—is clearly aimed at ending the position of inferiority in which Parliament finds itself by comparison with the Council and the Commission (it is not entitled to bring proceedings under Article 173 of the EEC Treaty or to act as a defendant under Articles 173 and 175). The amendment in question would make it possible to rectify the disparity between Article 173 of the EEC Treaty and Article 38 of the ECSC Treaty, which at least makes provision for the possible annulment of acts of the Assembly. There is another factor, however. Given that

the laws of the Union will result from the joint exercise of legislative power by the Parliament and Council of the Union (see Article 36), it is unthinkable that the Council by itself, without Parliament, should assume the role of defendant in proceedings for the annulment of a law. On this point, the organic law designed to implement the principle of equal treatment should be introduced as soon as possible after the creation of the Union.

Finally, it should be noted that the inclusion of the European Council as one of the institutions of the Union means that, logically, it is also subject to the abovementioned principle. However, this raises the serious problem of determining in which type of the existing types of proceedings the European Council could act as a defendant, given the specific nature of its activities.

5. The principle that the Court should have jurisdiction for the protection of fundamental rights *vis-à-vis* the Union raises numerous doubts. The Court of Justice of the Community has provided such protection for some years already but in the context of actions which are not based on any specific power of the Court but are part of proceedings for annulment or extra-contractual responsibility, actions by staff, or references for preliminary rulings. In other words, the Court has protected fundamental rights by considering them as principles of unwritten law taking priority over acts of secondary legislation and has enforced compliance with these principles whenever they have been threatened in actions for which the Court is competent. Now, however, it seems that an attempt is being made to introduce a new field of competence, but without specifying who would be entitled to institute proceedings (only individuals or States and Institutions as well?), what action by the Union could be the subject of proceedings (presumably legal acts, but what kind of acts; those with both general and specific application; irrespective of actual damage already produced?), or, finally, what the eventual outcome of such proceedings would be (annulment, compensation, or both?). There is no information on which to base a reply. The problem is also linked to the future regulations governing fundamental rights within the Union (see Article 4). At any event, there is a danger that this new power would interfere with or duplicate existing ones.

6. The fourth principle is primarily technical. Giving the Court jurisdiction to annul an act of the Union within the context of a reference for a preliminary ruling or of a plea of illegality merely implies altering

the nature of the decisions on the inapplicability of the act contested, which the Court is currently empowered to take pursuant to Articles 177 and 184 of the EEC Treaty. In other words, the consequences of declaring an act invalid are at present applicable only to the dispute in question. Under Article 43 they would be generally applicable and thus entail annulment of the act. The approach adopted by the Commission in fact shows that there is already a tendency in such cases to proceed as though the act had been annulled.

7.   The fifth principle is highly innovative; the right of appeal to the Court against the decisions of national courts of last instance which infringe the obligation to request a preliminary ruling from the Court (Article 177 of the EEC Treaty) or fail to comply with a preliminary ruling of the Court. The English text of the Treaty uses the term 'right of appeal'—the only appropriate expression in British legal terminology—but when the various language versions are compared the accepted idea is clearly that the Court may annul decisions made by national courts. This idea is totally alien to the concept accepted in the Community Treaties and would profoundly alter the nature of the relations between the Court of the Community and the national courts of the Member States. The aim is clearly to strengthen compliance with the obligations which are part of the preliminary ruling procedure; however, objections on principle and technical difficulties should not be underestimated. From the technical point of view, it does seem less troublesome to annul a national decision which disregards a preliminary ruling of the Court than to adopt the same remedy against a decision refusing to refer a case to the Court for a preliminary ruling. It is sufficient to note that failure to refer a case to the Court is frequently implicit but does not take the form of a refusal and that, in addition, this omission may be justified on one of the grounds recognized in the CILFIT judgment of 6 October 1982.[2] As for the procedure for any such appeal and its adaptation to national rules of procedure, this remains virgin territory.

8.   It would also be a considerable innovation to grant the Court jurisdiction to impose sanctions on a Member State failing to fulfil its obligations under the law of the Union (sixth principle). The terms used in some of the other languages of the Treaty could be understood in

---

[2] Case 283/81 [1982] ECR 3415.

the narrow sense of 'establishing the illegality of failure to fulfil obligations'. However, this cannot be the case since it would not represent any improvement on the procedure provided for in Articles 169-71 of the EEC Treaty, which simply serves to declare the existence of the offence. Logically, therefore, the expression must mean that, as the English text of Article 43 makes clear, the Court has jurisdiction to impose sanctions on Member States which have infringed Union law. This development would without doubt be both significant and desirable given that a major shortcoming of the EEC and EURATOM systems is the absence of provision for sanctions for failure by a Member State to fulfil its obligations, whereas the ECSC Treaty at least allows the Community executive to adopt the measures laid down in Article 88.

However, if the Court is to have the power to impose sanctions, there must first be a mechanism for this purpose governed by precise rules. The only mechanism of this kind provided for in the Treaty is that laid down in Article 44, which stipulates that the Court is responsible for establishing 'serious and persistent violation' whereupon the European Council is empowered to impose the sanctions described in that article. The aim of granting the Court the power to impose sanctions on Member States is therefore not feasible without a prior decision on what sanctions may be used and for what offences. Can provisions of such magnitude be introduced in the same law used to supplement the powers of the Court of Justice? There is legitimate cause for doubt; the necessary instrument should be an *ad hoc* organic law.

9.   The compulsory jurisdiction of the Court to rule on any dispute between Member States in connection with the objectives of the Union (final principle) immediately calls to mind Article 182 of the EEC Treaty (modelled on Article 89, second paragraph, of the ECSC Treaty), which states that any dispute between the Member States 'which relates to the subject matter of this Treaty' may be submitted voluntarily to the Court by agreement between the parties. Is the aim simply to turn an optional jurisdiction into a compulsory one? Everything depends on the importance attributed to the difference in the wording (in connection with the objectives rather than the subject matter of the Treaty); it seems that the wording used in Article 43 is more cautious and less extensive than in Article 182 of the EEC Treaty.

In addition, the future organic law will have to clarify whether disputes arising from supplementary agreements concluded among the Member States of the Union (or, hitherto, among Member States of the

Article 44

Sanctions

In the case provided for in Article 4 (4) of this Treaty, and in every other case of serious and persistent violation by a Member State of the provisions of this Treaty, established by the Court of Justice at the request of the Parliament or the Commission, the European Council may, after hearing the Member State concerned and with the approval of the Parliament, take measures:

— suspending the rights deriving from the application of part or the whole of the Treaty provisions to the State in question and its nationals, without prejudice to the rights acquired by the latter,

— which may go as far as suspending participation by the State in question in the European Council, the Council of the Union and any other organ in which that State is represented as such.

The State in question shall not participate in the vote on the sanctions.

Preparatory texts:

Doc. 1-575/83/B, De Gucht Report, p. 11.
Doc. 1-575/83/C, De Gucht working document, p. 16.
Resolution of 14 September 1983, paragraphs 26-7.

1. The wording of this article implies the need to distinguish between two categories of violations of the provisions of the Treaty by a Member State: on one hand, offences which are not serious and are committed sporadically, as it were, and, on the other hand, serious and persistent violations. With regard to the first category of offences, the Union could undoubtedly use the procedure currently laid down by Article 169 of the EEC Treaty, under which an action brought by the Commission before the Court leads merely to a declaratory judgment establishing that an offence has been committed. If a future organic law were to give the Court the power to impose sanctions for failure by the Member States to observe the law of the Union (see Article 43, sixth indent), it would be possible to obtain a condemnation of the State which had committed the offence. However, it has already been noted that this

would require not only a change in procedure but also a prior legal definition of the possible sanctions, which have yet to be specified.[1] In the case of serious and persistent violations, however, Article 44 does define both the nature of the sanctions and the procedure for applying them.

2.   Two remarks should be made concerning actions which are liable to sanctions. In the first place, the article under consideration places particular emphasis on serious and persistent violation of democratic principles or fundamental rights (referring to Article 4 (4)), yet it is clear that this would also constitute a violation of a provision of the Treaty, since it is implicit in Article 4 (4) that the Member States, each in their own sphere, are obliged to respect these principles and rights. Secondly, it should be remembered that during the preparatory work on the Treaty it was proposed that sanctions should be applied only when *fundamental* provisions of the Treaty were violated.[2] Although this idea was abandoned, it remains true that in assessing the gravity of an infringement account should also be taken of the importance of the provision infringed.

3.   The procedure laid down in Article 44 includes a first stage consisting of a declaratory judgment establishing that serious and persistent violation has occurred—the case being referred to the Court at the request of Parliament or the Commission—and a second stage consisting of a decision on the sanctions to be imposed, taken by the European Council, which is required to hear the Member State concerned and obtain the approval of Parliament. This procedure raises numerous doubts. Suffice it to say that rules are still required to govern the proceedings before the Court (from which it is unthinkable that the State accused should be excluded); the relationship between Parliament's opinion and the decision of the European Council (the need for the two to concur suggests that in practice Parliament would be the one to determine the sanction); the parliamentary majority required (under Article 17 a simple majority would be required, although this would be insufficient from a political point of view); and the influence of the declaratory judgment on the subsequent decision on sanctions. (Would it be possible not to apply sanctions despite the judgment?)

---

[1] See commentary on Article 43.
[2] See De Gucht Report, Doc. 1-575/83/B, paragraph 38.

It should also be pointed out that this is the only provision which provides for a vote to be held within the European Council, as indicated by the stipulation that the State in question may not participate in the vote on sanctions. This constitutes a restriction on the European Council's power to determine its own decision-making procedures (Article 32 (2)). In the final analysis, the subject ought to be covered by an organic law, although the article makes no reference to this. It could be held that Article 34 (2) would allow this course, since as a general rule it stipulates that the operation of the institutions should be governed by laws of this type.

4. The common feature of all the measures provided for by way of sanction is the suspension of certain of the subjective rights enjoyed by the offending Member State under Union law. In limiting itself to the suspension of rights, Article 44 implicitly excludes any possibility of expulsion, in contrast to the Charter of the United Nations and the Statute of the Council of Europe, which provide for both sanctions.

The scope of the suspension may vary widely and could involve either suspension of the rights deriving from the provisions of the Treaty as a whole or suspension of part of these rights (which part would have to be decided in each individual case). Logically, the suspension of all rights—which would amount to the suspension of the *status* of a member, although the obligations of membership would remain—ought also to include suspension of the right to participate in the institutions and bodies on which the State in question is represented as such, whereas partial suspension may or may not affect such participation (though it seems more logical that it should not do so).

5. With regard to the rights of citizens, the wording of the article suggests that these would necessarily be suspended together with the rights of the State concerned, whenever they both derive from the same provision of the Treaty. However, if it is possible for suspension to affect the rights of a State based on provisions of the Treaty from which individual rights are not derived, it would be reasonable to provide that suspension should concern only the rights of the State, without affecting the legal position of individuals. On the other hand, it is out of the question that suspension might affect only the rights of private citizens.

6. A particularly delicate problem is whether or not it would be possible to suspend the right of the individual members of an institution—

Parliament, Commission, or Court—or of an organ to participate in the activities of that body. This question would, of course, arise in the event of the suspension of the right of the State concerned to participate in the Institutions and bodies in which it is represented. The correct answer would seem that it should not be possible, for two reasons. First, because Article 44 considers the suspension of participation in Institutions and bodies as a last resort, applying only to the States, and secondly because the individual members of the Institutions and bodies of the Union occupy a position of independence in respect of their governments which overrides the ties that bind them to a particular State.

7. Finally, with regard to the suspension of the rights of citizens, it should be noted that the provision makes an exception of rights already acquired. This clarification, introduced during the final stage of drafting, is intended to prevent sanctions having a retroactive effect, in line with a principle which ought really to apply also to the Member States.

PART FOUR

THE POLICIES OF THE UNION

Article 45

General Provisions

1. Starting from the Community patrimony, the Union shall continue the actions already undertaken and undertake new actions in compliance with this Treaty, and in particular with Article 9 thereof.

2. The structural and conjunctural policies of the Union shall be drawn up and implemented so as to promote, together with balanced expansion throughout the Union, the progressive elimination of the existing imbalances between its various areas and regions.

Preparatory documents:

Doc. 1-575/83/B, De Gucht Report, pp. 13-26.
Doc. 1-575/83/C, De Gucht working document, pp. 25-88.
Resolution of 14 September 1983, paragraphs 12(b) and 29.

1. The most important of the principles underlying the policy of the Union are the notions of continuity with regard to the previous achievements of the Community and further development on this basis. The very first recital of the preamble enshrines the aim of '*continuing* and *reviving* the democratic unification of Europe, of which the European Communities, the European Monetary System and European Political Co-operation represent the first achievements'. In addition, Articles 7 and 9 respectively define how the law of the Union should 'take over' the Community patrimony and the objectives which the Union should set itself. Article 45 (1) highlights the link between the opening words of the preamble and the two articles mentioned and stresses that the Union intends to continue and extend the European experiment.

The paragraph speaks of the actions already undertaken and the new actions to be undertaken. These actions clearly refer to the various aspects of economic policy, policy for society, and international relations and the form which these policies will take can be inferred from the provisions appearing under the three Titles in the fourth part of the Treaty. According to the subject matter covered by each provision, the balance varies between, on one hand, policies already established and needing to be supplemented (e.g. Article 47) and, on the other, new policies needing to be launched (e.g. Article 53(c)). The overall activity of the Union will be a combination of these two elements.

2.   The second paragraph lays down two further principles on which the drawing up and implementation of the Union's policies should be based: balanced expansion throughout the Union and the elimination of regional imbalances. It is vital that equal weight should be given to both these principles and that one should not take precedence over the other. The notion of balanced expansion is significant not only from an economic but also from a social standpoint. Article 9 rightly refers to the aim of attaining both 'a humane and harmonious development of society' and 'the economic development' of the peoples of the Union. As to the elimination of regional imbalances, realistically envisaged as being a gradual process, Article 9 defines it as one of the bases for the development of society, though its role is more clearly defined in Article 45 (2). The Union must not confine itself to operating a specific regional policy (Article 58), but must devise and implement all its policies (even those whose effects are purely temporary) in such a way as to reduce regional imbalances gradually. Moreover, there is no doubt that the situation regarding the lack of harmonious economic development will improve or deteriorate depending on the decisions made in particular sectors, notably agriculture, industry, and transport.

Article 46

Homogeneous judicial area

In addition to the fields subject to common action, the co-ordination of national law with a view to constituting a homogeneous judicial area shall be carried out in accordance with the method of co-operation. This shall be done in particular:

— to take measures designed to reinforce the feeling of individual citizens that they are citizens of the Union,

— to fight international forms of crime, including terrorism.

The Commission and the Parliament may submit appropriate recommendations to the European Council.

Preparatory texts:

Doc. 1-575/83/B, De Gucht Report, p. 11.
Doc. 1-575/83/C, De Gucht working document, p. 16.
Resolution of 14 September 1983, paragraph 28.

1. A distinction must be made between the co-ordination of the Member States' laws, which is the subject matter of Article 46, and the approximation of laws, which is dealt with in Article 49. For although the desired result is technically the same—to make certain groups of the Member States' laws as similar in content as possible—the sectors concerned and the methods employed are different. The matters covered by the co-ordination of laws fall outside the sphere of common action, so that the relevant national laws will be co-ordinated by the method of co-operation, either through the conclusion of legally binding agreements between the Member States within the European Council or through the adoption of political understandings or joint resolutions. The approximation of laws, on the other hand, relates to matters which fall within the sphere of common action (specifically economic policy) and is achieved by means of framework laws which are intended to be implemented by the Member States.[1]

[1] See commentary on Article 49.

2. Article 46 sets the objective of creating a 'homogeneous judicial area'. The word 'judicial' in English does not correspond to the terms used in German, French, and Italian which are nearer to 'legal' and which seem more appropriate given that the measures in question concern the co-ordination of national laws. Irrespective of this terminological disparity, the expression carries a political emphasis disproportionate to its real significance. It is true that the European Council can decide freely on the fields in which it wishes to promote the co-ordination of laws (provided that it does not interfere with the sphere reserved for common action), but in practice the 'legal areas' are limited.

The article mentions two specific objectives to which the present European Council has already given consideration. It is apparent that the national laws which need to be co-ordinated in order to attain these objectives cover sectors which are limited in scope, but sensitive, and that as a result the task of co-ordinating them raises numerous difficulties. More precisely, the aim of taking 'measures designed to reinforce the feeling of individual citizens that they are citizens of the Union' would require an effort to co-ordinate the laws of the Member States, notably in a number of areas already mentioned in the European Parliament's resolution of 16 November 1977 on the granting of special rights to citizens of the European Community, including the right to stand for and vote at administrative or regional elections, the right to hold certain offices and functions, and so on.[2] The other objective—to fight international forms of crime, including terrorism—has also been under discussion for some time. This would require the co-ordination of penal and police laws and more extensive use of the extradition procedure, but previous experience in this field suggests that the Council of Europe is better able to act in these areas.

3. The final paragraph of Article 46 envisages the possibility of the European Council's initiatives to co-ordinate national laws being prompted by recommendations from the Commission or Parliament. Clearly, this type of act would constitute an appeal rather than a proposal and would therefore have very little power to influence agreements within the Council. Nevertheless, the Commission and Parliament will be in a position at least to suggest the areas in which co-ordination seems most appropriate and to point out to the Council the reasons why such action may be urgent. In formal terms, the provision is one

[2] See also the commentary on Article 3.

of those which illustrate that the method of co-operation should not exclude the collaboration of institutions other than the European Council.

Finally it should be noted that the subject-matter referred to in Article 46 is different from that covered by Article 11 (1) which means that the co-ordination of national legislation to be carried out in accordance with the method of co-operation may not become the subject of common action. This is explained by two factors, one relating to the text (Article 46 is applicable 'in addition to the fields subject to common action') and the other to the inherent restriction imposed by Article 49, which defines the areas in which the approximation of legislation may be carried out by the method of common action.

Article 47
Internal market and freedom of movement

1. The Union shall have exclusive competence to complete, safeguard and develop the free movement of persons, services, goods, and capital within its territory; it shall have exclusive competence for trade between Member States.

2. This liberalization process shall take place on the basis of detailed and binding programmes and timetables laid down by the legislative authority in accordance with the procedures for adopting laws. The Commission shall adopt the implementing procedures for those programmes.

3. Through those programmes, the Union must attain:

— within a period of two years following the entry into force of this Treaty, the free movement of persons and goods; this implies in particular the abolition of personal checks at internal frontiers,

— within a period of five years following the entry into force of this Treaty, the free movement of services, including banking and all forms of insurance,

— within a period of ten years following the entry into force of this Treaty, the free movement of capital.

Preparatory documents:

Doc. 1-575/83/B, Moreau Report, pp. 13-14.
Doc. 1-575/83/C, Moreau working document, pp. 32-3.
Resolution of 14 September 1983, paragraphs 30 and 31.

Provisions in force:

EEC Treaty, Articles 9–17, 30–7, 48–73.

1. Two essential sets of provisions of the Treaty establishing the EEC represent the foundation of this article, the basis on which the Union proposes to build further developments. These are the provisions governing the free movement of goods, contained in Part Two, Title I, and the whole of Title III, concerning the free movement of persons, services, and capital. There is no doubt that the Community has achieved notable successes in all the fields mentioned. The provisions of the Treaty of Rome have been and continue to be applied (although the extent of their application varies from one sector to another). The Union will take over this Community patrimony (in accordance with Article 7). The provisions in question will therefore become part of Union law and the acts promulgated by the Community institutions will remain in force.

However, if the process of liberalization is to be developed to the full, many remaining obstacles must be removed. That is why Article 47 does more than just confirm that particular provisions and acts of the EEC will be incorporated into Union law. It grants the Union the competence to complete and develop the four freedoms mentioned above, and not merely to ensure compliance with them. This competence is described as exclusive, which means that no intervention by national authorities is possible, except where it is provided for by a law of the Union (Article 12 (1)).

The subject-matter covered by this competence will clearly be all aspects of the free movement of persons, services, goods, and capital—concepts introduced by the EEC Treaty and further defined by Community acts deriving from it. However, the scope of the Union's competence is broader, at least with regard to the movement of persons. This is made clear by the explicit reference in paragraph 3 to 'the abolition of personal checks at internal frontiers', which should benefit all those crossing such frontiers, whether or not they meet the requirements set out in the EEC Treaty relating to freedom of movement (i.e. whether or not they are employed workers, professional people, craftsmen, businessmen, etc.). In this respect Article 47 confirms the tendency, already apparent under the Community system, to promote freedom of movement for individuals, even for purposes not of a strictly economic nature. Besides, the movement of tourists may be regarded as an extension of the free movement of services (a category which certainly includes tourism).

A particular problem arises in connection with trade between the Member States, mentioned at the end of paragraph 1 as the subject of exclusive competence on the part of the Union. All trade in goods within the present Community is covered by the customs union (see Article 9 of the EEC Treaty) and trade between the Member States has never yet been seen in any other light than that of the free movement of goods. For what reason then does Article 47 (1) mention trade between the Member States in addition to the free movement of goods? The answer might lie in the influence exerted by the American concept of the exclusive competence of the federal authority as regards trade between Member States. If that were the case, however, it would have been wrong to ignore the fact that this concept is going through a crisis and that the jurisprudence of the US Supreme Court seems to distinguish, in the mass of trade regulations, between those aspects reserved for the federal authority and those that are left to the competence of the individual states.[1]

2.   Paragraphs 2 and 3 of Article 47 lay down the procedure to be followed for completing the liberalization process as regards both acts and deadlines, in line with the needs of the various sectors. On the first point, provision is made for the legislative authority to lay down 'detailed and binding programmes and timetables' for liberalization, and for the Commission to adopt the implementing procedures for these programmes. In short, a law laying down programmes will form the basis for Commission regulations and decisions, and it seems incongruous that no provision is made for national measures based on framework laws, since the EEC Treaty makes extensive use of directives to implement freedom of establishment and the free movement of services and capital.

The deadlines set are of different lengths. The shortest (two years) relates to the sectors which are thought to have reached an advanced stage of liberalization (movement of persons and goods). The longest (ten years) relates to the movement of capital, which is undoubtedly far from being liberalized, and the intermediate one to the services sector. The rigidity of these deadlines may be incompatible with the objective difficulties involved, but it was considered that the deadlines constituted a necessary constraint for the Institutions.

---

[1] See V. Blasi, 'Constitutional limitations on the power of States to regulate the movement of goods in interstate commerce', in *Courts and Free Markets*, ed. T. Sandalow and E. Stein, Oxford, 1982, vol. I, pp. 174 ff.

In addition, it might have been preferable to separate the movement of workers from freedom of establishment, where progress has been much slower. Finally, there is some doubt as to what is meant in paragraph 3 by the expression 'attain the free movement'. It would seem that the intention is to attain both the final objectives laid down in the EEC Treaty for each of the four types of free movement, and the two specific aims set by this provision of abolishing personal checks at internal frontiers and liberalizing banking and insurance services prior to the liberalization of the movement of capital (despite the provisions of Article 61 (2) of the EEC Treaty).

The fact that Article 47 establishes an exclusive competence for the Union raises the question of the force of those provisions of the Community Treaties which allow for unilateral action by the States, such as Article 71 (2) of the EEC Treaty. It seems that those provisions form part of the Community patrimony, having the status of organic law (cf. Article 7). They may be amended only by an organic law. Article 12 does not exclude the possibility, within the framework of an exclusive competence, of intervention by the States when a law of the Union so provides.

Article 48

Competition

The Union shall have exclusive competence to complete and develop competition policy at the level of the Union, bearing in mind:

— the need to establish a system for the authorization of concentrations of undertakings based on the criteria laid down by Article 66 of the Treaty establishing the European Coal and Steel Community,

— the need to restructure and strengthen the industry of the Union in the light of the profound disturbances which may be caused by international competition,

— the need to prohibit any form of discrimination between private and public undertakings.

Preparatory documents:

Doc. 1-575/83/B, Moreau Report, p. 14.
Doc. 1-575/83/C, Moreau working document, pp. 34-5.
Resolution of 14 September 1983, paragraph 32.

Provisions in force:

ECSC Treaty, Articles 65-7.
EEC Treaty, Articles 85-94.

There is a certain parallel between Articles 47 and 48. Both relate to sectors in which the Community's achievements have been extensive and important, both relate to policies which the Union is to 'complete and develop' and both grant the Union exclusive competence for this purpose. In this article, however, exclusive competence covers competition policy at the level of the Union. There is therefore nothing to prevent the Member States from regulating competition at the purely national level, as they do at present.

It is clear that, by virtue of Article 7, the rules on competition contained in the ECSC and EEC Treaties, together with all the regulations of the Council and Commission of the Communities which have supplemented and extensively developed these rules, will form part of the law of the Union. Naturally, in exercising its competence, the Union will be able to supplement or amend provisions of Community origin as it sees fit. However, Article 48 draws attention to three needs which the Union will have to take into account when developing its policy in this field. The first is the need to establish a system for the authorization of all concentrations of undertakings, a long-standing objective of the Commission, which it has failed to achieve because the Council has not yet approved its proposals on the matter. The present provision offers a precise point of reference on which to base this system: the criteria laid down by Article 66 of the ECSC Treaty, relating to concentrations in the coal and steel sector.

The second need is to restructure and strengthen the industry of the Union in the light of the disturbances which may be caused by international competition. At first sight, it might seem that this provision is out of place here and ought rather to figure among the provisions on industrial policy (Article 53 (e)). However, the aim is to stress one of the constant concerns of competition policy, the need to remember that many oligopolies and groups of undertakings play a part in the struggle to compete adequately with powerful industries in third countries which are in competition with European industry. The objective is thus essentially to adapt competition policy to the need for European industry to develop a structure and a strength which will enable it to withstand external competition.

Finally, the third requirement is for public and private undertakings to be treated equally in matters of competition policy. Serious difficulties have been encountered in applying Article 90 of the EEC Treaty, which is based on the same principle. The Commission has been accused of being too timid in dealing with the Member States and the economic activities of public undertakings (in his working document on European Union Mr Moreau, the rapporteur, wrote that the Union must 'restore the authority of the common competition policy, particularly in relation to the public sector and to the Member States themselves').[1] This experience explains the strong wording used in the last indent of Article 48. Nevertheless, it would have been wiser to recognize that 'discrimination' between private and public undertakings is not always arbitrary and that in some cases different treatment may be justified (e.g. as provided for by Article 90 (2) of the EEC Treaty).

[1] See Doc. 1-575/83/C, paragraph 53.

Article 49

Approximation of the laws relating to undertakings and taxation

The Union shall take measures designed to approximate the laws, regulations, and administrative provisions relating to undertakings, and in particular to companies, in so far as such provisions have a direct effect on a common action of the Union. A law shall lay down a Statute for European undertakings.

In so far as necessary for economic integration within the Union, a law shall effect the approximation of the laws relating to taxation.

Preparatory documents:

Doc. 1-575/83/B, Moreau report, p. 15.
Doc. 1-575/83/C, Moreau working document, pp. 35-6.
Resolution of 14 September 1983, paragraph 33.

Provisions in force:

EEC Treaty, Articles 100-2, 54 (3)(g), and 99.

1. The words 'approximation of the laws' used in the title of this article, and the more precise expression 'to approximate the laws, regulations, and administrative provisions' which appears in the text of the article, are a faithful reproduction of the terms used in the EEC Treaty (Article 100). There is no doubt that the concept involved is also the same. Certain parts of the national law of the Member States need to be brought closer into line from the point of view of content so as to produce rules on particular subjects, which, if not uniform, are at least harmonized in the various countries belonging to the Union.

This type of operation, which under the Community system is achieved by directives for the approximation of laws (see Article 100 of the EEC Treaty), will be put into effect in the Union by means of framework laws designed to be implemented by the national legislatures or administrations.[1] It is in this sense that the phrase 'a law shall *effect*

[1] See commentary on Article 34 (1) as regards the concept of framework laws or laws laying down principles.

the approximation of the laws relating to taxation' should be understood. The phrase is clearly imprecise, however, since the approximation may be said to be effected as soon as the framework law is implemented in each of the Member States. As for 'measures' designed to approximate the laws, referred to at the very beginning of the article, it is difficult to see what form these could take, other than that of framework laws. In addition, the Treaty provides not only for the approximation but also for the co-ordination of national legislation, to be carried out by the method of co-operation (Article 46) using various measures (agreements between Member States, political understandings, joint resolutions). The subject-matter, too, is of course different: 'fields subject to common action' are excluded, which implies a radical distinction between the scope of Article 46 and that of Article 49.

2.   According to the article under consideration, the approximation is limited to the provisions relating to undertakings and in particular to companies, and provisions relating to taxation, in so far as they have an effect on the common action of the Union (this condition is stipulated for both sets of provisions in different, though substantially equivalent terms). Article 49 therefore has a more limited sphere of application than Article 100 of the EEC Treaty. Its immediate legal precedents are to be found rather in Articles 54 (3)(g) and 99 of the EEC Treaty, which are concerned respectively with the co-ordination of the safeguards required by companies to protect the interests of members and others and the harmonization of national laws on indirect taxation. This interpretation makes it possible to argue that, by virtue of Article 7, the law of the Union will also take in the wider objective laid down in Articles 3(h) and 100 of the EEC Treaty—the approximation of all the laws of the Member States which affect the functioning of the common market. In fact, this is not incompatible with Article 49 of the Union Treaty, provided the objectives of that article are not interpreted in a restrictive manner. Needless to say, the Community procedure must in any case be replaced by the use of organic laws, by virtue of Article 7 (3).

3.   A different subject altogether is that of the European undertaking, envisaged as a new type of undertaking which would be based on the law of the Union. The idea of a statute for European commercial companies, to be introduced on the basis of a regulation under Article 235, has been under discussion for many years in the EEC (it has been drawn

Article 50

Conjunctural policy

1. The Union shall have concurrent competence in respect of conjunctural policy, with a particular view to facilitating the co-ordination of economic policies within the Union.

2. The Commission shall define the guidelines and objectives to which the action of the Member States shall be subject, on the basis of the principles and within the limits laid down by laws.

3. Laws shall lay down the conditions under which the Commission shall ensure that the measures taken by the Member States conform with the objectives it has defined. Laws shall authorize the Commission to make the monetary, budgetary, or financial aid of the Union conditional on compliance with the measures taken under paragraph 2 above.

4. Laws shall lay down the conditions under which the Commission, in conjunction with the Member States, shall utilize the budgetary or financial mechanisms of the Union for conjunctural ends.

Preparatory documents:

Doc. 1-575/83/B, Moreau Report, p. 15.
Doc. 1-575/83/C, Moreau working document, pp. 36-8.
Resolution of 14 September 1983, paragraphs 34-7.

Provisions in force:

EEC Treaty, Articles 103-45.

1. The unsatisfactory functioning of the mechanisms provided for in the EEC Treaty for the co-ordination of Member States' economic policies led Mr Moreau, rapporteur on Economic Union, to state in his working document that 'the Union must therefore make considerable progress in this sector'.[1] The instruments to be used to achieve this progress are set out in Article 50, which confers on the Union concurrent competence in respect of conjunctural policy and provides that, in

---

[1] Doc. 1-575/83/C, of 15 July 1983, paragraph 64.

exercising this competence, the Union may promulgate laws and play an important executive role.

2.   The article highlights four objectives to be met by the legislative body: to define the principles and limits (the Resolution of 14 September 1983 referred to 'criteria') on the basis of which the Commission will guide the Member States' policies; to confer on the Commission the power to monitor implementation and to lay down the conditions governing the exercise of this power; to govern the possible utilization of the Union's budgetary and financial mechanisms for conjunctural ends and, finally, to determine whether and in what way the monetary, budgetary, or financial aid of the Union may be made conditional on compliance by the Member States with the Commission's decisions.

3.   Within limits which will be defined by a law, the Commission will be required to take measures designed to influence directly the actions of the governments by co-ordinating their economic policies. Some of these measures will be set out in regulations, others in decisions or in non-binding acts (recommendations, communications, opinions, etc.). The need for flexible, timely, and varied action will presumably be reflected in the type of instruments chosen. The tasks assigned to the Commission are without doubt both numerous and sensitive: to impose on the Member States specific guidelines and objectives for action in the conjunctural sector (paragraph 2), to ensure that national measures conform with these objectives (paragraph 3), to utilize the budgetary and financial mechanisms of the Union for conjunctural ends (paragraph 4) and possibly to make aid granted by the Union conditional on the extent to which the Member States concerned have complied with the Commission's decisions (paragraph 3).

4.   The possibility of using the budgetary and financial mechanisms of the Union for conjunctural ends involves consultations (the expression used is 'in conjunction with') between the Commission and the Member States. The law is unclear on this point. If such consultations are taken to be a stage in the procedure leading to the Commission's decision to use the budgetary and financial mechanisms, then the form they should take would simply have to be set out in the law provided for in paragraph 4. However, the expression could be taken to mean that these instruments of the Union are to be used in conjunction with the Member States, that is, that consultations are a prerequisite to the adoption of the measures envisaged. Thus the Commission would be empowered to use the budgetary and financial mechanisms of the Union for conjunc-

tural ends only in so far as the Member States made the equivalent national instruments available for the same purpose, and provided the deployment of these mechanisms and instruments was co-ordinated. The English text ('the Commission, *in conjunction with* the Member States . . .') points to the second interpretation.

5. If Article 50 of the Treaty of Union is compared with Article 103 of the EEC Treaty, the first obvious difference is that the decision-making power is assigned by the latter to the Council and by the former to the Commission. This innovative aspect reflects the spirit of the Treaty of Union, in which a reduction in the Council's powers is linked to the conviction that the egotistical attitude of the governments, which is given added strength by the unanimity rule, prevents any joint action. A further significant difference is that the measures covered by Article 103 are referred to in extremely wide and general terms (measures 'to be taken in the light of the prevailing circumstances' or 'appropriate to the situation'), whereas the content of Article 50 is relatively specific. Above all, however, while confirming that the Member States' economic policies should be co-ordinated and hence not pursued unilaterally, Article 50 is based on the idea that conjunctural policy could be guided and, in short, governed by the Union and thus lies entirely outside the system of co-operation which, on the other hand, is clearly accepted by Article 103 (1) of the EEC Treaty: 'Member States . . . shall consult each other and the Commission on the measures to be taken.'

Article 51

Credit policy

The Union shall exercise concurrent competence as regards European monetary and credit policies, with the particular objective of co-ordinating the use of capital market resources by the creation of a European capital market committee and the establishment of a European bank supervisory authority.

Preparatory documents:

Doc. 1-575/83/B, Moreau Report, p. 15.
Doc. 1-575/83/C, Moreau working document, pp. 38–41.
Resolution of 14 September 1983, paragraph 41.

1.   The detailed rules governing the European monetary policy referred to in Article 51 are set out in Article 52, which defines the most important aspects (the European Monetary System, monetary union and the Monetary Fund). In this connection, it should be recalled that, in the working document on Economic Union, the rapporteur, Mr Moreau, included under monetary policy all the common mechanisms for the regulation of exchange rates, that is, the European Monetary System.[1] This interpretation is open to criticism, since it seems too closely linked to the existing concept of monetary policy within the Community context.

2.   With regard to European credit policy, which is concerned primarily with the question of recourse to capital markets, the concurrent competence assigned to the Union involves co-ordination and to a certain extent institutionalization of the policy. The above working document on Economic Union mentioned, as the subject of co-ordination, the various mechanisms for collecting capital and granting loans currently available to the Community. These mechanisms should be amalgamated and Mr Moreau suggested that this could be carried out under the aegis of the European Investment Bank.[2] This matter should ultimately be dealt with in the organic law needed to govern the other tasks of the

[1] Doc. 1-575/83/C paragraph 65.
[2] Ibid., paragraphs 74 and 75.

Bank (see Article 33 (1)). On the other hand, the wording of Article 51—'co-ordinating the use of capital market resources'—does not exclude the possibility of other objectives being pursued, in addition to that of amalgamating the Community's credit mechanisms.

3. Finally, as regards the proposal to create new institutions in this sector, Article 51 refers to two bodies to be created (a European capital market committee and a European bank supervisory authority), but it leaves open the question of their nature, structure, and powers. Clearly, if these bodies were regarded as 'organs necessary for (the Union's) operation', an organic law would be required to set them up (see Article 33 (5)).

Article 52

European Monetary System

1. All the Member States shall participate in a European Monetary System, subject to the principles set out in Article 35 of this Treaty.

2. The Union shall have concurrent competence for the progressive achievement of full monetary union.

3. An organic law shall lay down rules governing:

— the Statute and the operation of the European Monetary Fund in accordance with Article 33 of this Treaty,

— the conditions for the effective transfer to the European Monetary Fund of part of the reserves of the Member States,

— the conditions for the progressive conversion of the ECU into a reserve currency and a means of payment, and its wider use,

— the procedures and stages for attaining monetary union,

— the duties and the obligations of the central banks in the determination of their objectives regarding money supply.

4. During the five years following the entry into force of this Treaty, by derogation from Articles 36, 38, and 39 thereof, the European Council may suspend the entry into force of the organic laws referred to above within a period of one month following their adoption and refer them back to the Parliament and the Council of the Union for fresh consideration.

Preparatory documents:

Doc. 1-575/83/B, Moreau Report, p. 15.
Doc. 1-575/83/C, Moreau working document, pp. 38–41.
Resolution of 14 September 1983, paragraphs 39–40 and 42.

1. One of the objectives of this Treaty, and one of the features which help to differentiate it, is the overcoming of the formal separation of the Community and the European Monetary System; the latter is included in the Union. It should be observed in this respect that the first sentence of the preamble, after stating the intention of 'continuing and reviving the democratic unification of Europe' mentions as the 'first

achievements' of that unification, in addition to the European Communities, the European Monetary System and European political co-operation, which are recognized as being distinct from the Communities. It should also be borne in mind that the European Monetary System, which was set up by the European Council by the Brussels Resolution of 5 December 1978 and came into force on 13 March 1979, is the result of an agreement made within the context of co-operation between the Member States of the Communities and has not yet been extended to Greece. The mechanism set up by that agreement is still outside the Community legal order and operates essentially by means of continual co-operation between the central banks of the countries taking part, which collaborate in order to ensure that the rates of exchange of the various currencies are stabilized.

2. Paragraph 1 of the article under consideration, which provides that all the Member States of the Union shall participate in the European Monetary System, lays down a rule which is the logical consequence of the granting of monetary competence to the Union (provided for under Article 51). This means that a situation such as that of Greece at present will no longer be permitted. However, another feature of this paragraph is that it is subject to the 'differentiated application' principle set out in Article 35. Under that article the implementation of certain legislative provisions may be subject to time limits or transitional measures 'which may vary according to the addressee' if the particular situation of one of the addressees is such as to make uniform application thereof difficult. This will enable the arrangements put into effect within the European Monetary System, under which special conditions apply to some Member States (at present the United Kingdom and Italy) to be maintained and possibly extended. However, the differentiation permitted by Article 35 is temporary and must ultimately lead to the uniform application of the law. The reference to the principle set out in Article 35 perhaps implies that the differentiation is only provisional.[1]

It should be observed that within the framework of Article 52 (1) the principle laid down in Article 35 is linked to the rule that all Member States shall participate in the European Monetary System rather than to rules laid down by law: this means essentially, that the fact that all the Member States participate is not incompatible with the laying-down of varying conditions. When the Treaty of Union comes into force, the previous European Monetary System regime will be retained at first:

[1] See Article 68 (2) and commentary.

Article 7 (4) provides as follows: 'the measures adopted within the context of the European Monetary System ... shall continue to be effective,
in so far as they are not incompatible with this Treaty, until such time
as they have been replaced by acts or measures adopted by the institutions of the Union in accordance with their respective competences.'
Thus any differentiated conditions which might be applied within the
European Monetary System when the Treaty of the Union comes into
force will continue to apply: the words 'subject to the principle set out
in Article 35 of this Treaty' ensure that they will be compatible with
the Treaty. However, when, at a later date, the institutions of the Union
become aware of the need to amend the European Monetary System
mechanism the legal instrument to be used will be a law; and it is clear
that, within the meaning of Article 35, any law may provide for different
treatment for the various States to whom it is addressed. If the intention
of Article 52 (1) had been to govern only this stage of the European
Monetary System it would have been superfluous to make it subject to
that reservation. The reservation is therefore justified only by reference
to a regime which has not been introduced by a law, which is the regime
which the Union will inherit, together with the whole of the Community
patrimony (Article 7 (4)).

3.   The rationale behind Article 52 (2), which merely provides that the
Union's concurrent competence is to be exercised with regard to a
specific objective (the progressive achievement of full monetary union),
is the grant to the Union under Article 51 of concurrent competence in
respect of monetary policy. As for the prescribed objective, this does
not rule out the possibility of a need to use that competence for any
amendments to the European Monetary System mechanism, including
those which do not constitute progress towards monetary union.

   With regard to the process of monetary union, when the European
Monetary System was set up it was expected that two very important
stages would be reached by March 1981: the creation of a European
Monetary Fund and the use of the ECU as a reserve currency and a
means of payment. This forecast turned out to be very optimistic. For
this reason the Treaty of Union, though confirming that the aim is 'full'
monetary union, acknowledges that this could only be achieved progressively. It will be for the legislature to determine the stages: this
follows expressly from the penultimate indent of Article 52 (3) which
provides that a subsequent organic law will lay down the procedures
and the stages for attaining monetary union.

Article 52 (3) also indicates specifically three matters to be governed by an organic law: the creation and operation of the European Monetary Fund, the new uses of the ECU, and the duties of the central banks of the Member States. With regard to the first point, it should be borne in mind that Article 33, to which express reference is made, includes the Monetary Fund as one of the organs of the Union, leaving it to an organic law to lay down the rules governing the competences and powers of those organs, their organization and their membership. From this point of view the first indent of Article 52 (3) does no more than repeat, with specific reference to the Fund, what follows in general from Article 33 (1) mentioned above: the fact that the term 'Statute' (of the Fund) is preferred to the word 'organization' probably takes into account the fact that the Monetary Fund has still to be set up. It should also be pointed out that an important characteristic of the Fund may be deduced from Article 33 (4); the autonomy required to guarantee monetary stability. The second indent of Article 52 (3) thus enables one of the most important tasks of the future Fund to be specified—the effective transfer to it of part of the reserves of the Member States—in that the conditions for that transfer must be laid down by an organic law to be adopted.

The new uses of the ECU, to which the third indent of paragraph 3 relates, constitute another decisive factor in the 'second stage' of the European Monetary System, which it was expected under the initial plan to have achieved as long ago as 1981. The ECU is in fact to be converted, on the basis of the organic law, into a reserve currency and a means of payment: in addition, its use may be extended subsequently. The provision takes care to describe this conversion as 'progressive', which is consistent with the idea that the monetary union will be achieved by stages. This wording shows an attitude of cautious realism on the part of the authors of the Treaty; moreover, they based the substance of the first three indents of paragraph 3 on the implied belief that, until the Union has been set up, the European Monetary System is not meant to go beyond the first stage in which it is at present.

It must also be observed that, according to the last indent of paragraph 3, the organic law will also lay down specific limits on the action of the central banks, binding them in the determination of 'their objectives regarding money supply'. This reflects the intention of introducing a framework of rules on national monetary policy beyond the field of exchange rates; and it cannot be denied that this course of action will be made necessary by the creation of the Monetary Fund and the conversion of the ECU.

4. Article 52 (4) outlines a special mechanism for including the European Council in the legislative process, by reference to the organic laws mentioned in paragraph 3. The objective of this provision is to ensure 'overall political control' over the process of achievement of the monetary union.[2] Essentially, as this matter is at present governed by agreements between the Member States, while the Treaty puts it within the framework of common action, the intention was that within the institution responsible for co-operation—the European Council—the Member States would still be able to decide to slow down the progress towards monetary union during the five years following the entry into force of the Treaty. The procedure devised is based on the suspension by the European Council of the entry into force of an organic law; subsequently the law is referred back to the legislative authority for fresh consideration (and therefore another vote) which will ultimately lead to the approval, amendment, or rejection of the law previously adopted.

The fact that the power of suspension granted to the Council may be exercised within one month from the adoption of the law gives rise to a problem: under Article 39 a law must be published in the *Official Journal* 'without delay' when it has been established that the legislative procedure has been completed. Thus an organic law may come into force when the period of one month mentioned above has not yet expired. On the other hand, it would be illogical and incongruous for the suspension of the entry into force of a law to affect law already in force which would therefore already have begun to produce its effects. One consideration which might help to solve the problem is that the provision in question derogates not only from Article 36 (legislative authority) and Article 38 (voting procedure for draft laws) but also from Article 39 (publication of laws). Bearing this in mind it is reasonable to suppose that when one of the laws referred to in Article 52 (3) is adopted, the President of the branch of the legislative authority which has taken the last express decision is authorized to delay publication of the law until the date on which the period of one month granted to the European Council to exercise its power of suspension has expired.

[2] The expression was used by the rapporteur, Mr Moreau: see Doc. 1-575/83/B, paragraph 59.

Article 53
Sectoral policies

In order to meet the particular needs for the organization, development or coordination of specific sectors of economic activity, the Union shall have concurrent competence with the Member States to pursue sectoral policies at the level of the Union. In the fields referred to below, such policies shall, by the establishment of reliable framework conditions, in particular pursue the aim of facilitating the decisions which undertakings subject to competition must take concerning investment and innovation.

The sectors concerned are in particular:

— agriculture and fisheries,

— transport,

— telecommunications,

— research and development,

— industry,

— energy.

(a) In the fields of agriculture and fisheries, the Union shall pursue a policy designed to attain the objectives laid down in Article 39 of the Treaty establishing the European Economic Community.

(b) In the field of transport, the Union shall pursue a policy designed to contribute to the economic integration of the Member States. It shall, in particular, undertake common actions to put an end to all forms of discrimination, harmonize the basic terms of competition between the various modes of transport, eliminate obstacles to transfrontier traffic and develop the capacity of transport routes so as to create a transport network commensurate with European needs.

(c) In the field of telecommunications, the Union shall take common action to establish a telecommunications network with common standards and harmonize tariffs. It shall exercise competence in particular with regard to the high technology sectors, research and development activities and public procurement policy.

(d) In the field of research and development, the Union may draw up common strategies with a view to co-ordinating and guiding national activities and encouraging co-operation between the Member States and between research institutes. It may provide financial support for joint research, may take responsibility for some of the risks involved and may undertake research in its own establishments.

(e) In the field of industry, the Union may draw up development strategies with a view to guiding and co-ordinating the policies of the Member States in those industrial branches which are of particular significance to the economic and political security of the Union. The Commission shall be responsible for taking the requisite implementing measures. It shall submit to the Parliament and the Council of the Union a periodic report on industrial policy problems.

(f) In the field of energy, action by the Union shall be designed to ensure security of supplies, stability on the market of the Union and, to the extent that prices are regulated, a harmonized pricing policy compatible with fair competitive practices. It shall also be designed to encourage the development of alternative and renewable energy sources, to introduce common technical standards for efficiency, safety, the protection of the environment and of the population, and to encourage the exploitation of European sources of energy.

Preparatory documents:

Doc. 1-575/83/B, Moreau Report, pp. 20-2.
Doc. 1-575/83/C, Moreau working document, pp. 49-58 and 64-5.
Resolution of 14 September 1983, paragraphs 44-54.

Provisions in force:

ECSC Treaty, Articles 46-8, 57-64, and 70.
EEC Treaty, Articles 38-47 and 74-84.
EAEC Treaty, Articles 1-2, 4-100, 194-7.

1.   The sectors of economic activity dealt with in Article 53 differ from each other considerably as regards their nature and scope and the type of rules appropriate to each of them. In that connection, two points

deserve particular emphasis: in the first place, the matters covered by
the article range from those which are already substantially covered by
Community law (agriculture and fisheries) to one which has so far been
the subject of hardly any common action (telecommunications), but in
most of the sectors Community experience is only partial (energy, for
example) and far from well defined (as in the case of transport, industry,
research and development); thus it is necessary for the Union to direct
considerable effort towards 'revival', to use the term appearing at the
beginning of the preamble to the Treaty. In the second place, the means
for implementing the various policies vary according to the sector: it is
foreseeable for example that agriculture and fisheries will continue to
be subject to copious and detailed rules, whereas the 'common strategies' to be drawn up (in the fields of research and development and
industry) will be reflected in the preparation of programmes (and it is
difficult to say whether this will be done by means of framework laws
or even by non-binding measures). At the same time, the promotion of
specific sectors will involve direct action on the part of the Union of a
technical nature (the provision refers to research in the telecommunications sector, as well as in the field of research and development) or
of a financial nature (in paragraph (d) financial support for joint
research is mentioned).

From the drafting point of view, it would have been preferable to
limit the content of Article 53 to the two initial propositions, which set
out the objectives of the various policies, and to replace paragraphs (a)
to (f) by six separate articles: it might thereby have been possible to
give clearer indications regarding the measures and action to be taken
in the various fields. As it stands, the article is both too long and rather
superficial; however, while the length of it is accounted for by the large
number of subjects covered, the particular criticism which must be
levelled against it is its lack of precision. Indeed, the main feature of
its lack of balance lies in the fact that with regard to certain sectors
the main emphasis is placed on the objectives to be pursued and not on
the legal means to be employed, while with regard to other sectors the
opposite is true.

2.   In all the sectors mentioned in Article 53, the competence of the
Union is concurrent. It is apparent from the preparatory documents that
initially the idea was considered of conferring exclusive competence
with regard to the common organization of the agricultural markets,
but since agriculture in its entirety was then adopted as a sector, it was

logical to treat that area as one to be the subject of concurrent competence.[1]

In those circumstances, the Union is given the power 'to pursue sectoral policies at the level of the Union'. In the Resolution of the European Parliament of 17 October 1983, the expression used in that connection referred to 'policies appropriate to the special circumstances in those areas' (paragraph 44); the basic idea therefore was to establish a correlation between the content and the means of implementing each policy and the actual situation in the sector in question. As regards the words 'at the level of the Union', they appear to be designed to reiterate the concept clearly laid down in Article 12 (2), that is to say that wherever there is concurrent competence the tasks entrusted to the Union are in particular those whose dimensions and effects extend beyond national frontiers (see also, in the last paragraph of the preamble, the reference to the principle of subsidiarity).

The needs on which the competence in question is based are the *specific* needs to organize, develop, and co-ordinate certain areas of economic activity. It is clear that the distinction between these three requirements reflects the various ways in which the Union is to act: where it organizes a particular sector, it is substituted for the Member States; where it merely develops or co-ordinates another sector, it promotes an activity and that activity continues to be carried on by the Member States. Once again, the choice of the method of action is determined by the conditions obtaining in each sector.

The article draws particular attention to one of the aims pursued by the sectoral policies: that of establishing reliable framework conditions so as to facilitate the decisions which undertakings must take concerning investment and innovation. The meaning of this phrase is that the undertakings are to play the role of protagonists in the economy, as is required by the principles of the market economy. The success or failure of undertakings must be the result of competition (note the emphasis on the competition facing undertakings), and therefore the authorities of the Union and the Member States must essentially concern themselves with the reliability of the 'framework conditions'; in other words, it is incumbent upon them to determine and maintain certain ground rules (legal provisions or other measures) on the basis of which undertakings may compete freely with each other. All this is consistent with the

---

[1] However, this cannot lead to a retreat from the *status quo* since, where the Union acts or the Community has already acted in a field of concurrent competence, the Member States may only legislate to the extent laid down by the law of the Union.

economic doctrine of the Union; but it must be pointed out that the statements are too vague and general to succeed in exercising any specific influence on conditions in the various sectors with which the article is concerned. (Compare, for example, the reality of the Common Agricultural Policy with the principles of the market economy!)

3. With respect to the policy of the Union in the fields of agriculture and fisheries, paragraph (a) merely refers to the objectives laid down in Article 39 of the EEC Treaty. Adherence to those objectives seems to imply that the instruments adopted for implementing the Common Agricultural Policy will be retained, in particular the machinery of the common organizations of the markets (Article 40 (2) and (3) of the EEC Treaty)—and the related machinery for regulating prices and grants—and that of the EAGGF (Article 40 (4) of the EEC Treaty). Moreover, by virtue of Article 7 ('Community patrimony') Articles 38 to 47 of the EEC Treaty are to constitute part of the law of the Union, and all secondary legislation on agricultural matters enjoys the same treatment. In practical terms, this means that the starting-point for the rules on agriculture in the context of the Union will be a very substantial inheritance.

In the working document prepared by the rapporteur, Mr Moreau, it is acknowledged that the agricultural sector 'has two advantages: a solid legal basis ... and the fact that the results of its activities are on the whole positive'; therefore it was envisaged that the problems arising for the Union would be only problems of 'adjustment'.[2] Mention was made in particular of the need for European production to be better adapted to the world agricultural situation and for the Common Agricultural Policy to reflect a more diversified approach, depending upon the characteristics of the various products. Moreover, the hope was expressed that the Union would seek to a greater extent to give incentive to national reorganization measures.[3] In more concise terms, the introduction to the Moreau Report entrusted to the Union the task of making, with regard to agriculture, 'the adjustments needed to correct and make good deficiencies or shortcomings in the present system'.[4]

This view clearly relates to the future trends of the Agricultural Policy. For the time being, from a legal point of view, it is sufficient to emphasize that in the sector of agriculture and fisheries the Treaty

[2] Doc. 1-575/83/C, paragraph 109.
[3] Ibid., paragraph 137.
[4] Doc. 1-575/83/B, paragraph 61.

establishing the Union fully adopts the criterion of continuity. Irrespective of the criticisms which are often levelled against the EEC agricultural rules, the Union seems bound to manage that sector without any innovations regarding matters of form.

4. It is recognized that in the field of transport the ECSC Treaty (Article 70) confines itself to dealing with specific points, particularly with respect to non-discrimination, while the EEC Treaty deals with the problem in more general terms, adopting a very broad approach and some detailed rules (see Articles 74–84 of that Treaty). However, by contrast with the area of agriculture, only a small part of the EEC Treaty provisions on transport has been applied: a true Common Transport Policy has not yet emerged.[5] In these circumstances, by entrusting to the Union policy in the field of transport the task of contributing 'to the economic integration of the Member States', Article 53(b) adopts the same approach as Article 74 of the EEC Treaty and by implication focuses upon the need to find a remedy for the fragmentary nature of Community action in recent years.

The Article then dwells upon the aims of certain aspects of Community action and here in part it is in line with the approach already adopted in the EEC Treaty (abolition of discrimination: see Article 71 of that Treaty), seeking moreover to achieve more far-reaching results (to put an end to *all forms* of discrimination). Furthermore, to some extent it lays down new objectives (to develop the capacity of transport routes). It should be pointed out that some objectives, although not specifically enunciated in the Treaty of Rome, at present form part of the programme of the Commission of the European Communities, which is endeavouring to persuade the Council to pursue those objectives; in that respect it has achieved some, albeit marginal, results. The areas in question are in particular the removal of obstacles to cross-frontier traffic and harmonization of the conditions for competition between the various types of transport.

It may indeed be said that the Union's future legislative activity regarding transport will have to be intensive and co-ordinated in order to make up for the inadequacy of Community legislation in that area. In Mr Moreau's Report it is specifically pointed out in that regard that it will be the Union's responsibility to 'provide for the genuine

---

[5] See the action brought by the European Parliament against the Council for failure to fulfil its obligations: Case 13/83 *European Parliament* v. *Council*, Judgment of 22 May 1985, not yet reported.

implementation of a transport policy covering all sectors ... and all aspects ..., in so far as it is in the common economic interest for the Union to intervene'.[6]

5. In the field of telecommunications—with which the EEC Treaty does not concern itself—the Community has so far confined itself to financing a number of research programmes (the Esprit Programme in particular may be mentioned: the European Strategic Programme for Research and Development of Information Technology). Article 53(c) provides that the Union is to undertake common action 'to establish a telecommunications network with common standards and harmonized tariffs'. Probably, if not necessarily, common action will concentrate on the establishment of 'common standards' (a term borrowed from Community language) and harmonization of tariffs, and it will be the responsibility of the Member States to establish the telecommunications network. In the same way, the public procurement policy referred to at the end of the paragraph will doubtless entail the issue of framework laws. But the enactment of legislation will have to be supported by research and development activity: and it is to this in particular that the term 'high technology sectors' must logically refer. The detailed arrangements for research and development activity will be adopted in accordance with the provisions of Article 53(d).

6. The problems of research have been taken into account, in Community law, both in the ECSC Treaty (Article 55) and in the EAEC Treaty (Articles 4-11): both lay down provisions for the co-ordination, financing, or conduct of research designed to meet the requirements of the coal, iron and steel, and atomic energy sectors. Subsequently, Community research activity extended into other fields: in particular those of energy, industry, health, and the environment, in which Community action concentrated on financing research activity. Article 53(d) describes how the competence of the Union will be exercised with regard to research and development (an expression which appears to refer to applied research, for the purposes of development). Essentially, it will act in two ways: by drawing up 'common strategies' for the Member States and also by direct participation in research projects.

The term 'common strategies' appears to imply, as stated above, a system of programming designed to ensure a convergent approach in

[6] Doc. 1-575/83/B, paragraph 62.

activities undertaken at national level: the provision expressly states that it has the object of 'co-ordinating and guiding national activities and encouraging co-operation between the Member States and between research institutes'. By means of framework laws, that system of programming could be made binding; but there is nothing to prevent a law from merely making the Commission responsible for ensuring co-ordination and providing guidance in the form of recommendations.

As regards the Union's participation in joint research—that is to say research in the common interest, based on joint initiatives whose scope extends beyond individual Member States—this may take the form either of financial support or responsibility for some of the risks involved: but the line separating these two possibilities is not clear. Finally, the Union may undertake research in its own establishments— something which has been going on at the EURATOM research centres for a considerable time.

7. Reference is also made to 'strategies' to be drawn up, more specifically 'development strategies' in connection with the industrial sector, provided for in paragraph (e) of the Article under consideration. The use of the same term reflects the parallel approach with regard to industry and research and development, in so far as in both fields there is a general awareness of the need for action to guide and co-ordinate the policies of the Member States, rather than for rules, and still less direct management, imposed by the Union. Of course, the questions dealt with above regarding the scope of the word 'strategies' again arise with respect to the industrial sector; but it is interesting to note that the arguments in favour of a non-binding system of programmes are reinforced by the reference in the working document prepared by Mr Moreau to 'co-operation plans which will provide points of reference for national operators'.[7]

Furthermore, account must be taken of the fact that the principle requiring recognition of the Community patrimony (Article 7) requires an approach to the problem of the coal and steel and nuclear industries which is different from that adopted for problems relating to other kinds of industries; the means of control and intervention available to the Union in the two areas indicated are based on the existence of much wider powers of the kind inherent in 'dirigisme'. It must also be pointed out that, even in the case of the industries which at present come within

[7] Doc. 1-575/83/C, paragraph 134.

the scope of the EEC, Community influence is exercised by means of legislative measures and not solely by means of co-ordination; however, the legislative measures in question derive from powers which are not specifically linked to industrial policy. In that connection, it is appropriate to mention, first of all, the competition rules applicable to undertakings and then the Community directives on the harmonization of company law and the approximation of tax laws, on public contracts and the elimination of technical obstacles to trade. This situation will continue to exist after creation of the Union; it will of course be possible to replace or supplement the directives by framework laws, and other applicable regulations or laws may come later on the basis of Articles 47, 48, and 49.

The provision under consideration here is intended to establish a criterion which may be used to define the field of competence of the Union in relation to the spheres of competence of the Member States. In fact, the guidance and co-ordination of the policies of the Member States must be limited to 'those industrial branches which are of particular significance to the economic and political security of the Union'. It can be readily seen that that criterion is so vague as to allow the institutions a wide margin of discretion. But let it not be forgotten that the question of the borderline between common action and action by the individual States is dealt with in general terms by the principle of subsidiarity, which is reiterated in Article 12 (2) with respect to all cases of concurrent competence.

In the second and third sentences of Article 53(e) two tasks are entrusted to the Commission: 'taking the requisite implementing measures', and submitting to the Parliament and the Council of the Union a periodic report on industrial policy problems. The first expression may give rise to confusion, but if it is compared with paragraph 51 of the Resolution of the European Parliament of 14 September 1983, it becomes apparent that the 'implementing measures' may take the form either of recommendations addressed to undertakings, Member States, and local authorities involved, or of co-operation schemes submitted to the European Council or, finally, of action of a legislative or financial nature on the basis of decisions taken by the legislative authority.

It is appropriate here to emphasize three points. In the first place, the possibility of schemes to be submitted to the European Council provides a sort of bridge between common action and co-operation, which is provided for by the Treaty in very few cases (cf. the last paragraph of Article 46 and Article 67 (1)) and is not taken into account by the provision concerning the competences of the Commission (Article 28). The question therefore arises whether the Commission is also in a position to submit schemes to the European Council on the basis of the general reference to 'requisite implementing measures'. A reply in the affirmative appears justified, in view of the fact that the primary objective is co-ordination of the activities of the Member States. In the second place, to consider that the measures which may be adopted by the Commission include 'action of a legislative ... nature' based on laws means concentrating attention on the executive phase, although the provision does not make clear which laws will require to be adopted. (Perhaps they will be such development strategies as may be drawn up by means of framework laws.) Finally, the reference to action of a financial nature ought to have been more specific, not only because it involves the legislative authority as well, but because today financing measures constitute an important aspect of Community activity in the industrial sector, undertaken at least in part, within the framework of the European Investment Bank or the Regional Fund.

8. At present, the energy sector is characterized by the existence of two complex Community structures in the case of coal and atomic energy (organizational and legislative structures which reflect the idea of a genuine common management of the two sectors) and by the total lack of Community provisions on other aspects of the energy problem. The Community institutions, spurred on by the oil crisis and the ever more evident need to research into the use of alternative energy sources, have in recent years promoted various kinds of co-operation, by recourse to a range of non-binding measures: resolutions of the Council or of the European Parliament, communications and reports by the Commission to the Council, and Council or Commission recommendations addressed to the Member States. At the same time, specific intervention measures have been undertaken, in the form of financial support for demonstration or research projects.

Article 53(f) confines itself to indicating a series of objectives to be achieved, but is silent regarding the means of so doing. It is clear that the ECSC and EURATOM legislation will become part of the law of the Union: the Resolution of 14 September 1983 of the European Parliament made this clear (paragraph 53), but in fact the provision under consideration has not reproduced that paragraph of the Resolution, so that the general principle that the Community patrimony is to be taken over, laid down in Article 7 of the Treaty, will apply. Coal and atomic energy will therefore continue to be subject to the legislation in force, and the present Community fields of competence in the two sectors will become competences of the Union. As regards problems relating to other sources of energy, the institutions of the Union will be able to exercise the concurrent competence provided for in the present Treaty, by the issue of laws and regulations, or to continue to rely upon non-binding measures and to use the mechanism of incentives. In the working document prepared by Mr Moreau, it was correctly pointed out that, in the Energy sector 'the principle of subsidiarity must be applied pragmatically, the Union chiefly performing a co-ordinating function but having the power to take common action in certain cases'.[8]

As regards the objectives of the energy policy, most of them are economic or technical in character; 'to encourage' results in conformity with those objectives implies above all, from the legal point of view, recourse to non-binding measures and financial support. It is rather in connection with the endeavours to ensure stability of the market or harmonization of prices—in so far as they are regulated at national level—that recourse to binding measures may be seen as appropriate, in particular in the form of framework laws; there is no doubt that the legislative authority of the Union is in a position to do this, on the basis of Article 12 (2).

[8] Doc. 1-575/83/C, paragraph 132.

Article 54

Other forms of co-operation

1. When Member States have taken the initiative to establish industrial co-operation structures outside the scope of this Treaty, the European Council may, if the common interest justifies it, decide to convert those forms of co-operation into a common action of the Union.

2. In specific sectors subject to common action, laws may establish specialized European agencies and define those forms of supervision applicable thereto.

Preparatory documents:

Doc. 1-575/83/B, Moreau Report, p. 22.
Doc. 1-575/83/C, Moreau working document, p. 67.
Resolution of 14 September 1983, paragraphs 55-6.

1. The principal examples of industrial co-operation structures established by certain Member States outside the framework of the Treaty are Ariane, the Airbus and CERN. They are referred to in the Resolution of the European Parliament of 14 September 1983 (paragraph 55) and in the working document prepared by Mr Moreau.[1] Those three initiatives relate respectively to the building and launching of a space vehicle, the manufacture of a commercial aircraft, and the management of a nuclear research centre. The paragraph of the Resolution of the European Parliament mentioned above appeared to be designed in the first place to establish that that kind of co-operation was compatible with the competence vested in the Union: it begins with the statement that 'the Union shall leave open the possibility for European or international ventures undertaken by certain Member States outside the legal framework of the Treaty ... where such action does not replace a competence of the Union.' However, immediately afterwards, in the same paragraph, it is envisaged that such activities may be subsequently 'integrated in a common policy of the Union'.

Article 54 (1) confines itself to this last aspect, stating that initiatives of the kind mentioned therein may be converted into common action of

---

[1] Doc. 1-575/83/C of 15 July 1983, paragraph 143.

Union, by decision of the European Council, *if the common interest justi-fies it*. This, therefore, is one of the two cases in which it is acknow-ledged that co-operation may be converted into common action, in accordance with Article 11 of the Treaty. But there is one factor which seems to have been left out of account: the participation of non-member States, and not only of some of the Member States of the Community, in the arrangements on which the existing industrial co-operation struc-tures are based. If it is assumed that that situation will remain un-changed when the Union comes into existence, no transition to the phase of common action would be possible unless two difficulties were surmounted: that of the attitude of the Member States which, today, are not involved in the forms of co-operation in question, and that of the attitude of the non-member countries, to which common action certainly cannot be extended. The first of these difficulties would dis-appear, by virtue of the consensus which would have to be achieved within the European Council in order to decide upon the 'transfer' of the structures mentioned above; but it is conceivable that the second difficulty might lead to the Union being substituted for its members as a partner in industrial co-operation with other non-member European States. Perhaps this possibility was perceived by the rapporteur, Mr Moreau, when he envisaged in his working document that the Union might 'if necessary, join in' ventures of the type under consideration here.[2]

2.   The purpose of paragraph 2 of the article is to provide for the possibility of establishing 'European agencies' specializing in sectors subject to common action (the German text uses, inappropriately, the term *Fachbehörden*, which refers rather to internal bodies). That could be brought about only by means of a law, and the law itself would have to regulate the manner in which the activities of such agencies were to be supervised. Among the examples given in the Moreau Report of sectors in which the use of this particular means of action might be envisaged are space, telecommunications, and transport; but only the last two fields of activity are subject to common action, under Article 53.

As regards points of reference within the Communities, mention may be made of the EURATOM supply agency, governed by Articles 52 to 76 of the EAEC Treaty and of the Statute thereon, adopted by the Council of the European Atomic Energy Community on 6 November

[2] Doc. 1-575/83/C, paragraph 144.

Article 55

General provisions

The Union shall have concurrent competence in the field of social, health, consumer protection, regional, environmental, education and research, cultural and information policies.

Preparatory documents:

Doc. 1-575/83/B, Pfennig Report, paragraph 69.

Doc. 1-575/83/C, Pfennig working document, paragraphs 1–16, 21–2.

1.   Title II, 'Policy for Society', provides for Union action in a wide range of fields, which are listed in the opening article of Title II, Article 55. The different fields are then provided for successively in the remaining articles of Title II, Articles 56–62.

The title 'policy for society' is used to indicate a new approach. The term 'policy for society', which appears only in the title of Title II itself, is far broader than the more specific term 'social policy', which appears in Article 55 as one policy among many and which is the subject of Article 56.

The choice of the term 'policy for society' is not explained in the Pfennig working document. Indeed, it is suggested (paragraph 14) that the term cannot be defined. It represents, however, the sum of the various separate policies which reflect a series of political choices and which embody shared European values.

2.   The policies provided for in Title II of the Treaty feature only to a very limited extent, if at all, in the Community Treaties, whose objectives were predominantly economic. In those Treaties, accordingly, the limited social policies were linked to an economic objective. In the present Treaty, while some of the policies listed in Article 55 are clearly linked with the economic competence of the Union, it seems equally clear that other policies have an independent justification, especially a concern with the 'quality of life'.

Even the EEC Treaty, which is the most developed of the Community Treaties in this respect, contains only certain relatively rudimentary provisions under the head 'social provisions' (Articles 117 ff. of the EEC Treaty). In respect of specific sectors, such as social security, the EEC Treaty contains provisions limited to social security arrangements for migrant workers (Article 51). Otherwise, and in all the other policies listed in Article 55 of the draft Treaty, Community action is possible only on the basis of the general provisions of Article 100 and/or Article 235 of the EEC Treaty. Under both Articles, unanimity is required. Under the present Treaty, the normal legislative majorities will suffice for Union action (Article 38).

3. Two further points are of general importance in Article 55 and in each of the remaining Articles of this Title. First, the competence of the Union is expressed as concurrent, not exclusive: consequently the provisions of Article 12 (2) are applicable. Secondly, in every case the starting-point of action by the Union is the 'Community patrimony': this is not expressed in the present Articles but follows from the general provision of Article 7. Consequently the existing corpus of Community legislation remains in force for the Union in each of the following sectors.

Article 56

Social and health policy

The Union may take action in the field of social and health policy, in particular in matters relating to:

— employment, and in particular the establishment of general comparable conditions for the maintenance and creation of jobs,

— the law on labour and working conditions,

— equality between men and women,

— vocational training and further training,

— social security and welfare,

— protection against occupational accidents and diseases,

— work hygiene,

— trade union rights and collective negotiations between employers and employees, in particular with a view to the conclusion of Union-wide collective agreements,

— forms of worker participation in decisions affecting their working life and the organization of undertakings,

— the determination of the extent to which citizens of non-member States may benefit from equal treatment,

— the approximation of the rules governing research into and the manufacture, properties, and marketing of pharmaceutical products,

— the prevention of addiction,

— the co-ordination of mutual aid in the event of epidemics or disasters.

Preparatory documents:

Doc. 1-575/83/B, Pfennig report, paragraphs 74 *et seq.*
Doc. 1-575/83/C, Pfennig working document, paragraphs 21 to 46.
Resolution of 14 September 1983, paragraphs 58–9.

1.   Article 56 is concerned with 'social policy' in the narrower sense.[1] It also includes certain aspects of public health. Article 56 spells out the sectors within the general area of social policy in which the Union may take action. Such detailed enumeration of the sectors in question may not seem in keeping with an instrument which in general is of a constitutional character; but it was considered valuable to specify in concrete terms those areas where Union action was particularly desirable.

2.   However, the indications given in Article 56 remain very general in character. In the first place, the sectors listed in the successive indents are, in effect, only examples. The inclusion in the opening of the Article of the words 'in particular', which gave rise to considerable controversy in the Institutional Committee and to further discussion in the plenary debate before the adoption of the text of the Treaty, shows that the catalogue enumerated in the Article is not exhaustive but only indicative.

Second, little practical and concrete detail is given of the content of the policies to be pursued: that is rightly to be left to the Institutions of the Union to work out.

Third, there is no precise indication of the methods by which the Union is to implement its chosen policies. Article 56 merely indicates, in its opening words, that the Union 'may take action'. Exceptionally, in relation to pharmaceutical products (indent 11), Article 56 refers to the 'approximation' of national rules, which recalls the language of Article 100 of the EEC Treaty and the harmonization directives adopted thereunder.[2]

3.   Otherwise, Article 56 leaves the choice of methods to the Union Institutions. In some cases, perhaps for example in determining the extent to which citizens of non-member States may benefit from equal treatment (indent 10), relatively detailed legislation may be found necessary. In other cases, 'framework laws' (*lois-cadre*) may be sufficient, or non-binding measures, such as recommendations, may be appropriate, e.g. for the prevention of addiction (twelfth indent). The Pfennig Report also envisaged, in this connection, other measures, such as a Union-wide campaign against the abuse of substances harmful to health, especially drugs, tobacco, and alcohol. The co-ordination of mutual aid

[1] See the commentary on Article 55, point 1.
[2] See the commentary on Article 46.

in the event of epidemics or disasters (final indent) will also require measures of a practical nature.

4. Despite the limited indications given in Article 56, it is clear that the Union's activities in the field of social policy will go far beyond the 'social provisions' of the EEC Treaty (Articles 117 to 122). While it was recognized at the Paris Summit of 1972 that 'vigorous action in the social field is as important as the achievement of the Economic and Monetary Union,[3] only limited progress has been made in implementing a Community social policy.[4]

The catalogue is based in part on Article 118 of the EEC Treaty (indents 1-2 and 4-8 of Article 56), but goes considerably further in extending the range of the Union's activities. Moreover, while Article 118 envisaged only 'close co-operation' between Member States, under Article 56 of the draft Treaty the Union has full legislative powers.

Equality between men and women (indent 3) generalizes a principle that has received particular applications in Community law. Article 119 of the EEC Treaty requires the application of the principle that men and women should receive equal pay for equal work, while the principle of equality between men and women has received legislative recognition in particular sectors in Council Directives 75/117, 76/207, and 79/7/EEC.

The ideas of worker participation and of equal treatment for citizens of non-member States (indents 9 and 10) have received support from the Commission of the European Communities and from the European Parliament but have not yet been given effect in Community legislation.

[3] EC Bulletin 10/1972.
[4] See The Social Policy of the European Community, European Documentation 3/1981.

Article 57

Consumer policy

The Union may lay down rules designed to protect the health and safety of consumers and their economic interests, particularly in the event of damage. The Union may encourage action to promote consumer education, information and consultation.

Preparatory documents:

Doc. 1-575/83/B, Pfennig Report, paragraphs 80-1.
Doc. 1-575/83/C, Pfennig working document, paragraphs 53-9.
Resolution of 14 September 1983, paragraph 60.

1. There is no specific provision in the Community Treaties for the adoption of measures for the protection or benefit of the consumer. It is true that, as early as the ECSC Treaty, the interests of the consumer were expressly recognized (see Article 3(b) of the ECSC Treaty). In the EEC Treaty, Article 86 includes among the examples of abuse of a dominant position, prohibited under that Article, 'limiting production, markets or technical development to the prejudice of consumers' (Article 86(b)). The case law of the Court suggests that national measures for the protection of the consumer may, exceptionally, justify under Article 36 of the Treaty restrictions on the free movement of goods which would otherwise be prohibited by Article 30.[1] Moreover, the *Cassis de Dijon* case[2] appeared to suggest that national measures for the protection of the consumer may in certain circumstances escape the prohibition of Article 30 altogether. However, *Community* measures for the protection or benefit of the consumer are nowhere expressly authorized by the EEC Treaty; they can be based only on the general provisions of Articles 100 and 235, each with its attendant limitations 'and each requiring the unanimous approval of the Council'.[3]

2. In April 1975 the Council adopted a Community programme for

---

[1] See e.g. Case 12/74 *Commission v. Federal Republic of Germany* [1975] ECR 181, P. Oliver, *Free Movement of Goods in the EEC*, London, 1982, pp. 147-50.

[2] Case 120/78 [1979] ECR 649.

[3] See G. L. Close, 'The legal basis for the consumer protection programme of the EEC and priorities for action', 8 *European Law Review* 1983, p. 221.

consumer protection and information[4] but few steps have been taken to implement the programme. A series of proposed directives from the Commission has been under consideration in the Council for some years, but only one directive has been adopted, and that one only very recently and in a form which fell far short of the Commission's proposal.[5]

The Pfennig Report recognizes that consumer policy concerns the quality of life of all Union citizens, and that 'the protection and perception of consumer interests are therefore a matter of concern for all.' It refers to previous consideration of consumer policy by the European Parliament,[6] and identifies the fundamental elements of that policy, which are set out in Article 57 of the draft Treaty. Of particular legal interest is the protection of the consumer in the event of damage, where the report envisages, among other things, the establishment of rules governing liability for defective products. Despite considerable work on the subject of product liability both in the Community (a draft directive) and in the Council of Europe (a draft convention), it has not hitherto proved possible to establish common European rules in this field. The legislative procedures of the Union can be expected to be more effective here.

[4] OJ C 92 of 25 April 1975.
[5] Directive 84/450/EEC, OJ L 250 of 19 September 1984, p. 17.
[6] O'Connell Report, Doc. 1-450/80, and the Resolution of the Parliament, OJ C 291, 16 October 1980, pp. 39 ff.

Article 58

Regional policy

The regional policy of the Union shall aim at reducing regional disparities and, in particular, the under-development of the least favoured regions, by injecting new life into those regions so as to ensure their subsequent development and by helping to create the conditions likely to put an end to the excessive concentration of migration towards certain industrial centres.

The regional policy of the Union shall, in addition, encourage transfrontier regional co-operation.

The regional policy of the Union, whilst supplementing the regional policy of the Member States, shall pursue specific Union objectives.

The regional policy of the Union shall comprise:

— the development of a European framework for the regional planning policies pursued by the competent authorities in each Member State,

— the promotion of investment and infrastructure projects which bring national programmes into the framework of an overall concept,

— the implementation of integrated programmes of the Union on behalf of certain regions, drawn up in collaboration with the representatives of the people concerned, and, where possible, the direct allocation of the requisite funds to the regions concerned.

Preparatory documents:

Doc. 1-575/83/B, Pfennig Report, paragraphs 47-52.
Resolution of 14 September 1983, paragraphs 61-4.

1. There is no specific provision in the Community Treaties for the adoption of a regional policy, perhaps because it was assumed that the disparities between the regions would be progressively lessened with the development of the common market. The desire to reduce such disparities is however mentioned in the preamble to the EEC Treaty,

while Article 2 describes the task of the Community as being 'to promote throughout the Community a harmonious development of economic activities'. Article 92 (3) allows that aids granted by States may be considered to be compatible with the common market if they are designed 'to promote the economic development of areas where the standard of living is abnormally low or where there is serious underemployment', and in recent years the Commission has sought to co-ordinate Member States' regional aid schemes.[1] The Community's own regional policy is still in its infancy.[2] Mr Mathijsen, the Commission's director-general for regional policy, has written:

Community regional policy is still in the developing stage; the very first steps have just been taken to arrive at a comprehensive approach to the problems created by the regional discrepancies within the Community. The means to implement such a policy are still extremely modest but the foundations have been laid which will allow the Community to remedy one of its most dramatic shortcomings.[3]

The Pfennig Report recognizes that, despite recent efforts by the Community in this field (especially through the European Regional Development Fund), the disparities between the regions have increased even further. The report, which refers to several earlier studies on the subject, proposes a number of specific remedies.[4]

2. Within the Union, regional policy will have a prominent place. The importance of the policy was continually emphasized in the Institutional Committee when the Treaty was drafted, and a special emphasis is given to it elsewhere in the Treaty.[5] Article 45 (2) places at the head of Part Four of the Treaty ('The Policies of the Union') the progressive elimination of the existing imbalances between the areas and regions of the Union, while Article 73 provides for a system of financial equalization to alleviate excessive imbalances between the regions. Taken together, Articles 45 (2), 58, and 73 clearly envisage a substantial shift of resources for the benefit of the less developed regions, a policy which will demonstrate a genuine sense of unity and a spirit of solidarity.

Article 58 of the Treaty substantially follows the terms of the Reso-

---

[1] See P. S. R. F. Mathijsen, A Guide to European Community Law, 3rd edn., London, 1980, p. 173 n. 31.
[2] Op. cit., pp. 177-86.
[3] Ibid., pp. 185-6.
[4] Paragraphs 49-52.
[5] See in particular Article 45 (2) and Article 73, and the comments thereon.

lution of the Parliament of 14 September 1983. The first paragraph gives general guidance as to the objectives of the regional policy, and as to the nature of the programmes which the Union is to encourage. The second paragraph makes specific reference to transfrontier regional co-operation, a subject in which there have been some developments within the Council of Europe: see the European Outline Convention on Trans-frontier Co-operation between Territorial Communities or Authorities (1980; European Treaty Series No. 106).

The third paragraph reflects the concern of the Institutional Com-mittee that the Union's regional policy should do more than provide additional funds for the individual regional policies of the Member States: it should pursue objectives for the benefit of the Union itself. That concern is also reflected, and is more fully spelt out, in the final paragraph.

The final paragraph makes it clear that the components of the Union's regional policy will include not only the co-ordination of national pol-icies within a European framework (first indent), but also the creation of an 'overall concept' designed at the level of the Union (second indent) and even, where appropriate, the implementation of the Union's own programmes (third indent). The programmes of Member States will thus be co-ordinated at the level of the Union, but the Union policy will not be wholly dependent on the national programmes: in some cases, national programmes and Union programmes may run side by side.

The Article omits, however, specific reference to the concept of addi-tionality which, in the Resolution, was to be the basis of the Union's regional policy. According to the Resolution (paragraph 64), the Union would base its regional policy on 'a concept of additionality determined not solely by quantitative criteria, but also by the development of specific Union policies which, while respecting national public expendi-ture targets and complementing national regional policies, shall be dis-tinguishable from the latter and shall conform to specific Union objec-tives'. The Treaty is less explicit in this respect: while Article 58 expressly requires that the regional policy should pursue specific Union objectives, the requirement of additionality was considered to be unduly restrictive.

Article 58 follows the Resolution in envisaging, to a greater extent than has proved feasible under the Community's regional policy, both the direct involvement of the regions themselves in the preparation of programmes and the direct allocation of funds, without the Member States acting as the intermediary in either respect. Moreover, the final

words of Article 58, referring to programmes drawn up with representatives of the *people* concerned (rather than representatives of the region
concerned) show an intention to involve the population of the region
directly. This idea reflects the Parliament's general concern that the
Union should be made a closer and more real phenomenon to the
ordinary citizen.

Article 59

Environmental policy

In the field of the environment, the Union shall aim at preventing or, taking account as far as possible of the 'polluter pays' principle, at redressing any damage which is beyond the capabilities of the individual Member State or which requires a collective solution. It shall encourage a policy of the rational utilization of natural resources, of exploiting renewable raw materials, and of recycling waste, which takes account of environmental protection requirements.

The Union shall take measures designed to provide for animal protection.

Preparatory documents:

Doc. 1-575/83/B, Pfennig Report, paragraphs 84–90.
Doc. 1-575/83/C, Pfennig working document, paragraphs 60–8.
Resolution of 14 September 1983, paragraphs 65–8.

1. Despite the absence of specific provisions in the Community Treaties, and despite certain early doubts about the competence of the Community in environmental matters,[1] the Community has adopted successive action programmes for the protection of the environment, and both the Pfennig Report and the Resolution of 14 September 1983 expressly adopt the objectives and subject-matter of the Community's programmes. No specific provision to that effect is necessary in Article 59, since the Community's programmes form part of the Community patrimony, which is taken over by the Union under Article 7.

The Community's activities, and the Treaty, recognize that environmental policy (perhaps more than any other policy) transcends national frontiers, since environmental pollution is increasingly transnational. The Treaty differs, however, from the drafting technique of the Resolution of September 1983. The Resolution (paragraph 65) envisaged that

---

[1] See, for example, House of Lords Select Committee on the European Communities, Session 1977-8, 22nd Report, considered by G. L. Close, *European Law Review* 1978, p. 461; compare the present view of the Select Committee, Session 1983-4, 1st Report.

the Union should prevent or redress loss or damage which

    (a) is of the same nature throughout the Union, or

    (b) occurs in more than one Member State, or

    (c) originates or terminates in the Union.

Article 59 simply refers to damage which is beyond the capabilities of the individual Member State or which requires a collective solution. While the criteria of Article 59 may seem at first sight more restrictive, it seems likely that they would prove adequate to cover any of the eventualities envisaged in the Resolution. In particular, since the second criterion must, according to standard principles of interpretation, be given a meaning different from the first, Article 59 should not be regarded as limited to damage which is beyond the resources of a particular Member State. It also provides a legal basis for environmental measures desirable in the Union interest, subject only to the principle of subsidiarity set out in the final recital of the preamble and reflected in Article 12 (2).

2.   Article 59 is unusual in embodying a specific legal principle, the 'polluter pays' principle, as a basis of liability for harm to the environment. That principle is increasingly recognized in some of the Member States and in some international conventions but is not yet fully reflected in Community law. However, the principle has in practice been recognized in Community law even in relation to the *prevention* of harm, since Community Directives in certain fields require industrial firms to take measures to prevent harm to the environment, which often require substantial expenditure on their part.[2] Because the Institutional Committee was unwilling to accept the 'polluter pays' principle as a universal principle, Article 59 provides only that the principle should be taken into account as far as possible.

The policies mentioned in the second sentence of the first paragraph, and in the second paragraph of Article 59 reflect the principal concerns of national environmental policy. Union action in respect of such policies would again be subject to the principle of subsidiarity.

---

[2] See for example the EEC Directives on titanium dioxide, e.g. Council Directive 78/176/EEC of 20 February 1978, OJ 1978, L54/19.

Article 60

Education and research policy

In order to create a context which will help inculcate in the public an awareness of the Union's own identity and to ensure a minimum standard of training creating the opportunity for free choice of career, job, or training establishment anywhere in the Union, the Union shall take measures concerning:

— the definition of objectives for common or comparable training programmes,

— the Union-wide validity and equivalence of diplomas and school, study, and training periods,

— the promotion of scientific research.

Preparatory documents:

Doc. 1-575/83/B, Pfennig Report, paragraphs 91-4.
Doc. 1-575/83/C, Pfennig working document, paragraphs 69-86.
Resolution of 14 September 1983, paragraphs 69-70.

1. The Community Treaties contain few provisions on education and research, and those provisions generally have a technical or economic purpose. The European Atomic Energy Community has as the first of the activities assigned to it to promote research and ensure the dissemination of technical information: see Article 2(a) of the EAEC Treaty and Title Two, Chapters I and II. However, it is clear from the terms and context of Article 60 of the present Treaty that this Article has wider aims. One of the activities of the Union will be the promotion of scientific research, and although that activity may be limited by the purposes specified in the opening words of Article 60, it is not limited by any technical purpose. Applied research falls within Article 53: see in particular Article 53(d). Article 60 is concerned with fundamental research.

2. Article 57 (1) of the EEC Treaty authorizes the adoption of directives for the mutual recognition of diplomas, certificates, and other evidence of formal qualifications, but such directives are limited by the terms of Article 57 (1) itself to qualifications for the activities of self-

employed persons, within the restricted context of attaining freedom of establishment. Moreover Article 57 (1) is limited to the mutual recognition of qualifications, while Article 60 of the draft Treaty envisages the Union-wide validity of professional and educational qualifications and experience.

3.   Finally (although mentioned first among the specific measures listed under Article 60) the Union is to define objectives for common or comparable training programmes. Again the aim is to enable qualified persons to work anywhere in the Union; there is however a necessary overlap with Article 56 of the Treaty, which governs the Union's competence in matters of 'vocational training and further training'.

Article 61

Cultural policy

1. The Union may take measures to:

— promote cultural and linguistic understanding between the citizens of the Union,

— publicize the cultural life of the Union both at home and abroad,

— establish youth exchange programmes.

2. The European University Institute and the European Foundation shall become establishments of the Union.

3. Laws shall lay down rules governing the approximation of the law of copyright and the free movement of cultural works.

Preparatory documents:

Doc. 1-575/83/B, Pfennig Report, paragraph 96.
Doc. 1-575/83/C, Pfennig working document, paragraphs 88–94.
Resolution of 14 September 1983, paragraphs 71–2.

1. Article 61 makes provision for various activities in the field of cultural policy which are not provided for in the Community Treaties.

The Pfennig Report advocated activity by the Union in three areas:

(i) representing cultural development within the Union and promoting cultural exchanges;

(ii) promoting cultural understanding between the citizens of the Union, and in particular establishing a European youth exchange programme;

(iii) improving the situation of 'persons active in the cultural sector', in particular by harmonizing copyright law in the Union and by freedom of movement for the cultural assets thereby created.

The Treaty follows the general lines of the report and Article 61 (1) makes provision for specific cultural programmes. The Report appears to seek a balance between, on one hand, the idea of the cultural unity of Europe and, on the other hand, the protection of ethnic and cultural diversity within a common European civilization. The report also recognizes the desirability of promoting cultural co-operation beyond the

Union's borders. These aims are reflected in Article 61 (1); in addition, Article 65 (1) provides for co-operation with the Council of Europe, 'in particular in the cultural sector'.

2.   Article 61 (2) incorporates the European University Institute and the European Foundation within the formal structure of the Union: both bodies are at present formally independent of the Communities, while having very close links with the Community Institutions. The term 'establishment' is used here (and in Article 53(d)) in contrast to the term 'institution' in Article 8 and the term 'organ' in Article 33.[1] (In the German text, the same term *'Einrichtung'* is used in Article 61 (2) as in Article 33.)

The Institute and the Foundation become establishments of the Union by virtue of the entry into force of the Treaty: no organic law (of the kind referred to in the last sentence of Article 33) or other law will be necessary for that purpose. The structure, operation, and finances of these establishments may be regulated by laws of the Union.

3.   The idea of an intergovernmental institution to extend European integration into the area of teaching and research was first launched in June 1955 at the Messina Conference of Foreign Ministers of the Six, which laid the foundations for the EEC and EAEC Treaties of 1957. The idea was not incorporated into those Community Treaties, although Article 9 (2) of the EAEC Treaty envisaged, in very general terms, the establishment of 'an institution of university status'. When the idea of establishing such an institution was finally approved at the Hague summit conference in December 1969, it was to be set up outside the framework of the Community Treaties, and the ensuing negotiations led to the signature by representatives of the Six, on 19 April 1972, of the Convention setting up the European University Institute. The Institute officially opened in 1976, and is housed near Florence.

While the Institute has established very close links with the Community, its status outside the Community structure has given rise to some difficulties. Such difficulties would be resolved by the incorporation of the Institute within the Union; such incorporation also appeared a logical consequence of the explicit extension of Union competence to cultural policy.

[1]   See further the commentary on Article 33.

4. The European Foundation for culture, education, and youth was being set up in 1985, with its headquarters in Paris. The Agreement establishing the European Foundation was adopted by the Heads of State and Government in 1982, but its entry into force requires ratification not only by all the Member States but by all of the German *Länder* and the two language areas of Belgium, which are competent under their respective constitutions in educational and cultural matters.

The task of the Foundation under Article 2 of the Agreement is to improve mutual understanding among the peoples of the European Economic Community to promote a better understanding of the European cultural heritage, both in its rich diversity and in the points it has in common, and to further a greater understanding of European integration.

The aims of the Foundation are thus closely related to those of the Treaty. Article 5 of the Agreement includes, among the Foundation's activities, promoting information on the efforts to unite Europe. Other aims are encouraging the study of the languages of the Community and fostering exchanges of persons within the Community, including professional exchanges and those concerning activities designed to increase understanding of the Community. Particular mention is made of programmes to meet the interests and requirements of young people. The Foundation is therefore well designed to help to achieve the aims of the Treaty, especially those set out in Article 61 (1).

5. Article 61 (3) envisages the harmonization of copyright law in the Union and the free movement of cultural works within the Union. The Pfennig Report refers in these respects to the Prout Report[2] and to the resolution of the European Parliament.[3]

The national copyright laws of the Member States were examined in the Dietz Report[4] but no steps have yet been taken towards their harmonization. The link with the free movement of books, recordings, works of art, etc., is apparent from Article 36 of the EEC Treaty, which recognizes that restrictions on the free movement of goods may be justified for the protection of 'industrial and commercial property'; the Court of Justice has held that that expression 'includes the protection conferred by copyright, especially when exploited commercially in the

---

[2] EP Doc. 1-558/80.
[3] OJ C 28, 9 February 81, pp. 82 ff.
[4] A. Dietz, *Copyright in the EEC*, Commission of the European Communities, Brussels, 1977.

form of licences capable of affecting distribution in the various Member States of goods incorporating the protected literary or artistic work'.[5]

The harmonization of national copyright laws will therefore itself facilitate the free movement of cultural property; in addition, Article 61 (3) of the Treaty envisages rules laid down at the level of the Union on such free movement itself. The scope of such rules is left entirely open, but it is apparent that they might include, for example, exchanges of works of art designed to further the aims set out in Article 61 (1).

[5] Cases 55 and 57/80 *Membran* v. *GEMA* [1981] ECR 147 at 161.

Article 62

Information policy

The Union shall encourage the exchange of information and access to information for its citizens. To this end, it shall eliminate obstacles to the free movement of information, whilst ensuring the broadest possible competition and diversity of types of organization in this field. It shall encourage co-operation between radio and television companies for the purpose of producing Union-wide programmes.

Preparatory documents:

Doc. 1-575/83/B, Pfennig Report, paragraph 95.
Doc. 1-575/83/C, Pfennig working document, paragraph 87.
Resolution of 14 September 1983, paragraphs 73–74.

1. The Pfennig Report makes explicit the link between freedom of information and the democratic character of the Union.

The guarantee of Union-wide freedom of information is essential for democracy in the Union. The qualitative variety of information, opinions, and ideas is essential for balanced development in the Union, which is based partly on the principles of pluralism, freedom of decision, and individual participation. The Union must facilitate an extensive, Union-wide exchange of information and access to information for its citizens.

The information policy provided for by Article 62 can thus be placed in a broader political context which recalls the 'commitment to the principles of pluralist democracy, respect for human rights and the rule of law' (recital 3 of the preamble to the Treaty). It also recalls the European Convention on Human Rights, especially Article 10 (which refers to the freedom to receive and impart ideas as well as information) and, within the framework of the Community, the Final Declaration of the European Summit in Paris, 1972.[1] Consequently, the relatively narrow term 'information' warrants a broad interpretation.

2. Both the report and Article 62 provide no express guidance on the extent to which the information policy is to be achieved by legislation

[1] Paragraph 1: Free movement of ideas, *EC Bulletin*, 10/1972.

as opposed to Union programmes of various kinds. However, it seems clear that the elimination of obstacles to the free movement of information, referred to in the second sentence of Article 62, will require legislative intervention. The report gives as examples 'the abolition of all barriers created on monopolistic grounds (e.g. in telecommunications), fiscal grounds (e.g. newspapers) or for reasons relating to tariffs, transmission, frequency, or satellite technology'. While Article 62 is less specific, the elimination of obstacles to the free movement of information in the widest sense will necessarily require a substantial legislative intervention.

Article 63

Principles and methods of action

1. The Union shall direct its efforts in international relations towards the achievement of peace through the peaceful settlement of conflicts and towards security, the deterrence of aggression, détente, the mutual balanced and verifiable reduction of military forces and armaments, respect for human rights, the raising of living standards in the Third World, the expansion and improvement of international economic and monetary relations in general and trade in particular, and the strengthening of international organization.

2. In the international sphere the Union shall endeavour to attain the objectives set out in Article 9 of this Treaty. It shall act either by common action or by co-operation.

Preparatory documents:

Resolution of 6 July 1982, paragraph 6.
Doc. 1-575/83/B, Prag Report.
Doc. 1-575/83/C, Prag working document.
Resolution of 14 September 1983, paragraphs 76-7.

Provisions in force:

EEC Treaty, Articles 3, 110-16, 228-34.
ECSC Treaty, Articles 71-5.
EAEC Treaty, Articles 101-06.

1. The section of the Treaty on international relations aims to combine the aspects of international relations provided for in the Community Treaties and the areas covered by European Political Co-operation. The object is to establish a uniform, coherent, and effective foreign policy for the Union. Nonetheless, there will still be situations in future in

which the Member States are also represented alongside the Union in areas in which they still have competence.[1]

This is made clear in Article 63, the introductory article to Title III, which first sets out the principles of the Union's foreign policy. Subsequent articles deal with the implementation of this policy by means of common action (Articles 64-5) and co-operation (Articles 66-8). In the area of common action an attempt is made to cover previous omissions in the field of the Community's foreign policy and to achieve a uniform foreign policy through the full exercise of parallel powers in the external field. Provision is made in particular for the European Parliament to play a more effective part in shaping this policy. All areas of the Union's internal competence will in future be covered by powers in the external field. Title III ends with provisions concerning the right of representation abroad. Other provisions of the Treaty relevant to international relations are contained in the preamble, Articles 2 (accession), 4 (3) (international covenants on fundamental rights), 6 (legal personality), 9 (objectives), 10 (methods of action), 21 (Council of the Union), 28 (Commission), and 82 (entry into force).

2. The first paragraph lists the principles of the foreign policy to be established by the Union. Reference is also made in paragraph 2 to the objectives set out in Article 9 of the Treaty, which to a large extent correspond to the principles listed in paragraph 1. Parliament considered it important to include a separate provision setting out the aims of foreign policy. The fourth paragraph of the Preamble was abridged on account of the presence of Article 63. Where the formulations differ in the three parts of the Treaty mentioned above, priority will be given to the specific principles of Article 63.

The key principles are the achievement of peace and security, which were essentially dealt with in the past within the framework of European Political Co-operation between the Member States. The reference to respect for human rights and the raising of living standards in the Third World reiterate aims which have already been described more fully in the last sentence of Article 9, but were not mentioned in the Community Treaties.

Whereas international trade and economic relations were referred to in the preamble and the first paragraph of Article 110 of the EEC Treaty, a new feature is an explicit reference to international monetary

[1] See commentary on Article 64.

relations (see Article 52). The 'strengthening of international organization' refers to an institutionalized improvement of international co-
operation. The fourth sentence of the preamble on the other hand refers
to strengthening 'international organizations'. There is no semantic difference.

3. The powers conferred on the Union by paragraph 2 in respect of
common action and co-operation correspond to the general provision
contained in Article 10 of the Treaty. They relate to the objectives set
out in Article 9, as illustrated by the principles of paragraph 1.

Article 64

Common action

1. In its international relations, the Union shall act by common action in the fields referred to in this Treaty where it has exclusive or concurrent competence.

2. In the field of commercial policy, the Union shall have exclusive competence.

3. The Union shall pursue a development aid policy. During a transitional period of ten years, this policy as a whole shall progressively become the subject of common action by the Union. In so far as the Member States continue to pursue independent programmes, the Union shall design the framework within which it will ensure the co-ordination of such programmes with its own policy, whilst observing current international commitments.

4. Where certain external policies fall within the exclusive competence of the European Communities pursuant to the Treaties establishing them, but where that competence has not been fully exercised, a law shall lay down the procedures required for it to be fully exercised within a period which may not exceed five years.

Preparatory documents:

Doc. 1-575/83/C, Prag working document, pp. 108 ff.
Resolution of 14 September, paragraphs 78-81.

Provisions in force:

EEC Treaty, Articles 3, 110-16.
ECSC Treaty, Articles 71-5.
EAEC Treaty, Articles 101-06.

1. The Community Treaties do not wholly succeed in defining the competence of the Community in the area of international relations. The Court of Justice of the European Communities has repeatedly been required to take decisions on the delimitation of powers in order to

close loopholes or eliminate contradictions between the Community's powers in the internal and external fields.[1]

2.   Paragraph 1 establishes the principle of parallelism between the powers of the Union in the internal and external fields (see Articles 65-7). The Court of Justice laid emphasis on this unwritten principle of Community law in the *ERTA* Case[2] and in Opinion 1/76.[3] Under paragraph 1, the Union has exclusive responsibility for international relations in all the areas for which it is given exclusive responsibility by the Treaty. The same applies to the areas of concurrent competence, where the Union's power to determine foreign policy is subject to the conditions laid down in Article 12 (2) of the Treaty. The Union may therefore take over responsibility in an area of concurrent competence by first acting in the field of foreign policy. As a result of such action, the Member States will also cease to have responsibility in the internal field. The principle that competence may first be exercised in the external field, which was developed by the Court of Justice in the *Kramer* Case,[4] is confirmed in paragraph 1.

3.   Paragraph 2 makes specific mention of commercial policy as an area of exclusive competence. The Treaty does not mark a departure from Article 113 (1) of the EEC Treaty here but goes further than the two other Community Treaties, which were limited in this respect. The term 'commercial policy' is to be understood in the wide sense defined by the Court of Justice, in consequence of the preservation of the Community patrimony, pursuant to Article 7.[5] Parliament considered it important to stress the exclusive competence of the Union in the field of commercial policy because of disagreements between the Communities and the Member States over the scope of the common commercial policy under the Community Treaties. The Union's area of exclusive competence should, in Parliament's view, include co-operation agreements, which until now have still been concluded by the Member States in some cases.

---

[1] Recent accounts of these cases can be found in: J.-V. Louis, P. Bruckner, *Le Droit de la Communauté économique européenne*, vol. 12: *Les Relations extérieures*, Brussels, 1980, pp. 94 ff., and J. Groux, Ph. Manin, *The European Communities in the International Legal Order*, European Perspectives, Brussels, 1984, pp. 103 ff.

[2] Case 22/70 *Commission* v. *Council* [1971] ECR 263.

[3] [1977] ECR 741.

[4] Cases 3, 4 and 6/76 [1976] ECR 1279.

[5] Opinion 1/78 [1979] ECR 2871.

That view is clear from Article 64 (4) of the Treaty[6] and from paragraph 79 of the Resolution of 14 September 1983. Under Article 70 (2) the Union will have financial competence for all aspects of commercial policy.

4. Paragraph 3 states that the development aid policy of the Union will progressively become the subject of common action during a transitional period of ten years. The text does not make clear whether this is to be an area of exclusive or concurrent competence. There is good reason to suppose that the Member States may continue to pursue national development aid policies after the ten-year transitional period has expired. According to the second sentence, the Member States continue to have the power to pursue independent policies during the transitional period at least, but only within the framework established for co-ordination with the progressive establishment of the development policy of the Union. The word 'continue' would appear, however, to relate also to the time subsequent to the expiry of the transitional period. In the long term there will therefore be co-ordinated action by the Union and the Member States in the area of development aid. There is no reason to suppose, from the preparatory work, that 'continue' was intended to have a more restrictive meaning and should relate only to the transitional period. It was never suggested that the Union should have exclusive competence in the field of development aid policy. Financial responsibility for development aid will in future follow from substantive responsibility (see Article 70 (2)), so that development aid granted by the Union will be paid for out of the Union's budget.

International commitments entered into by the Member States prior to or during the transitional period will continue to be observed during this period (paragraph 3, second sentence) and after the ten-year period has expired. In line with the principle laid down in Article 234 of the EEC Treaty, however, the Member States are required to take all appropriate steps to eliminate any incompatibilities with the policy of the Union.

5. In the context of the Community Treaties there still exist fields in which the Communities have not been able to exercise their exclusive competence (e.g. co-operation agreements, export credit policy, certain mixed agreements). Paragraph 4 expressly recognizes this situation and

[6] See below, point 5.

obliges the Union to adopt laws laying down procedures which will ensure that this competence can be fully exercised by the Union within a period of not more than five years. Paragraph 4 does not legitimize the previous usurpation by the Member States of Community competence in external fields, which runs counter to Community law, but simply provides a means by which the Union may be allowed to exercise its external competence uniformly. Observance of the time limit will also depend on the extent to which non-member states are prepared to recognize the powers conferred on the Union.

6.   The aim of Article 64 is to enable the Union to establish a uniform, coherent, and effective foreign policy. Past experience in the Community has shown that the achievement of this aim depends ultimately on the political will of the Member States and non-member countries. It is therefore questionable whether the deadlines are realistic. It would seem virtually impossible to give a more precise description of responsibilities in the field of external relations. National constitutions are also unable to define such responsibilities in detail. Even in the Union it will not be entirely possible to avoid mixed agreements involving participation by the Union in the framework of common action and participation by the Member States. Article 64 contains no provisions governing such cases. It therefore remains subject to the Community patrimony as provided for by Article 7.

Article 65

Conduct of common action

1. In the exercise of its competences, the Union shall be represented by the Commission in its relations with non-member states and international organizations. In particular, the Commission shall negotiate international agreements on behalf of the Union. It shall be responsible for liaison with all international organizations and shall co-operate with the Council of Europe, in particular in the cultural sector.

2. The Council of the Union may issue the Commission with guidelines for the conduct of international actions; it must issue such guidelines, after approving them by an absolute majority, where the Commission is involved in drafting acts and negotiating agreements which will create international obligations for the Union.

3. The Parliament shall be informed, in good time and in accordance with appropriate procedures, of every action of the institutions competent in the field of international policy.

4. The Parliament and the Council of the Union, both acting by an absolute majority, shall approve international agreements and instruct the President of the Commission to deposit the instruments of ratification.

Preparatory texts:

Doc. 1-575/83/C, Prag working document, pp. 109–11.
Resolution of 14 September 1983, paragraphs 82 and 86.

Provisions in force:

ECSC Treaty, Articles 71–5.
EEC Treaty, Articles 113, 228–31.
EAEC Treaty, Articles 101–06.

1. The exercise of powers in the field of external policy is largely the same as that provided for in the Community Treaties. The most important change is the increased involvement of Parliament, which must now approve all international agreements.

2.   According to the first sentence of paragraph 1, the Union is represented in its external relations by the Commission (see Article 28). The
scope of this representation is defined by the Union's international legal
capacity (Article 6, second sentence). The Community Treaties nowhere
expressly provide for representation by the Commission alone; the
fourth paragraph of Article 6 of the ECSC Treaty states that the Community may be represented by each of the institutions. The power of
representation extends to the accreditation of representatives from
non-member states; representations of the Union abroad can, however,
only be established with the approval of the Council of the Union
(Article 69).

The Commission is empowered to negotiate international agreements
(second sentence), a provision which corresponds to Article 228 (1) of
the EEC Treaty. The predominant view was that this power of negotiation extended only to the period preceding the initialling of agreements,
unless the Council's guidelines specified otherwise. The power to conclude agreements, which included the signing of them, lay with the
Council. Article 65 no longer gives the Council this power. As stated in
paragraph 4, the Council of the Union only approves 'international
agreements', i.e. agreements which have already been signed. It is the
President of the Commission who concludes agreements on behalf of
the Union.[1] This means that the Commission of the Union is responsible
for the initialling *and* signing of international agreements. Article 10(b)
of the Vienna Convention on the Law of Treaties refers in this connection only to the authentication of a text by signature.

The third sentence states that the Commission is responsible for liaison with all international organizations. These include the Council of
Europe, which is given special mention in paragraph 1. It is not the
Council of Europe as such which is singled out here, but rather the
particular field of cultural co-operation.

3.   The Council of the Union has a particularly important role in the
field of external relations. As specified also in the limited provision of
Article 113 (3), second sentence, of the EEC Treaty, the Council issues
the Commission, with guidelines for international actions. There is no
mention of constant consultation by the Commission of a committee
specially appointed by the Council, which was provided for in Article
113 of the EEC Treaty and has been widely used in practice, but this

---

[1] See below, point 4.

would remain possible in future. This would be covered by the Council's competence to issue guidelines.

The Council must issue guidelines by an absolute majority if the actions may create international obligations for the Union. Paragraph 2 refers specifically to the drafting of acts and the negotiation of agreements. The term 'acts' includes, *inter alia*, participation in decisions by international organizations where these can create obligations for the Union. There is no prejudice to the freedom of action which the Commission is allowed when fostering external relations (establishing contacts, preliminary talks, etc.). This is a question of Community patrimony (Article 7). It is noteworthy that, while Article 113 of the EEC Treaty gave the Council the possibility of issuing directives for negotiations to the Commission, Article 65 of the present Treaty transforms that possibility into an obligation.

4. The question of the European Parliament's involvement in determining external policy, which it has not been possible to settle satisfactorily in the past, is dealt with by the comprehensive but vague provision of paragraph 3. Parliament is to be informed 'in good time and in accordance with appropriate procedures' of all measures taken by the other institutions in the field of international policy. It will remain to be seen what this provision means in practice. Above all, the justified concern of confidentiality can be taken into account by 'appropriate' involvement (creation of a standing committee and similar measures). It does, however, correspond approximately to the statement made in the Solemn Declaration on European Union signed in Stuttgart on 19 June 1983.[2] It covers both consultation by the Council on the guidelines to be issued to the Commission and consultation by the Commission on its actions in the field of international relations.

5. Under paragraph 4, agreements signed by the Commission must be approved by the Parliament and the Council of the Union before the President of the Commission can deposit the instruments of ratification and the agreements can enter into force. The approval given by Parliament and the Council therefore authorizes ratification by the Commission and incorporates the provisions of the agreements into the law of the Union when they enter into force. This approval gives the agreement a democratic basis and support in the Member States. The Treaty does

---

[2] Paragraph 2.3.7.

not contain any separate provision governing simplified agreements (also referred to as administrative agreements), which means that a potentially large number of agreements of a technical nature must also be approved by Parliament and the Council. There would, however, seem to be scope for either an intra-institutional agreement on the delegation of power to the Commission by Parliament and the Council, or the introduction of a simplified procedure. The methods customary in the Member States may serve as examples.

The Commission thus has responsibility for the formal conclusion of agreements. Another possibility would have been to give this responsibility to the President of the Council of the Union, but by adopting the present solution the Union Treaty maintains the division between executive and legislative powers. The President of the European Council would also be unsuitable, in the European Parliament's view, since his institutional position is not directly comparable with that of a head of state (see further Articles 31 and 32 above).

The final stage of the process is publication of agreements in the *Official Journal*, to which the text of the Treaty makes no reference.

6.   As far as the conduct of common action in the field of international relations is concerned, the Commission is in general given a more important role than in the Community Treaties in the negotiation of international agreements concluded by signature. Parliament now has a greater part to play in the area of foreign policy, although the effectiveness of its power to approve international agreements is limited. Parliament's influence remains largely dependent on optional consultation, because decisions approving negotiated agreements cannot amend the texts of those agreements.

Article 66

Co-operation

The Union shall conduct its international relations by the method of co-operation where Article 64 of this Treaty is not applicable and where they involve:

— matters directly concerning the interests of several Member States of the Union, or

— fields in which the Member States acting individually cannot act as efficiently as the Union, or

— fields where a policy of the Union appears necessary to supplement the foreign policies pursued on the responsibility of the Member States, or

— matters relating to the political and economic aspects of security.

Preparatory documents:

Resolution of 6 July 1982, paragraph 10.
Doc. 1-575/83/C, Prag working document, pp. 99 ff.
Resolution of 14 September 1983, paragraphs 76, 84, and 86.

Provisions in force:

European Political Co-operation, Reports of the Foreign Ministers of the Member States of the European Community of 27 October 1970, 23 July 1973, and 13 October 1981.
Solemn Declaration on European Union of 19 June 1983, point 3.2.

1.   Article 66 essentially covers areas which were previously dealt with in the framework of European Political Co-operation. These areas are to be included in the field of co-operation, which is one of the Union's two methods of action provided for in Article 10 (1). The Union Treaty thus aims to ensure a coherent and consistent decision-making structure.[1] There is no intention to alter fundamentally the existing forms of co-operation (see Article 67). The scope of the powers provided for in Article 66 is limited to those areas of activity specified in the Treaty

---

[1]   See Tindemans Report, *EC Bulletin*, Supplement 1/1976, paragraph II A.

itself (Article 64) together with the areas specified in Article 68 for which the Union may subsequently assume responsibility. Other provisions relating to co-operation are contained in Article 10 (3) and Article 46 of the Treaty.

The wording ('shall conduct') appears to oblige the Union to exploit the potential area of competence in the field of co-operation. There are, however, no cogent grounds for this to be adduced from Parliament's preliminary work.

2. The 'Conduct of international relations' covers all action, from the conclusion of international conventions to ordinary diplomatic contacts.

3. Article 66 lists four areas in which matters not covered elsewhere in the Treaty are to be dealt with under the Union's common external policy by the method of co-operation.

Firstly, matters concerning the interests of several Member States of the Union are to be dealt with by co-operation. So too are fields in which the Member States acting individually cannot act as efficiently as the Union. This area seems the most significant, since it is hard to imagine any major issues of foreign policy in which the Union as a whole could not play a more effective role than an individual Member State. Emphasis is placed once again on the principle of subsidiarity which is set down as one of the basic principles of the Union in Article 12 (2).

There is also reference to the fields in which the Union can effectively supplement the foreign policies pursued by the Member States and, finally, matters relating to the political and economic aspects of security. It is likely in practice to prove difficult to distinguish between these matters and the areas of armaments, sales of arms to non-member States, defence policy, and disarmament, referred to in Article 68 (1). The term 'political and economic aspects of security' sought to exclude from co-operation all exclusively military problems (definition of a common strategy, organization of joint military exercises, a European army, etc.). Security was to be approached in the perspective of the co-ordination of foreign policy and industrial co-operation on armaments.

Article 67

Conduct of co-operation

1.   The European Council shall be responsible for co-operation. The Council of the Union shall be responsible for its conduct. The Commission may propose policies and actions which shall be implemented, at the request of the European Council or the Council of the Union, either by the Commission or by the Member States.

2.   The Union shall ensure that the international policy guidelines of the Member States are consistent.

3.   The Union shall co-ordinate the positions of the Member States during the negotiation of international agreements and within the framework of international organizations.

4.   In an emergency, where immediate action is necessary, a Member State particularly concerned may act individually after informing the European Council and the Commission.

5.   The European Council may call on its President, on the President of the Council of the Union, or on the Commission to act as the spokesman of the Union.

Preparatory texts:

Doc. 1-575/83/C, Prag working document, pp. 99 ff.
Resolution of 14 September 1983, paragraphs 84-7.

Provisions in force:

European Political Co-operation, Reports of the Foreign Ministers of the Member States of the European Community of 27 October 1970, 23 July 1973, and 13 October 1981.
Solemn Declaration on European Union of 19 June 1983, point 3.2.

1.   Article 67 specifies the roles of the Institutions of the Union in determining co-operation. Whereas hitherto this has been the responsibility of the Foreign Ministers of the Member States, it will now be primarily the European Council which will determine the policies to be pursued by the Council of the Union. The European Parliament is not given any specific role. The general provisions of Article 32 (1) and Article 21 are relevant in this respect in that they provide for Parliament

to be kept fully informed by the European Council and the Council of the Union and establish its right to table questions.

This will mean that the Member States will, as in the past, be responsible for fulfilling commitments entered into within the framework of co-operation. The Union has no responsibility for financing: see Article 70 (2).

2.   According to paragraph 1, the European Council has overall responsibility for co-operation. It will continue to take decisions unanimously, as the Member States will not depart from the present practice when deciding on the procedure to be adopted in the European Council (see Article 32 (2)). The Treaty tacitly accepts this. There therefore seemed to be no need for a proviso such as that contained in Article 23 (3) concerning 'vital national interests' in respect of the European council (see below, Article 68 (2)). Since the European Council will continue normally to meet only infrequently, the second sentence states that the Council of the Union, as a permanently operational institution, is to be responsible for the routine conduct of co-operation.

The Council of the Union is thus given a particularly prominent role. This reflects the importance attached to co-operation by the Member States. The text does not specify whether the Council of the Union may take measures in the field of co-operation without any prior decision of principle having been taken by the European Council. In practice, the European Council will in any case meet whenever new decisions have to be taken on basic matters of policy.

The Commission is for the first time given a comprehensive right of initiative and can propose 'policies and actions'. The Commission's proposals may be addressed to the European Council or to the Council of the Union, which may in turn instruct the Commission itself or the Member States to implement appropriate action. The text does not exclude the possibility of a Commission proposal being adopted and implemented by the Council of the Union itself. The present rules governing European Political Co-operation also provide for the 'full association' of the Commission.[1]

The text as a whole does not make clear whether decisions taken by the European Council or the Council of the Union impose direct obligations on the Union or the Member States. Article 10 (3) of the German text makes more explicit reference to the obligations ('*Verpflichtungen*') entered into by the Member States within the European Council. The

---

[1] See point 2.4. of the Solemn Declaration on European Union of 19 June 1983.

French and English texts, however, use the terms *'engagements'* and 'commitments' respectively. These suggest that, as in the past, no legally binding measures can be prescribed for the Member States in the area of co-operation. This view is supported by the lack of Union responsibility for financing, which follows from Article 70 (2).

3. According to paragraph 2, if co-operation is to take a coherent form, the foreign policies still pursued independently by the Member States must be consistent with the policies of co-operation. Responsibility for ensuring the consistency of 'international policy guidelines' lies with the Union, i.e. in principle the European Council and, on a routine basis, the Council of the Union. This provision does not impose any legal obligation on the Member States. However, the principle of loyalty to the Union, which is a fundamental principle of the Treaty (see Article 13), requires that the Member States take account of Union policies when adopting their national guidelines.

Paragraph 3 makes clear that the Member States still act officially in their own name in the areas of international policy coming within the sphere of co-operation. Agreements negotiated in these areas, whether directly or within the framework of international organizations, are officially concluded by the Member States. The Member States are, however, required to co-ordinate their positions within the Union beforehand. Nevertheless, 'co-ordination' does not mean that agreement is essential. Articles 6, 105, and 145 of the EEC Treaty similarly call for a harmonized approach but do not lay down that there must be agreement on material issues. Efforts within the European Council and the Council of the Union will therefore be directed towards harmonizing the negotiating positions of the Member States.

4. Paragraph 4 allows Member States the possibility of taking individual emergency measures in urgent situations. They are required to inform the European Council and the Commission before taking such measures. The inclusion of the Commission reflects its closer involvement in co-operation (see paragraph 1).

5. Under paragraph 5 the European Council may appoint as the spokesman of the Union in the field of co-operation its President, the President of the Council of the Union, or the Commission, which is the sole representative of the Union in the field of common action (Article 65 (1)).

Article 68

Extension of the field of co-operation and transfer from co-operation to common action

1. The European Council may extend the field of co-operation, in particular with regard to armaments, sales of arms to non-Member States, defence policy, and disarmament.

2. Under the conditions laid down in Article 11 of this Treaty the European Council may decide to transfer a particular field of co-operation to common action and external policy. In that event the provisions laid down in Article 23 (3) of this Treaty shall apply without any time limit. Bearing in mind the principle laid down in Article 35 of this Treaty, the Council of the Union, acting unanimously, may exceptionally authorize one or more Member States to derogate from some of the measures taken within the context of common action.

3. By way of derogation from Article 11 (2) of this Treaty, the European Council may decide to restore the fields transferred to common action in accordance with paragraph 2 above either to co-operation or to the competence of the Member States.

4. Under the conditions laid down in paragraph 2 above, the European Council may decide to transfer a specific problem to common action for the period required for its solution. In that event, paragraph 3 above shall not apply.

Preparatory documents:

Doc. 1-575/83/C, Prag working document, pp. 109 ff.
Resolution of 14 September 1983, paragraphs 84, 86, and 89.

1. Article 68 allows the Union, under the conditions laid down in Article 11 (1), the possibility of bringing areas of co-operation in international relations within its own competence. Provision is made for different procedures to take account of various hypotheses. Paragraph 1 specifies that the European Council may extend the field of co-operation to include questions of security and defence policy, which were previously the responsibility of the Member States. It may also transfer

areas of co-operation to the more intensive field of common action. In such cases, however, Article 68 provides that individual Member States may be granted exemption and that, by way of derogation from the principle established in Article 11 (2), the transfers may also be reversed. It is also possible to transfer a matter temporarily to common action for a predetermined period of time.

The procedures available in the field of international relations are therefore more extensive than the possibilities offered by Article 54 (1) of the Treaty in respect of industrial co-operation.

2. Under paragraph 1, the field of co-operation may, by unanimous decision of the European Council, be extended to include 'in particular' armaments, sales of arms to non-member States, defence policy, and disarmament. In relation to disarmament, Article 63 (1) prescribes the 'mutual balanced and verifiable reduction of military forces and armaments'.

Only military aspects of security are listed here, since the political and economic aspects of security are already included in the field of co-operation by Article 66. This list is not definitive; however, the principle of subsidiarity must always be respected even in this field.[1] Co-operation can also be extended to include other areas of foreign policy. The implications of this paragraph are considerable, since no provision is made for parliamentary participation in the decisions to extend co-operation. Neither the approval of the Parliament of the Union nor the approval of the parliaments of the Member States is required.

3. Only when additional matters are transferred to the field of common action, in accordance with paragraph 2, is the consent of the Parliament of the Union needed. Article 11 (1) is applicable in such cases. No provision is made for approval by the Member States, although this could lead to important shifts of power. Under national constitutional law, however, the consent of national parliaments will normally be required if decisions by the European Council amount in substance to a transfer of competence.[2]

Such possible transfers can involve any of the areas of co-operation in international relations for which the European Council has assumed

---

[1] See preamble, last sentence, and the commentary on Article 12 (2)).

[2] In addition, the European Council, when determining its own decision-making procedures in accordance with Article 32, could of its own initiative submit its decision to the States for their approval in accordance with their respective procedures.

responsibility in accordance with Articles 66 and 68 (1). The second sentence of paragraph 2 grants the representatives of the Member States the possibility, without any time limit, of invoking a 'vital interest'. This possibility is not only of relevance to unanimous decisions to transfer fields of co-operation to common action, it also applies in relation to measures taken subsequently in the context of common action, for which unanimity is not required (see Article 38). This concession is, however, only of limited significance; any vital interest must first be recognized as such by the Commission and the concession only allows for postponement of the decision and re-examination of the matter.

The third sentence facilitates the approval by the Member States of transfers to the field of common action by allowing for differentiated application. Article 35 introduced this possibility in respect of the laws of the Union. By decision of the European Council, one or more Member States may be exempt from certain measures in the field of common action. This form of 'opting out' practised in other international organizations differs in two respects from the differentiated application of laws provided for in Article 35. In Article 35 the differentiated application is subject to objective criteria concerning the situation of the Member State or Member States concerned and provision is made for a time limit. Since the 'principle' laid down in Article 35 is to be borne in mind, derogations pursuant to Article 68 (2) must also be aimed at facilitating the subsequent participation of all the Member States in the measures concerned. The third sentence specifies that such derogations are possible only in exceptional cases. Whether this restriction is sufficient to prevent fragmentation of the Union in international relations will depend on the political will of the Members of the European Council. The Member States not participating would still be able to act independently in international relations alongside the Union.

4. Paragraph 3 provides the possibility of restoring the areas transferred to common action pursuant to paragraph 2 either to co-operation or to the full competence of the Member States. Under Community law it has not been possible to reverse such transfers once responsibility has been assumed by the Community, except where the Community Treaties, which were concluded for an unlimited period, expressly provide for an exception.[3] The present provision should not be criticized on the

<hr />

[3] See Case 7/71 *Commission* v. *France* [1971] ECR 1003 at 1018.

grounds that it expressly provides in the Treaty for exceptions to the principle of 'no return'. It facilitates approval by the Member States of transfers of areas of co-operation to the field of common action. In no circumstances may transfers be reversed without respect for the rights of non-member states.

5. Paragraph 4 offers a further incentive for the transfer of a problem to common action. The European Council can decide beforehand that the transfer is to be for a limited period only. On expiry of the time limit or when the desired solution has been found, the matter is restored to the sphere of co-operation. This provision is intended to deal with specific and temporary crises which may require a united approach in the framework of common action. Decisions taken on such transfers by the European Council must also be approved by the Parliament of the Union.

Article 69

Right of representation abroad

1.   The Commission may, with the approval of the Council of the Union, establish representations in non-member states and international organizations.

2.   Such representations shall be responsible for representing the Union in all matters subject to common action. They may also, in collaboration with the diplomatic agent of the Member State holding the presidency of the European Council, co-ordinate the diplomatic activity of the Member States in the fields subject to co-operation.

3.   In non-member states and international organizations where there is no representation of the Union, it shall be represented by the diplomatic agent of the Member State currently holding the presidency of the European Council or else by the diplomatic agent of another Member State.

Preparatory document:

Resolution of 14 September 1983, paragraph 90.

Previous text:

Protocol on Privileges and Immunities of 8 April 1965, Article 17.

1.   In the context of the international legal capacity accorded to the Union by the second sentence of Article 6, Article 69 empowers the Union to establish representations abroad. The right to have representations of non-member states accredited to the Union (the right to grant accreditation) is already established under existing Community law (see Article 7 of the present Treaty and Article 17 of the Protocol on Privileges and Immunities of 8 April 1965).

2.   In the past only the Commission was represented by external offices in various non-member states. The Council was represented by the ambassadors of the Member State holding the presidency. There has not in fact been any normal diplomatic representation of the Community itself, although in principle the Community could be authorized to

establish representations and to grant accreditation. Article 69 (1) now
lays down the procedure for establishing representations of the Union.
With the approval of the Council of the Union, the Commission may
establish representations in non-member states and international organizations. It did not seem necessary to include a provision governing the
right to grant accreditation, since this right is unquestionably recognized
as part of the Community patrimony. It is clear from paragraph 2 that
paragraph 1 refers to representations of the Union itself and not just of
the Commission.

3. Paragraph 2 specifies that the Union is represented abroad only in
matters subject to common action. Representation in matters of co-
operation is still the responsibility of the diplomatic agents of the Member States themselves. The diplomatic activities of the Member States in
these areas are co-ordinated by the representations of the Union in
collaboration with the diplomatic agent of the Member State holding
the presidency of the European Council. Such co-ordination is not compulsory but is left to the discretion of the representations of the Union.

4. Representations can be established only if the Union has been recognized by the host state or international organization concerned. If
such recognition has not been granted or if the Union does not wish to
establish its own representation, paragraph 3 provides that it will be
represented by the diplomatic agent of the Member State currently
holding the presidency of the European Council. Under Articles 6 and
46 of the Vienna Convention on Diplomatic Relations, however, this
form of representation is also subject to approval by the host country
concerned.

5. The fact that this article relates only to the right of representation
abroad is a reflection of the effort made in the Treaty to include only
those areas for which there are no provisions under existing Community
law. Uniform provisions governing both the right of representation
abroad and the right to grant accreditation would, however, have emphasized the international legal personality of the Union and at the
same time complemented the list of the powers to be assigned to the
Union in the field of international relations under Articles 63 to 68.

PART FIVE

THE FINANCES OF THE UNION

Article 70

General provisions

1. The Union shall have its own finances, administered by its institutions, on the basis of the budget adopted by the budgetary authority which shall consist of the European Parliament and the Council of the Union.

2. The revenue of the Union shall be utilized to guarantee the implementation of common actions undertaken by the Union. Any implementation by the Union of a new action assumes that the allocation to the Union of the financial means required shall be subject to the procedure laid down in Article 71 (2) of this Treaty.

Preparatory documents:

Doc. 1-575/83/B, Seeler Report, pp. 33 ff.
Doc. 1-575/83/C, Junot working document, pp. 116 ff.
Resolution of 14 September 1983, paragraph 92.

1. Article 70 (1) embodies the fundamental principle of the financial autonomy of the Union. The principle is spelt out in the succeeding articles: all revenue and expenditure is exclusively within the jurisdiction of the Union's Institutions; and the Member States have no part in the Union's financial system. The financial system of the Union can be contrasted in that respect with the Community system, whereby any increase in the Community's own resources is subject to ratification by the Parliaments of the Member States. The total exclusion of the national parliaments from the Union's financial system is a remarkable innovation which underlines the Union's financial autonomy. The democratic control of the Union's finances will be the function of the Union's own Parliament.

2. The provision in Article 70 (1) that the Union's finances shall be 'administered by its institutions' may appear to suggest that a contrast is intended with Article 205 of the EEC Treaty, which provides that the Community budget shall be implemented by the Commission alone. That that is not the intention, however, is made clear by Article 78, which provides, in terms similar to those of Article 205 of the EEC

Treaty, that the budget shall be implemented by the Commission on its own responsibility under the conditions laid down by the Financial Regulation. No doubt the Financial Regulation may assign certain functions to the other Institutions, as in the Community system (cf. Article 205, paragraph 2), but the provision in Article 70 (1) that the Union's finances shall be 'administered by its institutions' should be interpreted as emphasizing the financial autonomy of the Union: compare the term 'originating in its institutions' in Article 10 (2) of the Treaty.

3. In the Union the budgetary authority consists of the European Parliament and the Council of the Union, the same Institutions which constitute the legislative authority of the Union. Hence any legislative activity of the Union can be expected to carry with it an allocation of any necessary funds. However, it is a fundamental principle in the financial and budgetary regime of the Union that, while overall expenditure and revenue must in principle be in balance, revenues must not be earmarked for specific purposes: see Article 75 (1).

4. Article 70 (2) envisages that the Union budget will be 'expenditure orientated'. Whereas under the Community system a ceiling on Community revenues, as explained below, effectively determines the limits on spending policies, in the Union financial system the adoption of policies will entail the raising of the necessary funds.

5. The first sentence of Article 70 (2) restricts the use of Union revenues: in principle they may be used only to finance common action, although the Union may also act by co-operation between the Member States, a distinction explained in Article 10. Article 10 (3) defines co-operation as 'all the commitments which the Member States undertake within the European Council'. It stipulates that the measures resulting from co-operation shall be implemented by the Member States or by the Institutions of the Union. Where they are implemented by the Member States, they will no doubt be financed by them. Where they are implemented by the Institutions of the Union, it seems that Union funds may, exceptionally, be used.

6. The second sentence of Article 70 (2) provides an important financial safeguard by requiring, as a condition of the implementation of any new Union action, the passage of an organic law, with the special

procedures laid down by Article 38, for the allocation of the necessary funds.

This provision, however, is not free from difficulty. It is difficult to suppose that its intention is to require an organic law for any new activity, even where the Union has previously decided to enter a new field so as to exercise a concurrent competence with the Member States. Article 12 (2) already requires, in all areas where the Union has a concurrent competence, the adoption of an organic law before the Union takes new action. It can hardly be supposed that a further organic law is required in such a case to provide the necessary funds. It is therefore natural to assume that, in such a case, the organic law which authorizes new action by the Union will at the same time make the necessary financial provision. There is no difficulty in reconciling that interpretation with the principle, referred to above under Article 70 (1), that revenues must not be earmarked for specific purposes, since the additional revenues will not be specifically allocated but will form part of the general budget. There must, however, be a decision allocating the necessary funds before the new action can be undertaken.

Article 71

Revenue

1. When this Treaty enters into force, the revenue of the Union shall be of the same kind as that of the European Communities. However, the Union shall receive a fixed percentage of the basis for assessing value added tax established by the budget within the framework of the programme set out in Article 74 of this Treaty.

2. The Union may, by an organic law, amend the nature or the basis of assessment of existing sources of revenue or create new ones. It may by a law authorize the Commission to issue loans, without prejudice to Article 75 (2) of this Treaty.

3. In principle, the authorities of the Member States shall collect the revenue of the Union. Such revenue shall be paid to the Union as soon as it has been collected. A law shall lay down the implementing procedures for this paragraph and may set up the Union's own revenue-collecting authorities.

Preparatory documents:

Doc. 1-575/83/B, Seeler Report, paragraphs 206 ff.
Doc. 1-575/83/C, Junot working document, paragraphs 32 ff.
Resolution of 14 September 1983, paragraphs 96-9.

Provisions in force:

EEC Treaty, Articles 201-03.
Council Decision of 21 April 1970 on the Replacement of Financial Contributions from Member States by the Communities' own Resources.

1. Under the Treaty establishing the European Coal and Steel Community, the Community was to meet its expenditure from its own resources, in the form of a levy on coal and steel production (Article 49). The revenue of the EEC and EURATOM, in contrast, was initially to include financial contributions from the Member States, but those contributions were to be replaced by the Communities' own resources. That step was taken by the Council Decision of 21 April 1970, while

the Budgetary Treaty of 22 April 1970 conferred certain budgetary powers on the European Parliament.

Since 1980, the Communities' expenditure has been entirely financed by the revenue from agricultural levies and customs duties on imports into the Community, together with a percentage of the value added tax levied by Member States, which is subject to a fixed ceiling. The ceiling was fixed at 1 per cent by Article 4 of the Decision on own resources of 21 April 1970 and can be raised only with the agreement of all Member States; agreement in principle was reached in 1984 that the ceiling should be raised to 1.4 per cent.

2.   Initially the revenue of the Union will be provided from the same sources. However the percentage of VAT will not be subject to a ceiling but will be fixed by the budget on the basis of the projected and actual expenditure of the Union under the financial programmes provided for by Article 74.

3.   Moreover Article 71 (2) empowers the Union, by an organic law, not merely to amend the nature or the basis of assessment of existing sources of revenue, but also to create new sources. The Union could therefore introduce new taxes to be levied by the Member States, or transfer existing national taxes to the Union, or even levy direct taxation on the citizens of the Union. In contrast with the Community system, ratification by national parliaments would not be required. This reflects the principle of the Union's financial autonomy. The absence of any limit on the Union's fiscal powers is, however, one of the most controversial features of the Treaty. The requirement of an organic law, adopted in accordance with the procedure laid down by Article 38, provides only a limited safeguard.

4.   Article 71 (2) also enables the Commission to be authorized to issue loans, within limits laid down in the annual budget (Article 75 (2)). This contrasts with the position of the Community, since the EEC Treaty conferred no formal borrowing powers.[1]

---

[1] See the Couste Report on the borrowing and lending activities of the Commission, OJ 1982 C 125/57, and see further the commentary on Article 75 (2) below. See also, on borrowing, John A. Usher, 'The financing of the Community', in *Thirty Years of Community Law*, European Perspectives, 1983, pp. 195 ff., and D. Strasser, *Les finances de l'Europe*, 1984, pp. 234 ff.

5.   While in principle, under Article 71 (3), the revenue of the Union is to be collected by the authorities of the Member States, the Union may, as was seen above, levy direct taxation. Such Union taxes could still be collected by the authorities of the Member States as agents of the Union. But Article 71 (3) goes further and provides for the possibility for the Union to have its own revenue-collecting authorities.

Article 72

Expenditure

1. The expenditure of the Union shall be determined annually on the basis of an assessment of the cost of each common action within the framework of the financial programme set out in Article 74 of this Treaty.

2. At least once a year, the Commission shall submit a report to the budgetary authority on the effectiveness of the actions undertaken, account being taken of their cost.

3. All expenditure by the Union shall be subject to the same budgetary procedure.

Preparatory documents:

Doc. 1-575/83/B, Seeler Report, paragraphs 209 ff.
Doc. 1-575/83/C, Junot working document, paragraphs 47 ff.
Resolution of 14 September 1983, paragraphs 102-04.

Provisions in force:

EEC Treaty, Article 202.

1. Under the Community's financial system, increases in expenditure are subject to two constraints: first, the ceiling on the Community's own resources,[1] and second, the maximum annual rate of increase in non-compulsory expenditure, which is fixed by the Commission on the basis of variations in the Community's gross national product, in the budgets of the Member States, and in the cost of living (Article 203 (9) of the EEC Treaty). In addition, the Community cannot finance any deficit by borrowing: Article 199 of the EEC Treaty requires that the Community's revenue and expenditure should be in balance.

2. In the Union's financial system there are no *a priori* constraints on the Union's expenditure; instead, the expenditure is determined by the costs of the Union's activities. Article 72 (1) of the Treaty refers forward to Article 74, which provides for a medium-term ('multiannual') finan-

[1] See the commentary on Article 71.

cial programme to be drawn up every five years and to be revised every year as the basis for the preparation of the (annual) budget (Article 75).

3. In the place of any artificial constraints on the Union's expenditure, Article 72 (2) provides for cost-benefit analysis of the Union's activities. The Commission, reporting to the budgetary authority, will supplement in this way the financial scrutiny by the Court of Auditors (Article 79).

4. Article 72 (3), in providing that all expenditure by the Union shall be subject to the same budgetary procedure, abolishes the distinction between compulsory and non-compulsory expenditure introduced by the Financial Treaty of 22 July 1975 (see Article 203 (4) of the EEC Treaty). In the Community system, the procedures are different for the two categories and the Parliament's powers are somewhat wider for the latter category than for the former. In consequence, the distinction between compulsory and non-compulsory expenditure has led to difficulties of definition and to conflict between the Council of the European Communities and the Parliament. The present Treaty provides for a uniform budgetary procedure.[2]

[2] See Article 76 and the commentary thereon.

Article 73

Financial equalization

A system of financial equalization shall be introduced in order to alleviate excessive economic imbalances between the regions. An organic law shall lay down the procedures for the application of this system.

Preparatory documents:

Resolution of 14 September 1983, paragraph 101.

1. The present financial system of the Community, based on its own resources, involves a method of taxation which is not progressive, or related to the relative wealth of the Member States or of particular regions of the Community. Indeed it may in some circumstances prove regressive and favour the more prosperous regions. The same is likely to be true of the finances of the Union in its initial stages, since the Union's revenues are initially to be of the same kind as the Community's (Article 71).

2. A system of financial equalization may therefore be necessary, at least until there is a fundamental reform of the Union's financial system or a greater measure of economic convergence within the Union. Article 73 provides for the adoption of a system of financial equalization, designed to reduce the financial burden on the less developed regions of the Union. The Resolution of 14 September 1983 (paragraph 101) envisaged that financial equalization should be applicable to both revenue and expenditure. Article 73 leaves this question open.

While it will 'alleviate excessive economic imbalances between the regions', the system will not by itself achieve the required degree of economic convergence within the Union: that is to be achieved by the Union's policies, especially the regional policy.[1]

3. The subject of financial equalization in the Community was examined in the McDougall report of April 1977, which considered the possibility of limiting the contribution of the least favoured Member States

---

[1] See Article 58 and the commentary thereon.

to 65 per cent of the Community average, while ensuring them a level of social and public services closer to that of the rest of the Community.[2]

4. Comparison may be made with Article 107 (2) of the Basic Law of the Federal Republic of Germany, which provides that federal legislation shall ensure a reasonable equalization between the *Länder*, and which also authorizes legislation providing for grants to be made from federal funds to financially weak *Länder*.

5. In comparison with the McDougall Report and other studies, Article 73, which gave rise to considerable controversy in the Institutional Committee, is very general in its terms and is limited to a decision of principle, the ways and means being left to be governed by an organic law, adopted in accordance with the procedure laid down in Article 38. In contrast with the McDougall Report and other earlier proposals, Article 73 refers to imbalances between regions of the Union rather than between Member States.

[2] See Report of the study group on the role of public finance in European integration, Brussels 1977; see also *The future financing of the Community*, COM (83) 10 final, 4 February 1983, Annex II.

Article 74

Financial programmes

1. At the beginning of each parliamentary term, the Commission, after receiving its investiture, shall submit to the European Parliament and the Council of the Union a report on the division between the Union and the Member States of the responsibilities for implementing common actions and the financial burdens resulting therefrom.

2. On a proposal from the Commission, a multiannual financial programme, adopted according to the procedure for adopting laws, shall lay down the projected development in the revenue and expenditure of the Union. These forecasts shall be revised annually and be used as the basis for the preparation of the budget.

Preparatory documents:

Doc. 1-575/83/B, Seeler Report, paragraph 111.
Doc. 1-575/83/C, Junot working document, paragraphs 89 ff.
Resolution of 14 September 1983, paragraphs 105–6.

1. The financial system of the Union starts from the principle that the size of the Union budget will be determined by the nature and scope of the tasks assigned to it. That principle is given effect by Article 74, which seeks to ensure that the Union budget reflects the decisions taken about the allocation of tasks between the Union and the Member States. Thus, the Commission's report provided for in Article 74 (1), to be submitted every five years when the new Commission takes office, might envisage some reallocation of the responsibilities between the Union and the Member States, which would be reflected in the financial programme provided for in Article 74 (2).

2. The responsibility for implementing common actions, as defined by Article 10 (2), in principle devolves on the Union rather than on the Member States, and will generally do so where the Union conducts its own policies. In some cases, however, the Union may act by measures such as framework laws or by non-legislative measures such as drawing

up strategies, programmes, etc.[1] Here the responsibility will devolve on the Member States individually.

3. Article 74 (1) is based on and substantially follows the Resolution of the European Parliament of 9 April 1981 on the Community's own resources.[2] That Resolution in turn was based on the Spinelli Report,[3] which envisaged that the European Parliament would examine, after each election, the current allocation of responsibilities and resources between Member States and the Community, and propose such changes as it considered desirable. The Commission would then draft a proposal for the creation of any new resources required. Such a proposal would require a qualified majority in the Council and a three-fifths majority in the Parliament. In the present Treaty the procedure is modified as there is no fixed ceiling on own resources, but the notion of a quinquennial report on the allocation of responsibilities between Member States and the Union is retained in Article 74 (1), while Article 74 (2) envisages a consequent multiannual financial programme.

4. Article 74 (2) introduces a system of medium-term planning for the Union's activities, designed, in the words of the Junot Report, 'to ensure the conscious, deliberate and coherent development of the Union'. For that purpose a multiannual financial programme, which has no counterpart in the Community system, is to be introduced; the programme will be adopted, on a proposal from the Commission, by the legislative authority, in accordance with the procedure for adopting ordinary laws (Article 38). The precise term of the financial programme is not specified, but in practice it will doubtless be found desirable to align it with the five-year term of the Parliament and the Commission and with the Commission's report provided for by Article 74 (1). The projections of revenue and expenditure laid down in the programme are to be revised annually, as part of the exercise of preparing the Union budget under Article 76.

[1] See, for example, Article 53 and the commentary on Article 56.
[2] OJ C 101 of 4 May 1981, p. 75.
[3] OJ C 101 of 4 May 1981, p. 75.

Article 75

Budget

1. The budget shall lay down and authorize all the revenue and expenditure of the Union in respect of each calendar year. The adopted budget must be in balance. Supplementary and amending budgets shall be adopted under the same conditions as the general budget. The revenue of the Union shall not be earmarked for specific purposes.

2. The budget shall lay down the maximum amounts for borrowing and lending during the financial year. Save in exceptional cases expressly laid down in the budget, borrowed funds may only be used to finance investment.

3. Appropriations shall be entered in specific chapters grouping expenditure according to its nature or destination and subdivided in compliance with the provisions of the Financial Regulation. The expenditure of the institutions other than the Commission shall be the subject of separate sections of the budget; they shall be drawn up and managed by those institutions and may only include operating expenditure.

4. The Financial Regulation of the Union shall be established by an organic law.

Preparatory documents:

Doc. 1-575/83/B, Seeler Report, paragraphs 112 ff.
Doc. 1-575/83/C, Junot working document, paragraphs 76 ff.
Resolution of 14 September 1983, paragraphs 108-9.

Provisions in force:

ECSC Treaty, Articles 76-8.
EEC Treaty, Articles 199-203.
EAEC Treaty, Articles 178-80.
Financial Regulation, Title I.

1. The provisions of Article 75 contain hardly any original features. For the most part, they simply reproduce the existing budgetary provisions to be found in the Treaties and the Financial Regulation. As is to

be expected, the key budgetary principles of unity, universality, and balance are given due prominence.

2.   In common with Article 199 of the EEC Treaty, Article 75 (1) establishes the principle of unity of the budget. For Parliament, which has repeatedly called for genuine unity, this principle implies—and paragraph 2 confirms—the need for the budgetization of borrowing and lending operations.

Article 75 (1) also establishes the principle of the annual frequency of the budget and the rule that the financial year must be coextensive with the calendar year.

Although the principle of balance mentioned in Article 199 of the EEC Treaty is also covered, the purpose is different from that of existing Community law, under which the intention is to prohibit borrowing as a means of financing the Community's activities. The Treaty establishing the Union does allow such borrowing in exceptional circumstances. Consequently, the principle of balance must be understood as having the meaning conferred on it by Article 110 of the Basic Law of the Federal Republic of Germany, which authorizes the inclusion of resources deriving from borrowing operations in the revenue section of the budget. Only this interpretation of the concept of balance, which is quite normal in the eyes of German parliamentarians, can explain the wording of Article 75 (2).

3.   Article 75 confirms the existence of supplementary and amending budgets, which will be subject to the same budgetary procedure as the general budget itself.

4.   Lastly, paragraph 1 reaffirms the principle established by Article 3 of the Financial Regulation that revenue may not be earmarked for specific items of expenditure. 'All revenue shall be used to cover all expenditure.' Paragraph 108 of the Resolution also forbids specific links between expenditure and revenue. It was considered that this rule was a matter for the Financial Regulation. The same could have been said of the principle that expenditure should not be earmarked for specific purposes.

5.   Paragraph 2 satisfies a long-standing demand by Parliament, namely that borrowing and lending operations should be budgetized, since the

maximum amounts for such operations are to be laid down by the budget. The second sentence covers the possibility of borrowing funds to meet expenditure requirements. This type of loan arrangement has nothing in common with the borrowing/lending system and, in the interests of greater clarity, it ought to have been covered by a separate paragraph. In principle, borrowing for purposes other than the financing of investments through on-lending is prohibited. Nevertheless, the Resolution envisaged the possibility of departing from this principle in periods of economic crisis. As Mr Junot writes in his working document:

It would therefore be appropriate to make provisions enabling the Union to complement its tax revenue by means of *borrowing* under precisely defined conditions.

It should be noted that this type of budgetary borrowing should remain separate from the Union's other borrowing and lending activities which are intended to finance specific measures outside the scope of the budget as such.[1]

Article 75 is, however, less restrictive than the working document since, while the raising of loans to finance operating expenditure is permitted in exceptional circumstances, the conditions under which this may be done are not spelt out, which means that the budgetary authority will be able to take a decision in accordance with the normal budgetary procedure.

6. The principle of dividing up expenditure according to its specific nature, which derives from Article 15 (2) and (3) of the Financial Regulation, is enunciated in Article 75 (3). The requirement that the expenditure of the Institutions other than the Commission should be presented in separate sections of the budget is in line with current practice (Article 203 (2) of the EEC Treaty and Articles 11 and 18 (2) of the Financial Regulation). The stipulation that these separate sections may include only administrative expenditure is also in line with current practice.

7. Whereas at present it is for the Council to adopt the Financial Regulation, acting unanimously on a proposal from the Commission

---

[1] Doc. 1-575/83/C, p. 130.

and after consulting the Parliament and obtaining the opinion of the Court of Auditors (Article 209 of the EEC Treaty), this power is conferred by Article 75 (4) on the legislative authority, acting by an organic law.

Article 76

Budgetary procedure

1. The Commission shall prepare the draft budget and forward it to the budgetary authority.

2. Within the time limits laid down by the Financial Regulation:

(a) on the first reading, the Council of the Union may approve amendments by a simple majority. The draft budget, with or without amendment, shall be forwarded to the Parliament;

(b) on first reading, the Parliament may amend by an absolute majority the amendments of the Council and approve other amendments by a simple majority;

(c) if, within a period of fifteen days, the Commission opposes the amendments approved by the Council or by the Parliament on first reading, the relevant arm of the budgetary authority must take a fresh decision by a qualified majority on second reading;

(d) if the budget has not been amended, or if the amendments adopted by the Parliament and the Council are identical, and if the Commission has not exercised its right to oppose the amendments, the budget shall be deemed to have been finally adopted;

(e) on second reading, the Council may amend by a qualified majority the amendments approved by the parliament. It may by a qualified majority refer the whole draft budget as amended by the Parliament back to the Commission and request it to submit a new draft; where not so referred back, the draft budget shall at all events be forwarded to the Parliament;

(f) on second reading, the Parliament may reject amendments adopted by the Council only by a qualified majority. It shall adopt the budget by an absolute majority.

3. Where one of the arms of the budgetary authority has not taken a decision within the time limit laid down by the Financial Regulation, it shall be deemed to have adopted the draft referred to it.

4. When the procedure laid down in this Article has been completed, the President of the Parliament shall declare that the budget stands adopted and shall cause it to be published without delay in the *Official Journal of the Union*.

Preparatory texts:

Doc. 1-575/83/C, Junot working document, paragraphs 82 *et seq.*
Resolution of 14 September 1983, paragraphs 110-13.

Provisions in force:

EEC Treaty, Article 203.

1. The budgetary procedure laid down by Article 76 of the Treaty takes account of the difficulties encountered in the application of Article 203 of the EEC Treaty and of the demands made by the European Parliament. The main innovation is the abolition of the distinction between compulsory expenditure and non-compulsory expenditure which, in the EEC Treaty, is the yardstick applied for the delimitation of the powers of Parliament and which deprives it of the right to impose its will on the Council except where non-compulsory expenditure is concerned.[1] The difficulties arising from the classification of expenditure have provoked several disputes over the budget and the joint declaration of 30 June 1982 established a procedure for the holding of a 'trialogue' between the Presidents of the Commission, the Council, and Parliament to settle arguments on the matter. Parliament has always held the classification to be artificial, so it is not surprising that Article 76 makes no reference to it.

Similarly, Article 76 makes no reference to the maximum rate of increase for non-compulsory expenditure which, under Article 203 of the EEC Treaty, restricts the powers of Parliament as one arm of the budgetary authority; instead, the preparation of the budget is based on the financial programmes introduced by Article 74.[2]

For the rest, the budgetary procedure is based on the same principles as the legislative procedure: establishment of a proper balance between the respective powers of Parliament and the Council and strengthening of the powers of the Commission. The obligation on each arm of the budgetary authority to take a decision within the time limits laid down,

---

[1] On the classification of expenditure, see D. Strasser, *Les finances de l'Europe*, 1984, pp. 73 ff.
[2] See above.

failing which it shall be deemed to have adopted the draft referred to it, has been maintained (Article 76 (3)). Similarly, the President of the Parliament retains the right to declare that the budget has been finally adopted (Article 76 (4)).

2. The Commission, which is required by Article 203 of the EEC Treaty to draw up a preliminary draft budget, is now made responsible for preparing the draft budget, in place of the Council. The purpose of this change is to turn the Commission into a genuine executive body. Nevertheless, in the performance of this new task, it must take due account of the financial programme adopted pursuant to Article 74.

In addition, at the end of the first reading the Commission is allowed fifteen days in which to register opposition to the amendments approved by the Council or Parliament. If it exercises this right, the amendments fall and may only be reinstated by the Institution concerned by a qualified majority on second reading. This procedure is similar in spirit to that laid down by Article 38, which empowers the Commission to deliver an unfavourable opinion on draft laws adopted at the end of the first reading. But whereas in legislative matters the unfavourable opinion relates to the text as a whole, in the budgetary field the opposition may be confined to individual amendments. The Commission wields considerable power because the qualified majority needed to overcome its opposition is difficult to achieve.[3]

3. On first reading, the draft budget is examined by the Council, which is empowered to amend it by a simple majority. Article 76 (2)(a) does not require the Council to vote on the budget as a whole at this juncture, since it refers only to its power to make amendments. Besides, a vote rejecting the budget would be illogical at this stage of the procedure because the Council has the opportunity to reshape it by way of amendment.

Parliament may also amend the budget by a simple majority and it may modify the amendments of the Council by an absolute majority. In the absence of modifications to the Council's amendments, the latter are deemed to have been adopted.

If the budget has not been amended or if the amendments tabled by the two arms of the budgetary authority are identical, and if the Com-

---

[3] Compare the qualified majority as applied to Parliament and the Council by Article 17 (2)(b) and Article 23 (2)(b) respectively.

mission does not oppose any amendment, the procedure is terminated without the need for a vote on the budget as a whole.

4. If these conditions do not apply, the budget is referred back to the Council, which may in turn modify by a qualified majority the amendments approved by Parliament as well as Parliament's modifications to its own amendments, since, in contrast to Article 203 of the EEC Treaty, Article 76 makes no distinction between the treatment of amendments and modifications. Lastly, the Council may by a qualified majority refer the budget back to the Commission and request it to prepare a new draft. Such a referral is tantamount to an outright rejection of the budget. This power, vested in Parliament by Article 203 of the EEC Treaty, is here vested in the Council, but the latter can exercise it only if it obtains a qualified majority of three-fifths of the weighted votes cast (see Article 23 (2)(b)).

If the budget is not referred back to the Commission, Parliament takes a final decision. It has the right, not to modify, but to reject by a qualified majority (a majority of its members and three-fifths of the votes cast), the amendments adopted by the Council. The Council is thus placed in a strong position from which it will not be easy to dislodge it.

Finally, the Treaty provides for the budget as a whole to be adopted by an absolute majority. Such a vote is not required under the EEC Treaty and its use was renounced by Parliament after it found that, owing to the adoption of amendments by differently constituted majorities, it could prove difficult to secure the majority needed to adopt the budget as a whole. The obligation to vote on the budget as a whole necessitates a measure of consistency during the votes on the budget amendments. When voting on these, Members of Parliament will no longer be able to treat them in isolation, but will have to consider the impact of their adoption on the vote on the budget as a whole and take care to avoid acting in a way that would make it impossible to obtain the majority needed to carry the budget.

Although nothing is said about the consequences of a rejection of the budget, the procedure would presumably have to be repeated from the beginning, with the Commission again taking the initiative.

5. Although Article 76 increases Parliament's budgetary powers, it cannot be claimed that Parliament would be in an omnipotent position. The powers of the Commission and the Council are clearly stated and

the Council is in a position to exert considerable influence both over the amendments and over the budget as a whole.

6.   As pointed out above, each reading before each Institution is subject to a time limit to be laid down by the Financial Regulation. By analogy with Article 203 of the EEC Treaty, Article 76 stipulates that if an Institution has not taken a decision within the prescribed time limit, it shall be deemed to have adopted the draft referred to it. The wording of Article 76 (3) is slightly different from that of Article 38 (5). Under the legislative procedure, expiry of the time limit signifies approval of the text where the institution has failed to put it to the vote; the procedure applicable to texts put to the vote but not adopted is laid down elsewhere in Article 38. In the budget section, the Treaty uses the phrase 'where one of the arms of the budgetary authority has not taken a decision'. This terminological difference is not, however, of fundamental importance since in all cases the purpose of the clause is to penalize inaction.

Failure by an Institution to vote on the budget or the amendments, as the case may be, may therefore amount to implicit acceptance. If no amendments are tabled, the expiry of the time limit automatically entails referral to the other arm of the budgetary authority. However, failure to secure the majority needed for the adoption of the budget is not, of course, the same thing as failure to take a decision, but amounts to a negative decision which dispenses with the need for a vote expressly rejecting the budget. To interpret such a negative decision as implicit adoption would be contrary to the requirement that the budget be expressly adopted and would deprive Article 76 (2)(f) of its significance.

Article 77

Provisional twelfths

Where the budget has not been adopted by the beginning of the financial year, expenditure may be effected on a monthly basis, under the conditions laid down in the Financial Regulation, up to a maximum of one-twelfth of the appropriations entered in the budget of the preceding financial year, account being taken of any supplementary and amending budgets.

At the end of the sixth month following the beginning of the financial year, the Commission may only effect expenditure to enable the Union to comply with existing obligations.

Preparatory document:

Resolution of 14 September 1983, paragraph 115.

Provisions in force:

EEC Treaty, Article 204.

1.   Article 77 contrasts with Article 204 of the EEC Treaty in its extreme brevity. Its purpose is to make it difficult for the Union to function with provisional twelfths and thus prevent the prolongation of a situation which should be short-lived: that of a Union without a budget. In this connection, the crisis experienced in 1981, following the rejection of the budget by Parliament, provoked concern among its Members and a desire to prevent the recurrence of a situation which caused the Community to operate for six months without a budget.

2.   If the budget is not adopted by the beginning of the year, one-twelfth of the budget appropriations for the preceding financial year may be spent each month by the Union. Article 204 of the EEC Treaty likewise provides that the twelfths must be calculated on the basis of the appropriations entered in the preceding budget, but it also stipulates that the appropriations may not be in excess of one-twelfth of those provided for in the draft budget in course of preparation. This further restriction is omitted from the Treaty establishing the Union, under

which only the budget of the preceding financial year and any supplementary and amending budgets may be taken into account. Accordingly, it also omits the clause in Article 204 which permits the authorization of expenditure in excess of one-twelfth.

3. The Treaty further provides that, after a period of six months, only expenditure needed to discharge existing obligations may be authorized. This provision, which is based on Article 111 of the German Basic Law, is intended to place the Union in an awkward position since, apart from meeting its obligations, it is debarred from engaging in any other activity.

Article 78

Implementation of the budget

The budget shall be implemented by the Commission on its own responsibility under the conditions laid down by the Financial Regulation.

Preparatory texts:

Doc. 1-575/83/C, Junot working document, paragraphs 97 *et seq.*
Resolution of 14 September 1983, paragraph 116.

Provisions in force:

EEC Treaty, Article 205.

1.   The text of Article 78 partially reproduces the first sentence of Article 205 of the EEC Treaty. For the rest, it refers to the Financial Regulation. Owing to its brevity, it fails to convey Parliament's earnest wish to restore total responsibility for the implementation of the budget to the Commission by abolishing the 'financing committees', modelled on the management committees, which are able to challenge the Commission's implementing decisions before the Council. The following comments in the working document on the finances of the Union are proof enough of Parliament's concern over this matter:

The Union's budget will be implemented independently and diligently by the Commission, which will be responsible to Parliament for its management—and indeed the whole of its operation.

The budget rules and the various policies will enable appropriations to be used freely and quickly. The other institutions will not attempt to intervene in budget management.[1]

Article 78 does not in fact solve the problem and a decision on the right approach will have to wait on the adoption of the Financial Regulation.

2.   Article 205 of the EEC Treaty provides that the Financial Regulation 'shall lay down detailed rules for each institution concerning its

[1] Doc. 1-575/83/C, p. 136.

part in effecting its own expenditure'. Does the omission of the clause from Article 78 reflect a desire to give the Commission sole responsibility for implementing the budget? This does not seem to have been the intention of the drafters of the Treaty. Indeed, Article 70 of the Treaty specifies that 'the Union shall have its own finances, administered by its institutions', which implies that Institutions other than the Commission may take part in the management of the budget. It could be argued that this provision does not necessarily mean that they are responsible for the actual implementation of the budget. Be that as it may, the most likely interpretation is that Institutions other than the Commission could be given responsibility for effecting their own expenditure, under the auspices of the Commission and under the conditions laid down by the Financial Regulation.

3. The Treaty has nothing to say about transfers of appropriations, whereas Article 205 of the EEC Treaty expressly provides for such operations. It must be assumed that this matter will be covered by the Union's Financial Regulation.

Article 79

Audit of the accounts

The Court of Auditors shall verify the implementation of the budget. It shall fulfil its task independently and, to this end, enjoy powers of investigation with regard to the institutions and organs of the Union and to the national authorities concerned.

Preparatory documents:

Doc. 1-575/83/C, Junot working document, paragraphs 100 ff.
Resolution of 14 September 1983, paragraph 117.

Provisions in force:

EEC Treaty, Article 206a.

1. Article 33 (1) of the Treaty provides that organic laws shall determine the responsibilities and powers of the Union's organs, which include the Court of Auditors. Article 79 merely stipulates that the Court shall verify the implementation of the budget. The essential change compared with Article 206a of the EEC Treaty is that the accent is placed on the powers of the Court, which are described as powers of investigation.

2. Whereas Article 206a provides that audits in the Member States shall be carried out in liaison with the national authorities, Article 79 makes no reference to joint verification of the implementation of the Union budget in the Member States. This matter will have to be clarified by the organic law specified in Article 33 and by the Financial Regulation.

Article 80

Revenue and expenditure account

At the end of the financial year, the Commission shall submit to the budgetary authority, in the form laid down by the Financial Regulation, the revenue and expenditure account which shall set out all the operations of the financial year and be accompanied by the report of the Court of Auditors.

Preparatory document:

Resolution of 14 September 1983, paragraph 119.

Provisions in force:

EEC Treaty, Article 205a.
Financial Regulation, Article 73.

1. Preceded by an analysis of the financial management, the revenue and expenditure account sets out all the operations of the preceding financial year. It must be submitted in the same form as the budget. It must be accompanied by the Court of Auditors' report and enable Parliament to exercise its powers of control.

2. Article 80 takes up only part of paragraph 119 of the Resolution of 14 September 1983. Matters not dealt with by the Treaty, such as the allocation of surpluses, will be covered by the Financial Regulation.

Article 81

Discharge

The Parliament shall decide to grant, postpone, or refuse a discharge; the decision on the discharge may be accompanied by observations which the Commission shall be obliged to take into account.

Preparatory texts:

Doc. 1-575/83/C, Junot working document, paragraphs 101 ff.
Resolution of 14 September 1983, paragraph 118.

Provisions in force

EEC Treaty, Article 206b.

1.   Article 81 makes only one fundamental change to the procedure laid down by Article 206b of the EEC Treaty. It abolishes the role played by the Council. At present, the Council, acting by a qualified majority, makes a recommendation to Parliament. The Council cannot therefore encroach on the powers of Parliament, but the latter is able to take account of its observations. It is regrettable that Article 81 omits this stage of the procedure, since it enhances the debate on the discharge without affecting Parliament's freedom of decision.

2.   For the rest, Article 81 reaffirms Parliament's power to postpone the granting of a discharge. This power has been exercised by Parliament in the past as a means of obtaining additional information from the Commission.

3.   As under the existing Treaties, refusal to grant a discharge is a political act without legal consequences. It is up to the Commission to put its house in order. It was thought that resignation was one possible remedy, but in November 1984 the Commission continued to perform its duties even though the refusal to grant a discharge amounted to a vote of no confidence in its administration. The only way of forcing the Commission to resign would be to follow up the negative discharge decision with a motion of censure.

4. Article 81 also provides that the discharge decision may be accompanied by observations which must be taken into account by the Commission. But such an obligation is not backed up by any kind of sanction, and it is in any case doubtful whether failure to take due account of an observation would affect the validity of any subsequent measure relating to the implementation of the budget. The only possible sanction would be to call into question the Commission's political responsibility.

PART SIX

GENERAL AND FINAL PROVISIONS

Article 82

Entry into force

This Treaty shall be open for ratification by all the Member States of the European Communities.

Once this Treaty has been ratified by a majority of the Member States of the Communities whose population represents two-thirds of the total population of the Communities, the Governments of the Member States which have ratified shall meet at once to decide by common accord on the procedures by and the date on which this Treaty shall enter into force and on relations with the Member States which have not yet ratified.

1. The first paragraph of this article indicates the States which will have the opportunity to become parties to the Treaty: namely 'all the Member States of the European Communities'. This implies, on the one hand, that every international subject which has the standing of Member State of the Community will be free to express its wish to become a contracting party to the Treaty of the Union; if and when it decides to do so, it must have recourse to ratification (see Articles 11 and 14 of the Vienna Convention on the Law of Treaties). It is sufficient if the party in question has that standing at the time of ratification: therefore not only States which are present Members of the European Communities may become parties to the Treaty but also those which become Members in the future, without any time limit other than the existence of the Communities. On the other hand, a state which is not a member of the Communities will be able to become a party to the Treaty of the Union only after that Treaty has entered into force and the Union has started to function; in fact, a state in that position may apply to become a Member of the Union (provided that it is a democratic European state: Article 2 of the Treaty), but in order to do so it must wait until the Union is operational, so that it can negotiate the requisite treaty of accession with the Union.

The provision under consideration also implies that the stage of signature is not envisaged in the procedure for concluding the Treaty of Union. Under international law, this is of course possible: it is true that many treaties are first signed and then ratified, but signatures are generally regarded as superfluous where the text of a treaty has been prepared by an international organization. The principle adopted by the Vienna Convention is that the consent of a state to be bound by a treaty may be expressed in the form of a signature, or by ratification or by other means (Article 11 of the Convention); the preliminary function of authentication of the text may, or may not, be assigned to the signing thereof (Article 10(b) of the Convention).

From a political point of view, the reason for making the Treaty open for ratification by all the Member States of the Community—all of those States, and no others—is clear. The Union is to be created with a view to 'continuing and reviving the democratic unification of Europe' commenced by the European Communities (see first paragraph of the preamble), and its creation is therefore a further stage in Community integration: this is confirmed by the Union's taking over the Community patrimony (Article 7 (1)). The political reason for which signature of the Treaty is not contemplated is also clear: this formality generally marks the end of negotiations conducted by governments, while here the text has been prepared by the parliamentary Institution of the Communities rather than by means of inter-governmental negotiations.

2.   It is appropriate to consider the procedure which would have to be followed to secure ratification by each Member State. Three stages are outlined in the Resolution whereby on 14 February 1984 the European Parliament approved the draft Treaty:[1] in the first place, that text was to be presented by the President of the European Parliament to the parliaments and governments of the individual Member States (paragraph 1 of the Resolution), and that has been done; in the second place, the national parliaments would consider the draft, possibly organize contacts and meetings with representatives of the European Parliament elected in June 1984, and state their views and make comments (paragraph 2 of the Resolution); finally, it will be the responsibility of the European Parliament 'to take account of the opinions and comments of the national parliaments' (ibid.). After this third stage, no details are given of the further developments. It is easy to infer from the Resolution that the European Parliament by implication reserved the right to amend the draft, taking account of the results of the discussions in the national parliaments. It is logical to conclude that the national parliaments should be requested to adopt laws authorizing ratification of the draft

[1] OJ C 77 of 19 March 1984, pp. 53-4.

thus amended; in the event of a positive vote, the Heads of State would be in a position to ratify the Treaty.

There are grounds for asking what role would be played by the governments of the states involved in following this procedure. The fact that the Resolution of 14 February 1984 provides for direct dialogue between the European Parliament and the national parliaments shows that the mistrust felt by the European Parliament towards the national governments—which is fully justified by the lack of success of the earlier attempts to make progress towards European union—is such that it would prefer to achieve ratification of the Treaty by the will of the national parliaments, entrusting to the governments no task other than that of conforming with the will thus expressed. But that is an abstract approach; from the formal point of view, it is sufficient to bear in mind that it is normally the government which submits to the parliament of a state draft laws whose purpose is to authorize ratification of international treaties, and that more generally the management of foreign policy is entrusted to the executive.

The events following the resolution of the Parliament of 14 February 1984 indicate that, irrespective of what was envisaged therein, the European Council of Heads of States and Governments has initiated a procedure capable of affecting the fate of the draft Treaty. That procedure, which was decided upon on 26 June 1984 by the European Council at Fontainebleau, is based on the creation of an *ad hoc* committee made up of personal representatives of Heads of State and Governments: this new committee is to present (to the European Council) 'suggestions for the improvement of European co-operation, in the Community sphere and in that of political co-operation, or others'. The Committee first met on 28 September 1984 and completed its report for the meeting of the European Council at Brussels in March 1985. The European Council meeting in Milan in June 1985 decided to convene a conference of representatives of the Governments of the Member States, with a view to amending the EEC Treaty in accordance with Article 236 of that Treaty, but to a far more limited extent than is envisaged by the Parliament.

3. The second paragraph of Article 82 is concerned with the conditions for the entry into force of the Treaty. The preliminary condition is that a certain number of ratifications must be obtained: the Treaty must be ratified by a majority of the Member States of the Community, whose population represents at least two-thirds of the total population of the

Communities. Since the number of the Member States of the Communities and of their inhabitants may undergo changes during the period necessary for that condition to be fulfilled, it is necessary to ask what date is to be taken as a reference point for calculating what constitutes a majority of the States and the ratio between the population of the ratifying States and the total population of the Community. The answer seems to be that for each ratification the reference point must be the situation existing when the ratification takes place; therefore the decisive point will be reached when a ratification takes place by virtue of which the position is that a majority of the Member States of the Community at that date have ratified and the population thereof represents two-thirds of the total population of the Communities at that date.

The consequence of reaching the 'threshold' prescribed in the second paragraph of Article 82 is not, by contrast with the position under numerous multilateral treaties, the automatic entry into force of the Treaty; rather, the consequence is that a meeting of the Governments of the States which have ratified must be convened immediately, and they must reach agreement on two kinds of problem: the procedure for and date of entry into force of the Treaty, and relations with the Member States of the Community which have not yet ratified. The range of options in the former case includes the fixing of a date for entry into force within a short period (limited, of course, to the States which have already ratified) or, on the contrary, a decision to defer the entry into force until a later date, or until the number of ratifications increases. It is impossible to rule out procedures providing for consultation of Community Institutions (for example, the European Parliament) or even recourse to referendums to decide whether or not to bring the Union into operation with a number of Member States lower than the number of members in the Community.

At the same time, the decision concerning relations with the Member States which have not yet ratified is intended to influence the solution of the problems relating to the entry into force of the Treaty establishing the Union. It is quite clear that the States which have already ratified the Treaty will only be in a position to offer the other Member States of the Community a basis for negotiations: definition of the relations between them and the Union will be possible only by means of an agreement. It may be imagined that the purpose of the negotiations will be above all formally to bring the Communities to an end, with the consent of all the Members thereof, so as to enable the Union to start functioning without the virtually insurmountable obstacles which would result from coexistence with the Community structures in their present form (the prospect of duplicating institutions, authorities, powers, and measures is almost inconceivable). Moreover, the negotiations in question would have to seek to establish between the Union and the states which decided to remain outside a kind of external link with the Union, so as to protect at least some common interests. Finally, in theory it is impossible to rule out the possibility of agreement being reached on reorganization of the Communities, which would enable them to continue to exist as a form of integration embodying only the Member States opposed to participating in the Union; in such a case, it would be a question of agreeing to approve the 'secession' of a majority of the Members.

4. The hypotheses discussed in the foregoing paragraph cannot be considered in greater depth from the legal point of view because their becoming reality depends upon a number of political factors which are unforeseeable at the present time. Also, the rationale of the second paragraph of Article 82 is clearly political: the intention was to prevent the unfavourable attitude of a minority of the Member States of the Communities from being sufficient to block the entry into force of the Treaty establishing the Union, while on the other hand it was not considered appropriate to prescribe as of now that the agreement of a majority would be sufficient to give rise to the entry into force of the Treaty.

In fact, the best political and legal solution would be for all the states mentioned above to consent: indeed, in paragraph 3 of the Resolution of 14 February 1984, the European Parliament expressed the hope that the Treaty 'will ultimately be approved by all the Member States'. It would not be out of the question for that solution to be arrived at over a long period of time, by a progressive increase in the number of ratifications: that is why the possibility is left open that, after the threshold for the requisite majority regarding ratifications is reached, the States which have ratified may be free further to defer the date of entry into force.

However, another hypothesis which is also worthy of consideration is that even if majority ratification is achieved, the other Member States adopt an attitude which is clearly and radically opposed to their participation in the Union. That would make it necessary to lay down a pattern for relations between the two groups of States. Both groups would have to consent to the extinction of the Communities or to a radical transformation thereof (to permit the departure of the majority group). In the absence of such an agreement, the creation of the Union would amount to an unlawful breach of the provisions of Community law, since the Institutions, competences, and acts of the Union are clearly intended to take the place of Institutions, competences and acts of the Communities. But in fact, the risk of a serious (political and legal) dispute regarding such a breach is reduced to a minimum by the well-conceived combination of the decision to be taken regarding entry into force of the Treaty, with the decision on relations between the two groups of States, separated by their respective attitudes towards ratification: in other words, it may be assumed that the Union would come into existence only after the matter of those relations had been settled.

Article 83

Deposit of the instruments of ratification

The instruments of ratification shall be deposited with the Government of the first State to have completed the ratification procedure.

1. It is well known that instruments of ratification must be exchanged, deposited, or notified in order to take effect (see Article 16 of the Vienna Convention on the Law of the Treaties). Article 83 adopts the solution of deposit of the instruments of ratification, which is very often adopted in multilateral treaties, and provides that the instruments are to be deposited with the Government of the first State to have completed the ratification procedure. This provision raises the question of determining that the first ratification has taken place. It is certainly not conceivable that the first State which ratifies would merely retain the instrument of ratification in its possession, but on the other hand Article 83 takes no account of the special position of that State and therefore does not prescribe any procedure for informing the other Member States concerned.

It would seem that a solution may be found in the provision of the Vienna Convention which describes the functions of depositaries (Article 77): that is, in fact, the capacity which attaches to the first State to ratify. The depositary has, *inter alia*, the duty of 'informing the parties and the States entitled to become parties ... of acts ... relating to the Treaty' (paragraph (e)). In the present case therefore it will be sufficient if all the Member States of the European Communities are officially *informed* by the first State to ratify that the constitutional formalities regarding its own ratification have been completed by it.

Article 84

Revision of the Treaty

One representation within the Council of the Union, or one-third of the members of Parliament, or the Commission may submit to the legislative authority a reasoned draft law amending one or more provisions of this Treaty. The draft shall be submitted for approval to the two arms of the legislative authority which shall act in accordance with the procedure applicable to organic laws.

The draft, thus approved, shall be submitted for ratification by the Member States and shall enter into force when they have ratified it.

Preparatory document:

Doc. 1-575/83/C, De Gucht working document, paragraphs 75 ff.

Provisions in force:

ECSC Treaty, Article 96.
EEC Treaty, Article 236.
EAEC Treaty, Article 204.

1. The procedure for amending the Treaty is based on the previous procedures provided for, *inter alia*, in Article 236 of the EEC Treaty. Under Article 84, however, the roles of the institutions involved reflect the changes in the relative importance of the institutions of the Union. the procedure is to be followed in the case of both amendments to the Union Treaty itself and amendments to the provisions of the Treaties establishing the European Communities which concern their objectives and scope (see Article 7 (2)). The institutional provisions of the Community Treaties which remain valid may, on the other hand, be amended by a simplified procedure through organic laws (see Article 7 (3)).

2. By way of derogation from Article 37, a draft law amending the Treaty may be proposed by any Member State ('one representation within the Council of the Union'), one-third of the Members of Parlia-

ment, or the Commission. The working document by Mr De Gucht recommended that such proposed amendments should require the support of at least three representations within the Council to ensure that they are more likely to be approved. Parliament has, however, maintained its position and given every Member State the right to propose amending laws in order that all political forces may exercise an influence. Under the Community Treaties, Parliament does not have any right of proposal. The fact that 'one-third of the Members' may now propose amending laws means that groups without majority support, but representing a considerable political weight, may also initiate the procedure for amending the Treaty.

3. Amendments to the Union Treaty are 'approved' by the two arms of the legislative authority (see Article 36) in accordance with the procedure applicable to organic laws. Article 38 specifies that the Parliament and the Council of the Union are to take their decisions by a qualified majority. Whereas in the past the text of amendments had to be determined by a conference of the Governments of the Member States, responsibility is thus transferred to the Institutions of the Union.

4. Following approval by the legislative authority of the Union, the amendments must be ratified by all the Member States. This is also a requirement under Community law. Article 84 does not specify that the ratification by the Member States must be 'in accordance with their respective constitutional requirements' but this addition is unnecessary since only the individual national laws can determine the conditions for ratification.

5. All the political forces in the Institutions of the Union and all the Member States may thus participate in the procedure for amending the Treaty. The aim is to ensure a 'balanced system guaranteeing the defence of the interests of the Member States and the Union'.[1] As a result, the Union Treaty does not provide for amendment by the Member States alone.

The Union Treaty contains no provisions other than Article 7 (3) and Article 84 for a simplified amendment procedure, such as that provided

---

[1] Working document by De Gucht, paragraph 75.

Article 85

The seat

The European Council shall determine the seat of the institutions. Should the European Council not have taken a decision on the seat within two years of the entry into force of this Treaty, the legislative authority shall take a final decision in accordance with the procedure applicable to organic laws.

Provisions in force:

ECSC Treaty, Article 77.
EEC Treaty, Article 216.
EAEC Treaty, Article 189.
Merger Treaty, Article 37.
Decision of the Representatives of the Governments of the Member States of 8 April 1965 on the provisional location of certain Institutions and Departments of the Communities.

1. A final decision has still to be taken on the seat of the Communities. Under the Community Treaties, this decision is the responsibility of the Member States, who, in their decision of 8 April 1965, simply determined the 'provisional places of work'. While the Court of Justice of the Communities has pointed out that it is the duty of the Member States to take a final decision on the seat, it has not yet taken any steps in the light of their failure to do so.[1] Article 85 empowers the European Council to determine the seat of the Institutions of the Union. This does not substantially change the existing legal situation, since it is likely that the European Council will take its decision by unanimity (see Article 32 (2)).

2. Since the European Parliament clearly expects that the European Council will not take a decision, the second sentence of Article 85 provides that two years after the entry into force of the Treaty the power to take the decision will be transferred to the legislative authority. The decision is then to be taken in accordance with the procedure applicable to organic laws, which means that the Parliament and the Council of the Union are to act by a qualified majority (Article 38).

[1] Case 230/81 *Grand Duchy of Luxembourg* v. *European Parliament* [1983] ECR 255.

3.   Article 85 refers only to the seat of the Institutions. Article 33 does not contain any provisions relating to the seat of the other organs, but simply deals with their competences, powers, and organization. These do not include determination of the seat. It would seem appropriate, for reasons of consistency, if Article 85 were also to empower the European Council to determine the seat of the organs. This power would in any case be transferred to the legislative authority after two years, with the result that the situation would then be the same: both Article 33 (1) and Article 85 provide for organic laws.

4.   The European Parliament discussed and rejected the following alternatives: establishing the seat of the political Institutions in Brussels (proposal by Mr Eisma), excluding any reference to the controversial question of the seat (proposal by Mr Seitlinger and others) or specifying that this matter was the exclusive responsibility of the European Council (proposal by Mr Kallias). In contrast to the provisions of the Community Treaties, the present Article 85 suggests that it will be possible to reach a final decision on the seat. The terms used in this article do not imply a choice in favour of a single seat for all the Institutions or for separate seats for each Institution. It will be for the competent authority to make that choice.

Article 86

Reservations

The provisions of this Treaty may not be subject to any reservations. This Article does not preclude the Member States from maintaining, in relation to the Union, the declarations they have made with regard to the Treaties and Conventions which form part of the Community patrimony.

1. Article 86 specifies that ratification of the Treaty may not be subject to reservations on individual provisions. This accords with Article 19(a) of the Vienna Convention on the Law of Treaties which expressly permits the exclusion of reservations. Even without this formal exclusion, any reservations on the part of individual Member States would run counter to the aims of the Treaty, which is a 'constituent instrument of an international organization' (Article 20(3) of the Vienna Convention). The Community Treaties did not contain any provision corresponding to Article 86. However, as a result of the conclusion in 1969 of the Vienna Convention on the Law of Treaties, which has already entered into force in some Member States, it was necessary to include this specification in Article 86, since a number of doubts could otherwise have arisen with regard to the admissibility of reservations.

2. The principle of safeguarding the Community patrimony (Article 7) is the basis of the second sentence, which allows the Member States to maintain, in relation to the Union, individual declarations which form part of that patrimony. This concerns nearly all the Member States, as is shown by the declarations on the three Community Treaties, the Accession Treaties, and the other Community agreements concluded by the Member States. A particular reason for making this provision explicit was the need to ensure the future application of the declarations made on successive occasions by the Federal Republic of Germany on the subject of Berlin and the responsibilities of the four powers in relation to Germany as a whole.

Article 87

Duration

This treaty is concluded for an unlimited period.

Provisions in force:

ECSC Treaty, Article 97.
EEC Treaty, Article 240.
EAEC Treaty, Article 208.

Whereas the ECSC Treaty was concluded for a period of fifty years, Article 87 is modelled on the other two Community Treaties and specifies that the Union Treaty is to be concluded for an unlimited period. This provision excludes the possibility of unilateral termination for arbitrary reasons. As in the past, the question of whether the Treaty may be terminated for important reasons or whether a State may withdraw or be excluded from the Union remains unresolved. The Union Treaty itself is to be concluded independently of the amendment procedures provided for in the three Community Treaties. The European Parliament takes the view that conclusion 'for an unlimited period' does not exclude the possibility of concluding a new treaty, provided that the degree of integration already achieved is extended and not diminished by the new treaty.[1]

---

[1] See commentary on Article 82.

Conclusions

THE draft Treaty which is the subject of this commentary essentially represents a means, proposed by the European Parliament, of resolving the protracted crisis in the process of integration, a process which began in 1951 with the creation of the ECSC. The objective of the Treaty is clearly indicated in the first line of the preamble: 'continuing and reviving the democratic unification of Europe', that is, to give fresh impetus to this process while maintaining continuity with the results already achieved.

The situation that prompted the need for a 'revival' is well known. Although the existence of the European Communities may be regarded nowadays as well established, the original direction has been abandoned. European integration was conceived as a dynamic process. The transfer of powers from the Member States to the Community Institutions was to have increased progressively, and the supranational method (admittedly with the 'corrections' to the 1951 Treaty of Paris, introduced in the Treaties of Rome) was to have been consolidated so as increasingly to limit the prerogatives of each sovereign State. This process was hindered by the shift in the institutional balance envisaged in the Treaties establishing the Communities and in particular by the emergence of four factors: the failure to apply the majority rule in the Council, the proliferation of instances of national interference in the management of common policies, the undermining of the Commission's effective independence, and the predominance of the role assumed by the European Council and hence of the method of co-operation between governments.

Was there any possibility of going back to the beginning, of applying once again all the rules of the game and breathing new life into the spirit of the Community Treaties? The authors of this draft Treaty thought not. They felt that in order to resume the path towards 'an ever closer union among the peoples of Europe' (referred to in the preamble to the EEC Treaty), it was necessary to renew the institutional framework. The substitution of the word 'Union' for 'Community' may also help to make clear this wish for renewal.

An account has already been given in the Introduction of the series of events which marked the European Parliament's initiative concerning the Union. It took this initiative primarily for two reasons. First, in one particular respect Parliament felt directly the failure to proceed with integration: the difficulty in resolving the contradiction between the strict limits on its powers and its role as a body representing the will of the people. Second, in a democratically balanced structure the two repositories of power are usually the Parliament and the executive body and control is exercised by the former over the latter. In the Community system, the task of combating a crisis provoked by the intrusion of the executive body should thus logically be the prerogative of the parliamentary Institution, all the more so after it had gained greater strength and prestige through the direct election of its members.

There is thus no doubt that the European Parliament had valid political reasons to draw up a draft text designed to influence the future of European integration. However, its initiative must also be assessed from a legal point of view. In this respect, it is obvious in the first place that the procedure for amending the Community Treaties was not followed (Articles 96 of the ECSC Treaty, 236 of the EEC Treaty, and 204 of the EAEC Treaty). In addition, the preparation of draft treaties does not fall within the powers explicitly conferred on the European Parliament. Faced with these difficulties, however, one can point out, on one hand, that Parliament went beyond the mechanism for amending the Community Treaties by proposing to the Member States that they conclude a treaty which differed in form from those of Paris and Rome and, on the other hand, that the power to adopt political resolutions which has come to be recognized in the European Parliament is sufficiently broad to include the possibility of adopting draft treaties. In addition, although the draft is worded in such a way as to enable it to be transformed into a treaty as soon as the conditions laid down in Article 82 are met, paragraph 2 of the accompanying resolution provides implicitly for further reflection in Parliament on its contents. It would thus not be correct to describe it as a final text requiring only the necessary ratifications to render it binding, as is the case for texts 'adopted' by the organs of other international organizations empowered to prepare draft agreements (for example, the United Nations Assembly or the ILO General Conference).

An important problem of quite a different kind concerns the content of the draft. The question inevitably arises as to whether the broad lines of the proposed text offer an adequate solution to the problems brought about by the crisis in the process of European integration. To answer that question it is necessary to identify the principal characteristic of the draft and that is, without doubt, a new vision of the Institutions, their powers, and their relations with each other. By comparison, the provisions governing the policies of the Union, which nevertheless contain some important innovations, may on the whole be described as more broadly inspired by a desire for continuity and gradual development. Under these circumstances, it would seem justified to hold that the introduction of structural innovations could succeed in overcoming the crisis in the policy of integration, both because this policy was inaugurated and rendered feasible in the first place by the creation of a power structure *sui generis* (the ECSC High Authority), and because the major aspects of the crisis have led to structural imbalances (principally as regards the relationship between the Council, to which was subsequently added the European Council, and the Commission). Moreover, while it is clear that the crisis cannot be resolved without the political will of the countries of Europe, it is equally clear that this will must find expression in a specific type of agreement, and it has already been pointed out that an agreement simply to reinstate the original rules of the game is, to be realistic, less likely (as well as less effective) than a pact of Union which contains new rules.

Still in connection with the principal characteristics of the draft, there are those who believe that it reveals aspects of a federal or quasi-federal concept of the Union. Reference is made in support of this argument to the rules on citizenship of the Union (Article 3) and on its territory, and in particular to the provisions which describe the Parliament and Council as the two arms of the legislative authority (Article 36) and the budgetary authority of the Union (Article 70 (1)); the article which specifies that Union law takes precedence over national law (Article 42); the provisions concerning sanctions (Article 44); and the tasks conferred on the Union with regard to the protection of fundamental rights (Article 4). This seems to herald the reopening of a debate which had closed: whether or not the ECSC had the characteristics of a 'partial' federal body. Now as then, it is doubtful whether terminology borrowed from state theory can contribute towards a better understanding of a different concept with characteristics resembling those of any entity created by international agreement (in particular, in the draft Treaty of the Union, the functions of the European Council). In the final analysis, the Union as set out in the present draft Treaty can not be reduced to an embryonic federal state. In order fully to understand its distinctive characteristics, it must be studied without reference to the federal model which could distort the picture. The only valid point of comparison is the experience of the European Communities, and, if there is felt to be a need to classify the Union, it should therefore be placed in the category of supranational organizations.

The content of the draft could also be assessed with a view to determining in what respects and to what extent it could be improved or indeed might require correction. For this purpose it would be necessary to carry out an analysis of the text which would be inappropriate in this context; reference should be made to the observations on each article contained in this commentary. In general, certain technical improvements would be welcome, particularly with regard to the competences of the Union. For example the distinction between exclusive and concurrent competence should be made clearer, above all with regard to the scope for action by the individual Member States up to the point where the Union exercises competence. As regards the areas covered by the two sections on economic policy and policy for society, areas whose extension is in many cases too vaguely referred to, the question of the relationship between the competences conferred on the Union and those retained by the individual Member States does not appear to have been adequately resolved. The question of which fields are to be the subject of co-operation should also be examined more closely in order to establish how to define their boundaries.

These comments do not of course have any bearing on the further question of the political desirability of certain aspects of the draft, opinions on which may vary considerably. Moreover, an assessment of the advantages and disadvantages of the options chosen by the authors of the draft would go beyond the scope of these conclusions. What can be stated is that the European Parliament's Committee on Institutional Affairs has endeavoured to reconcile innovation, and in particular the need to outline a more effective and more democratic structure, to quote once again the terms of the preamble, with a realistic acknowledgement of the influence which the Member States, and hence the Institutions composed of their representatives, will continue to exert in the life of the Union. Several aspects of the draft can be cited to confirm the accuracy of this statement: first, the system of joint decision-making (by the Parliament and Council of the Union) in the exercise of legislative and budgetary powers, and second, the statement of the principle of subsidiarity in relation to competences. To this must be added the role to be played by the European Council in the transfer from co-operation to common action (which includes as an exception the possibility of the reverse process in the field of foreign policy: Article 63 (3)), and in the appointment of the President of the Commission and the adoption of sanctions, and the clause allowing for a vote in the Council of the Union to be postponed when a government invokes a 'vital national interest'. The European Parliament can thus not be accused of having created the concept of a Union which takes little account of the Member States' sovereignty and its implications.

A number of events which may influence the fate of the draft Treaty have occurred since its adoption by the European Parliament. By decision of the European Council in Fontainebleau (26 June 1984) an *ad hoc* committee, consisting of personal representatives of the Heads of State or Government (the Dooge Committee), was instructed to make suggestions 'for the improvement of the operation of European co-operation in both the Community field and that of political, or any other, co-operation'. In its report to the European Council in Brussels (29–30 March 1985), this committee proposed that a conference of the representatives of the Governments of the Community Member States be convened to negotiate a draft European Union Treaty. This draft should be based on the Community patrimony, the Committee's report and the Stuttgart Solemn Declaration and should be 'guided by the spirit and method of the draft Treaty voted by the European Parliament'. The latter should be closely involved in the work of the conference, the results of which should in any event be submitted to it.

The European Parliament's initiative, which led to the preparation and adoption of the draft Treaty discussed in this commentary, has thus achieved considerable success, although in a different direction from that originally envisaged. Its success lies not only in having made a decisive contribution towards ensuring that the need to revive the process of integration is recognized by the representatives of the Member States' Governments (or at least by a majority of them), but also in the fact that the possibility of creating a Union has been discussed, that the February 1984 draft has become a factor which must be taken into account not least at government level, and that there is an intention to involve the European Parliament in the work of the proposed conference. The less successful aspects, however, include the fact that the governments have manifested a determination to retain control over future developments in the construction of Europe by preparing to follow the usual channel of a diplomatic conference. This has brought to nothing the hope, or perhaps the illusion, that was implied in the parliamentary resolution adopting the draft treaty—that, by addressing them directly, the European Parliament could give priority to the role of the national parliaments in the work of finalizing the draft. This does not, however, exclude the possibility that the fundamental ideas reflected in the document of February 1984, and perhaps even many of its more specific aspects, may ultimately be confirmed and enshrined in the text of the Treaty of Union which the governments intend to draw up, since some of them already appear in the report of the Dooge Committee. The balanced quality of Parliament's draft inspires confidence in its ability to act as a valid basis for future negotiations. In any event, the Parliament will be able to continue its own course, by strengthening its contacts with the national parliaments in order to find the greatest possible measure of agreement on a text which is realistic and which inspires further development.

Bibliography

I. BOOKS

BIEBER, R., JACQUÉ, J.-P., and WEILER J. (ed.), *An Ever Closer Union*, Brussels, European Perpectives, 1985.

DASTOLI, P.V., and PIERUCCI, A., *Verso una costituzione democratica per l'Europa*. Marietti, 1984.

LOUIS, J.-V. (ed.), *L'Union europénne avant le Conseil européen de Milan*, journée d'études, 27 avril 1985. Institut d'Etudes européennes, Université libre de Bruxelles, 1985.

——*L'Union européenne: le projet du Parlement européen après Fontainebleau*. Journée d'études, 17 novembre 1984. Institut d'Etudes européennes, Université libre de Bruxelles, 1984.

——*L'Union européenne: le projet de traité du Parlement européen*. Journée d'études, 22 octobre 1983. Institut d'Etudes européennes, Université libre de Bruxelles, 1983.

Parlement Européen, Bilan, Perspectives, 1979-1984. Collège d'Europe, Bruges, De Tempel, Bruges, 1983, esp. pp. 71-212.

SCHWARZE, J., and BIEBER, R. (ed.), *Eine Verfassung für Europa: von der Europäischen Gemeinschaft zur Europäischen Union*. Nomos Verlag, Baden Baden, 1984.

WILLIE, E., *L'Unione europea*. Edizioni scientifiche italiane, Naples, 1984.

II. ARTICLES

CATALANO, N., 'Le Traité d'Union européenne: légitimité juridique et institutionelle', in *Crocodile: lettre aux members du Parlement européen*, no. 11, June, 1983.

——'Parere sul progetto di Unione Europea', *Affari sociali internazionali*, no. 1, 1984.

CECOVINI, N., 'L'Unione europea: utopia o Malta?' *Affari sociali internazionali*, no. 1, 1984, pp. 163-72.

CONSTANTINESCO, Vlad., 'Le projet de traité créant l'Union européenne, analyse et perspectives,' *L'Europe en formation*, April-June 1984, pp. 53-63.

EVERLING, U., 'Zur Rechtstruktur einer Europäischen Verfassung', *Integration*, 1/1984, pp. 12 ff.

FRANZMEYER, Fr., 'Wirtschaftspolitische Ziele der Europäischen Union', *Integration*, 1/1984, pp. 25 ff.

FREDIANI, C.M., 'Il progetto di trattato sull' unione europea', *Affari esteri*, 1984, lxiii, pp. 314-27.

GROEBEN, H, VON DER, 'Plädoyer für einen Ausbau der Gemeinschaft', *Integration*, 1/1984, pp. 25 ff.

HERAUD, G., 'Union européenne et fédération', *L'Europe en formation*, April–June 1984, pp. 63-73.

JACQUÉ, J.-P., 'Le Traité d'Union européenne et les Traités Communautaires', in *Crocodile: lettre aux membres du Parlement européen*, no. 11, June 1983.

——'The Draft Treaty Establishing the European Union', *Common Market Law Review*, 1985, pp. 19-42.

LODGE, J., 'Some Problems of the Draft Treaty on European Union', *European Law Review*, 1984, pp. 387 ff.

——'European Union and the First Elected European Parliament: the Spinelli Initiative', *Journal of Common Market Studies*, 4/1984, pp. 377-404.

LODGE, J., FREESTONE, D., and DAVIDSON, S., European Union and Direct Elections 1984', *The Round Table*, 1984, pp. 57 ff.

NICKEL, D., 'Le projet de traité instituant l'Union européenne élaboré par le Parlement européen', *Cashiers de droit européen*, 1984, pp. 511-42.

——'Der Entwurf des Europäischen Parlaments für einen Vertrag zur Gründung der Europäischen Union', *Integration*, 1/1985, p. 11.

NICKEL, D., and CORBETT, R., 'The Draft Treaty Establishing European Union', *Yearbook of European Law*, 1984.

ORSELLO, G., 'Note sul progetto di trattato istitutivo dell'unione europea', *Affari sociali internazionali*, no. 1, 1984, pp. 53-79.

——'Prime considerazioni in ordine alla proposta del Parlamento Europeo per le predisposizione di un trattato istitutivo dell'Unione europea', *Annuario di diritto comparato et di studi legislativi*, series 4, lv, 1984, (*Volume unico* 1982), pp. 41-82.

PERNICE, I., 'Verfassungsentwurf für eine Europäische Union', *Europarecht*, 2/1984, pp. 126-42.

PIERUCCI, A., 'Il progetto di trattato che istituische l'unione europea', *Affari sociali internazionali*, 1/1984, pp. 195-209.

SAINT-MIHIEL, P. DE, 'Le projet de traité instituant l'union européenne', *Revue du Marché commun*, no. 276, April 1984, pp. 149-52.

SCHNEIDER, H., 'Europäische Union durch das Europäische Parlament—Zur initiative des Institutionellen Ausschusses', *Integration*, 4/1982, pp. 150 ff.

SCHWARZE, J., 'Mitgliedschaft in einer zukünftigen politischen Union', *Deutsches Verwaltungsblatt*, 15 March 1985, pp. 309-17.

SPINELLI, A., *Towards the European Union*, sixth Jean Monnet lecture, European University Institute, Florence, 13 June 1983.

——'Reflessioni nel Trattato-costituzione per l'Unione Europea', *Annuario di diritto comparato et di Studi legislativi*, 1984, pp. 21-40.

THOMASIS, G. DE 'Le projet d'union européenne à la veille de la campagne pour les deuxièmes élections européennes', *Revue du Marché commun*, no. 277, May 1984, pp. 212-15.

WEIDENFELD, W., 'Europäische Verfassung für Visionäre?', *Integration*, 1/1984, pp. 33 ff.

WESSELS, W., 'Der Vertragsentwurf des Europäischen Parlaments für eine Europäische Union: Kristallisationspunkt einer neuen Europadebatte', *Europa Archiv*, 8/1984, pp. 239 ff.